Freedom Church
of the Poor

Freedom Church of the Poor

Martin Luther King Jr.'s Poor People's Campaign

Colleen Wessel-McCoy

LEXINGTON BOOKS/FORTRESS ACADEMIC
Lanham • Boulder • New York • London

Published by Lexington Books/Fortress Academic
Lexington Books is an imprint of The Rowman & Littlefield Publishing Group, Inc.
4501 Forbes Boulevard, Suite 200, Lanham, Maryland 20706
www.rowman.com

6 Tinworth Street, London SE11 5AL, United Kingdom
Copyright © 2021 by The Rowman & Littlefield Publishing Group, Inc.

British Library Cataloguing in Publication Information Available

Library of Congress Cataloging-in-Publication Data

Names: Wessel-McCoy, Colleen, 1979– author.
Title: Freedom church of the poor : Martin Luther King Jr.'s Poor People's
    Campaign / Colleen Wessel-McCoy.
Description: Lanham : Lexington Books/Fortress Academic, [2021] | Includes
    bibliographical references. | Summary: "In Freedom Church of the Poor:
    Martin Luther King Jr.'s Poor People's Campaign, Colleen Wessel-McCoy
    roots King's political vision solidly in his theological ethics and
    traces the spirit of the campaign in the community and religious leaders
    who are responding to the devastating crises of inequality today"—
    Provided by publisher.
Identifiers: LCCN 2021020888 (print) | LCCN 2021020889 (ebook) | ISBN
    9781978710238 (cloth) | ISBN 9781978710245 (epub) | ISBN 9781978710252 (pbk)
Subjects: LCSH: King, Martin Luther, Jr., 1929-1968. | King, Martin Luther,
    Jr., 1929–1968—Religion. | Poor People's Campaign—History. | Religion
    and politics—United States. | Church and social problems—United
    States. | Civil rights movements—Washington (D.C.)—History—20th
    century. | Minorities—United States—Economic conditions—20th century.
    | Poor—United States—Social conditions—20th century. |
    Minorities—Civil rights—United States—History—20th century. | United
    States—Race relations—History—20th century.
Classification: LCC E185.97.K5 W46 2021 (print) | LCC E185.97.
    K5 (ebook)
    | DDC 323.092—dc23
LC record available at https://lccn.loc.gov/2021020888
LC ebook record available at https://lccn.loc.gov/2021020889

Contents

Acknowledgments   vii

Introduction   xi

Chapter 1: King's Vision for a Campaign of the Poor   1

Chapter 2: Organizing a New and Unsettling Force   23

Chapter 3: The Poor Come to Washington   41

Chapter 4: Assessing the Campaign   67

Chapter 5: Theologies of the Poor People's Campaign   95

Chapter 6: King's Theological Ethics   113

Chapter 7: Movement as Church   127

Chapter 8: Freedom Church of the Poor Today   139

Conclusion   165

Bibliography   169

Index   185

About the Author   193

Acknowledgments

The ember of the Poor People's Campaign has been tended by several generations of organizers and poverty scholars. This book is an attempt to trace how and why the political and theological thought and action in 1968 has remained so relevant to human rights organizing and Christian ethics.

Among the ember-keepers are those who shared their stories of 1968 with me: Hy Thurman, Annie Chambers, Carlos Raúl Dufflar, Al McSurely, Arvernetta Henry, Judy Sanders, Sammie McCray, Chuck Fager, John Alexander, and Michael Kline. All of them continue to organize for justice today.

I was a master's of divinity student when Willie Baptist, the Poverty Scholar in Residence at Union Theological Seminary, first shared with me the political vision he draws from Martin Luther King Jr's last years. Baptist is part of a network of poverty scholars organizing in the tradition of the Poor People's Campaign. They had commemorated the thirty-fifth anniversary by retracing the steps of the Mule Train by foot, organizing other poor people along the way around human rights. The theological significance of this history brought Baptist and Liz Theoharis to Union. I am deeply grateful for his mentorship.

Gary Dorrien and James Cone helped me turn this commitment to the lessons of the Poor People's Campaign into a dissertation and shaped me as a student of Christian ethics. I am grateful for their time, corrections, and support in learning how to bridge research and organizing, drawing from their deep legacies of socially engaged scholarship. Cone lives on in the hearts and minds of the many religious leaders he developed and the lives his theology changed. Dorrien is an adviser who calls his students to write dissertations only they could write. He could see where I was trying to go with mine before I could and helped me find my way. His support and enthusiasm are backed by the breadth and depth of his own scholarship. I am grateful not only for the time he spent advising me but also for my many colleagues he shaped who are now at work in the world.

The ember of 1968 ignited the fire of the Poor People's Campaign: A National Call for Moral Revival, cochaired by Liz Theoharis and William J. Barber II. I am grateful to both of them for mentorship in organizing and scholarship. Thanks also goes to Barber for serving on my dissertation committee.

I am grateful to the faculty of Union Theological Seminary who contributed to my development and shaped my research, including Brigitte Kahl, Aliou Niang, David Carr, Sam Cruz, Jan Rehmann, John Thataminil, Cornel West, Andrea White, Sarah Azaransky, Roger Haight, Su Yon Pak, Daisy Machado, Mary Boys, and Kelly Brown Douglass. Thanks also to Courtney Bender of Columbia University for serving on my dissertation committee.

I am also grateful to the staff of Union Theological Seminary, whose labor makes the mission of the institution possible. In particular I thank those who have been strong supporters of the Kairos Center and me as a student, including David Bryan, Ann Marie Spencer, Joyce Dompreh, Fredia Pagan, Calvin Mason, Alex Tamariz, Maurice Samuel, Hector Batista, Mel Hamil, Rudy Hoyos, Fouad Moussa, Juver Londono, Michael Orzechowski, Alberta McCants, Lisa Simon, Beth Bidlack, Luke Henderson, Damione Harrington, Steven Bie, Bass Diop, Marcus Mortise, and Donald Joshua.

Many thanks to Vicky Furio, assistant to James Cone, and Charmeine Fletcher, assistant to William Barber II.

Thanks for research assistance goes to Elaine Hall and Cynthia Lewis of the King Library and Archives, Betty Bolden of the Burke Library, Don Davis of the American Friends Service Committee Archives, and the staffs of Special Collections at Smith College, Rose Archive at Emory University Library, and the Paley Center for Media.

I am lucky to have had a supportive cohort of PhD peers who shared genuine enthusiasm for each other's success, including Nkosi Anderson, Charlene Sinclair, Derrick McQueen, Amy Meverden, Ashley Hufnagel, Joe Strife, Foster Pikney, Nixon Cleophat, Angela Parker, Kerri Whipple, Damien Wheeler, Jamal Calloway, Jorge Juan Busone Rodríguez V, Aaron Stauffer, Jason Wyman, Carolyn Klaasen, Joshua Samuel, Isaac Sharp, Todd Willison, Esther Parajuli, and Ruth Batausa.

Among the network of organizers who have contributed to the study of King and the Poor People's Campaign, I wish to acknowledge Marian Kramer, Maureen Taylor, Guida West, Ann Rall, and Mary Bricker-Jenkins of the National Welfare Rights Union; Savina Martin, Tony Prince, Moses Hernandez McGavin, and Kristin Colangelo of the National Union of the Homeless; Nijmie Dzurinko, Jae Hubay, Phil Wider, and Tammy Rojas of

Put People First—PA; Sarah Monroe, Aaron Scott, and Mashyla Buckmaster of Chaplains on the Harbor; Roz Pellez, Alvin Jackson, Clinton Wright, Laurel Ashton, Rob Stephens, and the staff of Repairers of the Breach; Avery Book and Kate Kanelstein of Vermont Workers Center; Alicia Swords, Arelis Figueroa, Joe Paperone, and Becca Forsyth and the New York Poor People's Campaign; Kenia Torres-Alcocer of Union de Vecinos; Ciara Taylor and Claudia de la Cruz of the Popular Education Project; Carolyn Baker of the General Baker Institute; Erica Williams of Set It Off Ministries; Anu Yadav; Tonny Algood of United Methodist Inner City Mission; Catherin Coleman Flowers of The Center for Rural Enterprise and Environmental Justice; Karenna Gore of the Center for Earth Ethics; Keith Bullard and Ben Wilkins of Rise up 15; and the many leaders of the state organizing committees of the Poor People's Campaign.

I have deep gratitude for those who have built the Kairos Center, including Charon Hribar, Shailly Gupta Barnes, Adam Barnes, Nic Laccetti, Jessica Chadwick Williams, West McNeill, Amy Miller, Heather West, Noam Sandweiss-Back, Paul Chapman, Gayle Irvin, Larry Cox, Solita Riley, more than a decade of Kairos fellows, the Reading the Bible with the Poor Cohort, and the kids who bring so much joy to the work, Indi, Jack and Michael Barnes, Sophia and Luke Caruso, Kenji Vasquez, and Annabella Vargas-Figueroa.

Thoughtful feedback and edits were offered by Chris Caruso, Liz Theoharis, Shailly Barnes, Adam Barnes, André Daughtry, Nancy Taylor, and the economics group of the University of the Poor, including Tim Shenk, Joyce Brody, Lenny Brody, Dan Jones, Bruce Perry, and Marilyn Hunter. I am also grateful to Neil Elliott and Gayla Freeman of Lexington/Fortress Academic.

I am grateful for the friendships Heather Branham, Stephen Wiseman, and Sarah Gillooly. There are generations of people who have been mentored by Tina Pippin, and I am proud to be one of them. Thank you also to the 1996 cohort of the Youth Theology Initiative at Candler Theological Seminary, including Helen Blier. I am sustained by the lifelong friendships of Tracy Bender, Katy Stout, Julie Reeves, and Katie Frazier.

Particular gratitude goes to Carolyn Baker, Erica Williams, Jessica Williams and Amy Meverden for encouragement and support during the writing process.

My family has given me lots of love and lots of childcare, including Mary and Walter Wessel and my parents Mike and Mary Ann McCoy. My mom in particular traveled from Atlanta to New York countless times to watch the kids and welcomed me home for writing retreats. This book would not exist without her labor and support.

John Wessel-McCoy falls in many of the categories of acknowledgment above. He is also my historian-in-residence, first-draft editor, and cheerleader.

I am inspired every day by our kids, Myles, Josephine, and Harriet. I hope to live up to Josephine's wish at age seven that this will be "the best writing that anyone has ever seen."

The Neely Visiting Professorship in Religion and Public Policy at Arizona State University's School Of Public Affairs provided me with research time and support for the completion of this book.

Introduction

In December 1967, Martin Luther King Jr. called the poor of all races and ethnicities to converge on the nation's capital to start a Poor People's Campaign. This is what he was tirelessly organizing when he was assassinated four months later. Reeling from that loss, caravans of the poor set off a few weeks later, traveling from across the United States to demand a response to malnutrition, slum housing, unchecked police brutality, and the many hardships of poverty. Delegations included a Western caravan, Appalachian caravan, and a mule-and-wagon procession from Marks, Mississippi. When they arrived in the capital, they constructed a tent encampment between the Lincoln Memorial and Washington Monument and pointedly named it Resurrection City. Its 6,000 residents occupied the parkland for six weeks. They were ten blocks from the White House and seventeen blocks from Congress. It was a position of confrontation. But the campaign dissolved, never reaching the mass civil disobedience that was part of the original plan to create a crisis that would force the hand of Congress and transform the lives of the forty million poor people in the richest nation in the world.

Doug "Youngblood" Blakey was among the poor whites from Chicago's Uptown neighborhood who traveled by bus to Resurrection City. When he reflected on the experience, he said it wasn't the, "petitioning of the government to address themselves to the problems of the deprived in the country," that made the campaign significant. Instead it was "what is happening to the poor people who are there and are learning what is going on." By coming together from across the nation and "having all of the things they've never had before (food, clothes, medicine, all of which is free) . . . they're redefining themselves as to what their lives should be about."[1] In a country proud of its ascending productivity and wealth, the persistence of poverty was a contradiction. In the Poor People's Campaign that absurdity was on display not only for the nation, but for the poor themselves. It broke their isolation and exposed the expansiveness of poverty. Aleah Omeja, a campaign participant from New York, said in the richest nation in the world, Resurrection City, "shouldn't have to exist."[2]

By coming together from across the country, the poor saw that poverty was not limited to their own neighborhood, geography, race, ethnicity, or occupation. The encampment included poor Native American families from reservations in the West and Pacific Northwest, poor Black families evicted from mechanized cotton farms of the South, poor white families from coal-rich Appalachia, poor white and Black families from the urban ghettos of the industrial North, poor Mexican American families from contested territories of the Southwest, and poor Puerto Rican families from the Northeast. And if poverty crossed all those boundaries, it meant those who were interested in ending poverty were a larger force than they had realized.

When King visited Albany, Georgia on March 22, 1968, for a mass meeting to recruit participants for the Poor People's Campaign, he told the congregation gathered there, "We aren't going to solve our economic problem until we confront this nation massively and militantly." He insisted they were on firm moral ground in making this demand. "We are going to Washington to say that all of God's children are significant." Their occupation of the capital to "demand jobs and income" was rooted in their belief that, "because we are God's children . . . God loves all of us, and he wants us to have the basic necessities of life."[3] This assertion of human dignity had galvanized the Civil Rights Movement as it toppled the violently policed racial segregation of the southern United States. But as the legislative victories of the Civil Rights Era began to be implemented, King saw that civil rights could not be fully realized in a society infected with racism, militarism, and poverty. He discerned that these three evils were knotted together structurally. Abolishing them would require a "radical restructuring of the architecture of American society." At first speaking only with his closest advisers and staff, he said they must not be afraid to seek hard answers to big questions. Assessing the "State of the Movement" with SCLC staff, he said, "We must begin to ask, why there are 40 million poor people in a nation overflowing with such unbelievable affluence? We must begin to ask, why has our nation placed itself in a position of being God's military agent on earth and intervene recklessly in Vietnam and the Dominican Republic?"[4]

Where the Civil Rights Movement had called the nation to expand existing political and social rights to Black people who had been systematically denied those rights, King argued the work ahead was not to "seek to integrate [Black people] into all the existing values of American society." Instead they needed to challenge the United States to "release itself from many things that for centuries have been held sacred." The nation would need to do so not on behalf of marginalized subset of the population, but for the entire nation's "very survival." King said, in the coming era, "we must not consider it unpatriotic to raise basic questions about our national character. . . . For the evils of racism, poverty and militarism to die, a new set of values must be born. Our economy must become more person-centered than property-centered and profit-centered. Our nation must depend more on its moral power than on its military power."[5]

When King more publicly articulated his opposition to the war in Vietnam and called for an examination of the structural roots of the persistence of poverty and racism, he quickly lost allies who had been important for his past work, including white liberals and established Black civil rights leaders. But King also discerned that, as in past struggles, those who were most affected by the problem at hand would need to put forward its solutions. "The only real revolutionary, people say, is a man who has nothing to lose. There are millions of poor people in this country who have very little, or even nothing, to lose. If they can be helped to take action together, they will do so with a freedom and a power that will be a new and unsettling force in our complacent national life."[6]

He saw that the poor, across race and geography, could be the social force capable of initiating this change. They not only had the impetus and mass, but if they could be organized and united, their "freedom and power" to take action could direct the nation "to a higher destiny, to a new plateau of compassion and a more noble expression of humanness." In describing the Poor People's Campaign, King said, "The dispossessed of this nation—the poor, both white and [Black]—live in a cruelly unjust society. They must organize a revolution against the injustice, not against the lives of the persons who are their fellow citizens, but against the structures through which the society is refusing to take means which have been called for, and which are at hand, to lift the load of poverty."[7]

This revolution of the poor against the structures that maintain poverty would require new forms of organizing, moving beyond ones that depend on mobilization alone. King argued they needed to develop sustained organizing relationships, supported by greater degrees of political education that could yield shared strategic analysis. In the era of human rights, the "supreme task" would be "to organize and unite people so that their anger becomes a transforming force."[8] King called the organized force he sought to build a "nonviolent army . . . of the poor" and a "'freedom church' of the poor."[9]

This book draws from King's insight about how a campaign of poor people across race and ethnicity would be central to a social movement response to the enmeshed structural evils of society.[10] It seeks to understand how King proposed that the poor, if organized and united, could be the social force capable of and compelled to initiate a "revolution of values" to transform society. It seeks to discern the theological and ethical concepts that lead to that political strategy, as well as understand how theological and ethical principles undergird a social movement and sustain its leadership. And it seeks to learn from academic, religious, and community leaders of today who have recalled the Poor People's Campaign in their commitments to the elimination of poverty, racism, state violence, and environmental devastation.

King was born on January 15, 1929 in Atlanta, Georgia, to a middle-income African American family.[11] Both his father ("Daddy King") and his maternal grandfather were preachers. He was formed in the Black church tradition, inculcated in its theology, culture, and ties to a long history of Black religious thought and struggle. He was formally educated at Booker T. Washington High School and Morehouse College and attended graduate schools in the North. At Crozier Theological Seminary he was immersed in liberal theologies including Social Gospel and Christian Realism, and in the doctoral program at Boston University he studied Personalist philosophy and theology. He moved to Montgomery, Alabama when he was twenty-five with his new wife, Coretta Scott, to be pastor of Dexter Avenue Baptist Church. There he was soon drawn into a leadership position in the organizing work of the local NAACP by Rosa Parks and others at the start of the 1955 Montgomery Bus Boycott.

King became the founding president of the Southern Christian Leadership Conference (SCLC) in 1957 and organized protests across the South, meeting a ferociously violent police and public with radical nonviolence and garnering national and international media attention. The 1963 March on Washington became a landmark moment in American history, and in 1964 King was awarded the Nobel Peace Prize. To accomplish the feats of this decade, King tapped into centuries of struggle in the Black church and abolition freedom churches, including Howard Thurman. He drew from W. E. B. Du Bois' lessons of Radical Reconstruction and the organizing work of the Black communities in the 1930s and 1940s. He was trained politically by Bayard Rustin and Glenn Smiley and gained political and philosophical resources from Gandhi and the nonviolent Indian Independence Movement.[12]

Although King's organizing genius and martyrdom are often most remembered, we misunderstand him if we fail to see him as a theologian. Scholars of theology sometimes make the opposite mistake, failing to allow King's political strategy to impact the way we interpret his theological writings. As James Cone observes, "King doesn't write theology from behind his desk, but out of the decisions he makes in the movement."[13] Cone says we underestimate King's theological contribution when we fail to see (or refuse to see), "the struggle for freedom is the only appropriate context for doing theology."[14] While it is true that the conditions of the historical moment helped drive the movement, King understood that moment theologically and was able to develop a consciousness that was both political and moral, creating a power-ful theological social ethic that gave the historical moment vision and spirit.[15] His theology was developed as he organized. Nonviolent boycotts, sit-ins, and freedom rides were the movement's innovative tactics for dismantling legalized segregation and voter suppression. In that rapidly unfolding political situation, King developed a theology that brought together the Black church, social gospel, personalism, Christian realism, American civil religion, and Gandhian nonviolence. King's emphasis on human dignity, sacrifice, love, and beloved community were not simply moral ideas to be applied interper-sonally. Those concepts were simultaneously (and inseparably) theology and political strategy. They were a method for social change that took seriously the imbalance of power and the transformative force of the powerless taking action together.

In King's understanding, the Poor People's Campaign represented a shift in strategy from the Civil Rights Movement to a human rights movement. He argued it was a first step in building a multiracial leadership for a human rights movement that could end racism, poverty, and war. The leadership of the poor demanding a response to the manifestations of poverty in the United States was not a prioritizing of one evil over another. It was a strategy for attacking all three: "We must see now that the evils of racism, economic exploitation and militarism are all tied together. And you really can't get rid of one without getting rid of the others. . . . The whole structure of American life must be changed."[16] King identified the violence of war, the arrogance of American exceptionalism, and the exploitation of neo-colonialism as related to the violence of capitalism the poor experienced domestically. By respond-ing to the violence of poverty within the United States, a movement would develop that could join the larger revolution against the global manifestations of the triple evils.[17]

In the decades that followed his assassination, King was enshrined as the patron saint of community service and color-blind meritocracy. Corporate and government forces employ him as a champion of the American Dream.[18] He has been used to say that we should respond to oppression with perseverance, not social transformation. Rarely seen is the King who said, "The fact is that capitalism was built on the exploitation and suffering of black slaves . . . and continues to thrive on the exploitation of the poor, both black and white, both here and abroad. . . . The way to end poverty is to end the exploitation of the poor."[19] We rarely hear of his proposal for a guaranteed annual income that "would benefit all the poor, including the two-thirds of them who are white." And those who sanctify property hide the King who pointed to a growing world revolution of values.

If we are to get on the right side of the world revolution, we as a nation must undergo a radical revolution of values. We must rapidly begin the shift from a "thing-oriented" society to a "person-oriented" society. When machines and computers, profit motives and property rights are considered more important than people, the giant triplets of racism, materialism and militarism are incapable of being conquered.[20]

King believed the shift from a "thing-oriented" society to a "person-oriented society" was materially possible because of the growing productivity of technological innovation. And it was politically possible because the freedom struggles across the world were creating a global revolutionary leadership. Together the material, political, and moral conditions could lead to a shared abundance and rejection of war.[21]

This revolution of values that would transform society is something very different from moral suasion and appeals to ethics. The movement for human rights would require grappling with evil structures and the redistribution of economic power.[22] King perceived that much of the resistance to "a restructuring of the architecture of American society," would be the powerful in society whose earlier support of the Civil Rights Movement stemmed more from a concern for "tranquility and the status quo than about justice and humanity."[23] He knew that there would be no tensionless or voluntary establishment of justice, but he also argued emancipation would not come from violent rebellion.[24] The scale of change required meant that racially isolated organizing would be insufficient. "We can get more organized together than we can apart. And this is the way we gain power. Power is the ability to achieve purpose, power is the ability to affect change, and we need power."[25] Led by this vision, the Poor People's Campaign was organized as a national, multiracial campaign that drew together not individual poor people but existing religious and community leaders and the communities they were organizing, across lines of difference. And this is why King drew lessons from revolutionary processes across the globe, seeing that in these "revolutionary times," the poor around the world "are revolting against old systems of exploitation and oppression and out of the wombs of a frail world new systems of justice and equality are being born."[26]

It is common today to think that the poor are poor because something went wrong. Some people say poverty comes from economic accidents, e.g., industry shifts (layoffs, offshoring), recessions, natural disasters, pandemics, or geographic isolation (urban or rural). Some people say poverty comes from people being left behind by social and political failings, e.g., the denial of adequate education, intrusive government regulation, or job-destroying taxes. And some people say poverty comes from personal failings, e.g., laziness, spending beyond one's means, not saving for rainy days, cultural habits, or addiction. These explanations for poverty cross lines of left and right, but they share a common assumption: unless something goes wrong, a stable, middle-income life can be assumed and depended upon. In this line of thinking, the poor are a minority subset of the US economy, and according to most of these ideas, poverty is something a determined poor person could have prevented.[27]

Our perception of the cause of poverty directs our sense of the appropriate response to poverty. The poor can be pitied, despised, or offered compassion. We can argue for bootstrap austerity, private charity, education and job training, or expanded welfare. But across these responses there is a shared assumption: the future of the poor is separate and different from that of the majority and overall health of the economy.

In reality, even when the federal poverty rate is at record lows, four in ten people in the United States are poor or low income.[28] It is far from a small minority of the population. And what is missed even within these high poverty rates are the number of families who cycle in and out of these categories. Census figures capture a single moment, but longitudinal studies suggest that as many as four in five US adults will experience a period of extended joblessness, rely on welfare, or fall below 150 percent of the poverty threshold before they turn sixty.[29] Half of all children will qualify for Supplemental Nutrition Assistance Program (SNAP) at some point before they turn twenty, including nine out of ten African American children.[30] In another measure of economic instability, a Federal Reserve Board study found that only 47 percent of US households could afford a $400 emergency without selling something or borrowing money.[31] These measures point to the reality that a large portion of the United States' population is in a situation of paycheck-to-paycheck insecurity. This indicates not only the reach of poverty but the vulnerability of our livelihoods, even for middle income families. Only a small percentage of people have financial wealth that would enable them to afford prolonged job loss.

While the reality is that poverty affects four out of ten people in the United States, the stigma of being poor comes from the narrative that poverty only happens when something goes wrong, and most often, when you do something wrong. Even those of us who struggle to meet basic needs sometimes think of ourselves as "middle class" or "working class," with the poor being someone different. This is especially true when compounded by narratives that racialize, criminalize, and feminize poverty, tactics that further subdivide the poor as different from one another.[32]

King pointed out that in 1968 people could work and still be poor. This is even more so today. One can work full time or hold multiple jobs and still not cross the poverty threshold. Many workers cannot meet their basic needs or the needs of their family. The minimum wage in 1968 was $1.60 per hour.

If that wage had grown with inflation over the following fifty years, it would have been $11.20. Yet fifty years later the federal minimum wage was just $7.25, nearly $4 less than the 1968 equivalent.[33] But a failure to pin the minimum wage to inflation is only part of the story. In 1973 incomes stagnated and there was a break in the relationship between productivity and hourly wages.[34] If the minimum wage had kept pace with productivity it would have reached $19.33 in 2018.[35]

The large-scale introduction of automation, just-in-time production, and other strategies of increasing profits by decreasing labor costs are more and more impacting farms, factories, the service sector, and even white-collar fields, like legal and financial services. These shifts not only affect existing jobs but put downward pressure on all wages. As robots and artificial intelligence become cheaper than human labor, large sections of the population, domestically and globally, are poised to become superfluous to the market economy:[36] This is an explosively dangerous development in a society where value is based not on inherent human dignity but one's economic production, making increasing segments of the population superfluous and disposable. And the commonly held expectation that the poor in developing economies will follow the ladder of growth through industrial development is proving false. Even low-waged, unskilled global labor is more expensive than labor-replacing technology.[37]

None of this is to say that there aren't natural disasters, underfunded schools, and bad public policies to blame for poverty, but accidents, bad habits, and bad policies cannot fully explain its reach. The commonality within diverse experiences of poverty is the connection of poverty to wealth. That relationship exposes as false the narratives that isolate the poor as a minority identity or an economic error within an otherwise healthy economy. Poverty is the product of capitalism's normal functioning in the twenty-first century and is intimately tied to the concentration of wealth.

Fifty years after the Poor People's Campaign of 1968, the wealthiest people commandeered an increasingly vast portion of our resources. The three wealthiest people in the United States--Jeff Bezos, Warren Buffett, and Bill Gates—owned more wealth than the bottom half of the United States combined. The top 10 percent of families commandeered 77 percent of wealth. The next 40 percent of families held 22 percent of wealth, a rate that was actually down from 30 percent thirty years earlier. And the bottom half of families owned only 1 percent of wealth.[38]

If the nation's wealth was distributed equally, each person would have around $339,375. Yet the bottom half of families have an average of just $11,000 per family.[39] That group has seen its wealth cut nearly in half over the last thirty years. One in ten families have zero wealth, meaning we owe more than we own.[40] If you don't count the value of the family car, the number of zero-wealth families doubles to one in five US households.[41]

Looking at global inequality, fifty years after the Poor People's Campaign, the 3.8 billion people who make up the poorest 50 percent of humanity owned just 1 percent of global wealth and lived on less than US $5.50 per day. This devastating poverty comes with deadly vulnerability to curable diseases, malnutrition, high maternal and infant mortality, and frontline exposure to the effects of our environmental crisis. For many this is compounded further by the steady increase of war and conflict, including 70.8 million people forcibly displaced by violence, persecution, and poverty, including 25.9 million refugees, over half of whom are under the age of eighteen. At the same time globally there were 2,208 billionaires.[42]

This trend toward a bifurcated economy, domestically and globally, has been accompanied by policies of austerity. In the 1980s the World Bank and global capital imposed structural adjustment programs on developing economies that required massive cuts to social spending, privatized natural resources, added trade and labor policies that favored businesses, and prioritized the payment of foreign debts. Those austerity measures are increasingly being imposed on developed economies. The concentration of wealth makes the economy susceptible to crisis due to disease pandemics, political turmoil, and climate events. These crashes are followed by recoveries that further concentrate wealth in the hands of the few. Lower revenues hollow out state and local treasuries, leading to budget cuts. This erosion of social programs is deepened by failing democratic accountability, voter suppression, and greater violations of civil liberties. Rising white nationalism, racism, xenophobia, and domestic terrorism grow and are emboldened by these conditions. Rather than resulting from a real scarcity of wealth and productivity, policies of austerity are indicative of a deeper economic dysfunction created by inequality.

Theologically and economically King refused the idea that we are governed by scarcity rather than abundance.

God has left enough and to spare in this world for all of his children to have the basic necessities of life, and God never intended for some of his children to live in inordinate superfluous wealth while others live in abject, deadening poverty. And somehow I believe that God made it all . . . (and) because God made it . . . I believe firmly that the earth is the Lord's and the fullness thereof. I don't think it belongs to Mr. Rockefeller. I don't think it belongs to Mr. Ford. I think the earth is the Lord's, and since we didn't make these things by ourselves, we must share them with each other. And I think this is the only way we are going to solve the basic problems and the restructuring of our society which I think is so desperately needed.[43]

In calling for a Poor People's Campaign, King was moving toward solving the desperately needed restructuring of our society. And in the midst of this planning he was assassinated, but its lessons remain relevant for the conditions of today.

Almost weekly I hear the argument that people don't want to be called poor because it's demeaning. Instead of avoiding the language of "poor" and "poverty," we must challenge the idea that being poor is to be less than human. An economy that creates poverty is what denigrates human dignity. By focusing on the basic needs that are systematically denied--health care, education, debt, child care, due process, housing, voting rights, freedom from mass incarceration and police violence--and reframing those basic needs as unfulfilled rights, we broaden the conversation about who is poor and what it means to be poor. Beyond a narrow and isolating definition, we can insist that anyone who does not securely have access to those rights is poor.

This book is written out of a commitment to the abolition of poverty, racism, and state violence[44] and a belief in the agency and intelligence of the poor and dispossessed as the social force capable of leading a moral revolution to realize that possibility. This commitment leads to a scholarly interest in the role of theology, ethics, and religious leadership in the history of social change.[45]

I bring to this research two decades of congregational, student, and community organizing. I was a cofounder of Kairos: The Center for Religions, Rights and Social Justice at Union Theological Seminary and its predecessor, the Poverty Initiative. Kairos is committed to education as essential to the development of movement leaders, and that knowing history, economics, and the Bible is particularly important for discerning our best chance of success today. The 1968 Poor People's Campaign is a period that offers many lessons for this task. This study of the last years of King grew in response to a network of grassroots organizations and religious communities wanting to know more about this history and what King meant by a "moral revolution of values." It coincided with the fiftieth anniversary of the original campaign, when the Kairos Center's Rev. Dr. Liz Theoharis joined with Rev. Dr. William J. Barber II to launch A Poor People's Campaign: A National Call for Moral Revival (PPC:NCMR). Drawing from the triple evils King identified—racism, poverty, and war—the PPC:NCMR added environmental devastation and distorted moral narratives as interrelated crises that must be confronted together, rather than as isolated issues. Launched with forty days of action in thirty five states and Washington D.C. exactly fifty years after Resurrection City occupied the National Mall, the PPC:NCMR was an expansive and sustained wave of nonviolent civil disobedience not seen in a generation. It laid groundwork for state-based leadership in building power for poor people across lines race, age, gender, ability, religion, and geography for years to come.

The first two chapters of this book spend time with the planning period before King was assassinated. Chapter 1 explores King's strategic vision for the Poor People's Campaign. How was it possible, given the almost unimaginable victories of the landmark legislation of the early and mid-1960s, that at the end of the decade the economic plight of most Black people worsened by several measures, with a widening racial wage gap, deteriorating urban slums, pervasive rural unemployment, and persistently segregated schools?[46] King argued that greater structural change was needed than they had initially endeavored to undertake, and so a movement for human rights must develop a strategy capable of tackling the roots rather than the branches of oppression. King believed a Poor People's Campaign was the first step in the new era.

Picking up with King's efforts to organize the Poor People's Campaign, chapter 2 examines organizations and organized communities King approached to collaborate on a campaign for jobs and income. Groups like the National Welfare Rights Organization and American Friends Service Committee were responding to similar conditions and social questions. They were critical to pulling off the Poor People's Campaign after King's assassination. The chapter ends with King's assassination.

Chapter 3 traces what transpired when thousands of poor people caravanned to the National Mall and lived in Resurrection City for six weeks. The story is both powerful and heartbreaking. It demonstrates genius and tenacity among those who organized it. But it also reveals how the campaign fell far short of the vision for it. Chapter 4 examines elements that contributed to the campaign's legacy as a failure, including internal factors like strategic differences among campaign leadership and external factors like rain and FBI infiltration. But it also sees the real gains of the campaign and its lessons for today.

Turning to King's theological ethics, chapters 5, 6, and 7 look to the theological ideas behind a campaign of the poor, and in particular seek to understand why King called it a "freedom church of the poor." Chapter 5 finds echoes of theological, biblical, and ethical ideas in the life of Resurrection City after King's assassination. It also traces the history of the first freedom church traditions from the abolition of slavery and history of the Black church. Chapters 6 and 7 move through concepts at the heart of King's theological ethics—human dignity, kingdom of God, love, power, and justice—looking to understand them in new ways in relationship to the work of the Poor People's Campaign. These chapters point to how Kings' theological ideas are inseparable from King's organizing strategies and vice versa.

Chapter 8 puts the history and theological ethics of the Poor People's Campaign in conversation with those who claim its legacy as they are calling forward similar revolutions of values today: Womanist ethicist Keri Day, the rural, poor congregation of Chaplains in the Harbor in western Washington State, and the Poor People's Campaign: A National Call for Moral Revival taking hold in states across the country. The chapter discerns the lessons they draw from that history and seeks to understand how the crises their communities face led them to that history. How are today's religious and community leaders taking up King's ideas as they fight for our lives and world? And how does King's vision call us even further?

NOTES

1. Doug Youngblood, "Letter from Youngblood," in *The Movement: 1964-1970*, ed. Clayborne Carson and Martin Luther King, Jr. Papers Project (Westport, CT: Greenwood Press, 1993), 434. Parentheses in original.
2. Gordon Mantler, *Power to the Poor: Black-Brown Coalition and the Fight for Economic Justice, 1960-1974* (Chapel Hill: University of North Carolina Press, 2013), 141.
3. Martin Luther King Jr., "Address at Mass Meeting" (Eutaw, AL, March 20, 1968), 3, King Speeches, Series 3, Box 13, King Center Archives.
4. Martin Luther King Jr., "State of the Movement" (Frogmore, SC, November 28, 1967), 9, King Speeches, Series 3, Box 13, King Center Archives.
5. King, "State of the Movement," 9. See also Jose Yglesias, "Dr. King's March on Washington, Part II," in *Black Protest in the Sixties*, ed. August Meier, John H. Bracey, and Elliott Rudwick (New York: M. Wiener Pub., 1991), 279–80.
6. Martin Luther King Jr., *The Trumpet of Conscience* (New York: Harper & Row, 1968), 60.
7. King, *Trumpet of Conscience*, 59–60.
8. Martin Luther King Jr., "Honoring Dr. DuBois," *Freedomways* 8, no. 2 (Spring 1968): 109.
9. King, *Trumpet of Conscience*, 60.
10. A distinction is made between campaigns and movements. Campaigns are concrete organizing efforts. You can build a campaign. Movements are not directly built or organized. They are composed of forms of collective action that alert, educate and mobilize to move large segments of society in response to conditions. Their sum is greater than their parts. Campaigns and leadership development are projects that contribute to social movements.
11. This short biographical introduction moves quickly toward the book's focus, the last years of King's life, hoping readers will turn to the many excellent biographies of King as well as his own extensive writing, preaching, and speaking. See in particular the following, Vincent Harding, *Martin Luther King, the Inconvenient Hero* (Orbis Books, 2008); Taylor Branch, *Parting the Waters: America in the King Years 1954-63* (Simon & Schuster, 1989); David J. Garrow, *Bearing the Cross: Martin Luther King, Jr., and the Southern Christian Leadership Conference* (Quill, 1999); Gary Dorrien,

Breaking White Supremacy: Martin Luther King Jr. and the Black Social Gospel (Yale University Press, 2017); James H. Cone, *Martin & Malcom & America: A Dream or a Nightmare* (Orbis Books, 1992). For King's works, see Martin Luther King Jr., *The Radical King*, ed. Cornel West (Beacon Press, 2015); Martin Luther King Jr., *A Testament of Hope: The Essential Writings and Speeches of Martin Luther King, Jr.*, ed. James M. Washington (HarperOne, 1991)., and *The Papers of Martin Luther King Jr.*, edited by Clayborne Carson, et al. at the King Research and Education Institute at Stanford University.

12. For more on the development of King's thought and organizing model, see Dorrien, *Breaking White Supremacy*; Rufus Burrow, *Extremist for Love: Martin Luther King Jr., Man of Ideas and Nonviolent Social Action* (Fortress Press, 2014); James H. Cone, *The Cross and the Lynching Tree* (Orbis Books, 2011).

13. James H. Cone, "Systematic Theology 393: Malcolm and Martin" (Lecture, Union Theological Seminary, New York, NY, March 28, 2006).

14. James H. Cone, "The Theology of Martin Luther King, Jr," *Union Seminary Quarterly Review* 40, no. 4 (1986): 21.

15. Larry L. Rasmussen, "Life Worthy of Life: The Social Ecologies of Bonhoeffer and King," in *Bonhoeffer and King: Their Legacies and Import for Christian Social Thought*, ed. Willis Jenkins and Jennifer M. McBride (Minneapolis: Fortress Press, 2010), 58.

16. Martin Luther King Jr., "Speech at Staff Retreat" (Frogmore, SC, May 1967), King Speeches, Series 3, Box 13, King Center Archives.

17. For a concise collection of King's thought on questions of internationalism, see Cornel West's edited volume, *The Radical King* (Beacon Press, 2015), especially the section, "Prophetic Vision: Global Analysis and Local Action."

18. Garrow, *Bearing the Cross*, 26–29.

19. Martin Luther King Jr., "The Three Evils of Society" (National Conference for New Politics, Chicago, IL, August 31, 1967), 7, King Speeches, Series 3, Box 13, King Center Archives.

20. Martin Luther King Jr., "A Time to Break Silence," in *A Testament of Hope: The Essential Writings and Speeches of Martin Luther King, Jr.*, ed. James M. Washington (San Francisco: HarperOne, 1991), 231–44.

21. Martin Luther King Jr., *Where Do We Go from Here: Chaos or Community?* (Boston: Beacon Press, 2010), 196.

22. Yglesias, "Dr. King's March on Washington, Part II," 280–82.

23. Martin Luther King Jr., "The Other America," in *The Radical King*, ed. Cornel West (Boston: Beacon Press, 2015), 235–36.

24. King, *Where Do We Go from Here: Chaos or Community?*, 95.

25. Martin Luther King Jr., "All Labor Has Dignity," in West, *The Radical King*, 173.

26. King, "A Time to Break Silence," 242.

27. This mapping of the ideas about poverty in the United States is drawn from William Goldsmith and Edward Blakely, *Separate Societies: Poverty and Inequality in U.S. Cities*, 2nd Edition (Philadelphia: Temple University Press, 2010) adapted by Chris Caruso.

28. The US Census calculated that in 2018 there were 41.4 million people living in families with incomes below the federal poverty threshold. That was 12.8% of the population, the lowest rate since 2008. But the federal poverty threshold is woefully inadequate. An individual with income of $12,491 and a family of four with income of $25,751 are considered to be above the poverty thresholds. Even families who make it on so little are left with little room for accidents and life changes. A better picture of poverty comes from looking at the number of families living at under twice the federal poverty threshold. That includes a further 28.6% of US families, often called low-income. Taken together the share of poor and low-income US families reaches 41.5%. For children these rates are higher, with 45.7% below twice the poverty threshold, 8. These rates use the Census' Supplemental Poverty Measure. The formula used to calculate this threshold was developed in 1965 by the Social Security Administration and multiplied the cost of adequate food by three, using an 1855 US Department of Agriculture study that found families spent 1/3 of their income on food. The poverty threshold has been adjusted for inflation, but has not been adapted to changes in the cost of living. Food takes up a significantly smaller portion of spending while other expenses--like health care, housing, and education--have increased dramatically, making the official federal measure a rather arbitrary number. Most developed nations use a ratio to median income to define poverty, with the poor being those who make below 50 or 60% of the median income after taxes and social benefits. Using this calculation would raise the US poverty rate significantly. "Annual Update of the HHS Poverty Guidelines" (Department of Health and Human Services, January 18, 2018), https://www.federalregister.gov/documents/2018/01/18/2018-00814/annual-update-of-the-hhs-poverty-guidelines.

29. Hope Yen, "4 in 5 in USA Face Near-Poverty, No Work," *USA Today*, September 17, 2013, http://www.usatoday.com/story/money/business/2013/07/28/americans-poverty-no-work/2594203/.

30. Mark R. Rank and Thomas A. Hirschl, "Estimating the Risk of Food Stamp Use and Impoverishment During Childhood," *Archives of Pediatrics & Adolescent Medicine* 163, no. 11 (November 2, 2009): 994–99, https://doi.org/10.1001/archpediatrics.2009.178.

31. Neal Gabler, "The Secret Shame of Middle-Class Americans," *The Atlantic*, May 2016, http://www.theatlantic.com/magazine/archive/2016/05/my-secret-shame/476415/.

32. Poverty is compounded by race, ethnicity, gender, citizenship status, and sexual and gender identity. Using the supplemental poverty measure and including those who live within twice the official poverty threshold, the number of poor and low income people include six in ten Black and Hispanic families (58.3% and 63.2%), four in ten Asian families (40.7%) and more than 1 in 3 white non-Hispanic families (36.2%). Because non-Hispanic whites make up 62.8% of the overall population, about half of poor and low income people are white (75 million people). Women and children are disproportionately affected, with over half of children below the federal threshold living in families headed by women. (Liana Fox, "The Supplemental Poverty Measure: 2018" [The United States Census Bureau, October 2019], 26; "2017 American Community Survey 1-Year Estimates" [The United States

Census Bureau, 2017], https://factfinder.census.gov/faces/tableservices/jsf/pages/productview.xhtml?src=bkmk.) The criminalization of poverty similarly encourages the idea that the poor are different from the whole and that poor life choices cause poverty. In the fifty years after the Poor People's Campaign the incarceration population went from less than 200,000 to 1,489,400. (Jennifer Bronson and Ann Carson, "Prisoners in 2017" [Bureau of Justice Statistics, April 2019], https://www.bjs.gov/index.cfm?ty=pbdetail&iid=6546). This escalation was particularly steep in the 1980s, not because of higher crime rates, but new laws and policies. As a percentage of the overall population, Black males are incarcerated at a rate six times that of white males. (Michelle Alexander, *The New Jim Crow: Mass Incarceration in the Age of Colorblindness* [New York: New Press, 2012], 54–58.) The pre-incarceration median income of incarcerated people was $19,650 for men and $13,890 for women. (Bernadette Rabuy and Daniel Kopf, "Prisons of Poverty: Uncovering the Pre-Incarceration Incomes of the Imprisoned" (Prison Policy Initiative), July 9, 2015, https://www.prisonpolicy.org/reports/income.html.)

33. "A Strong Minimum Wage Can Help Working Families, Businesses and Our Economy Recover" (New York: National Employment Law Project, January 2011).

34. Josh Bivens and Lawrence Mishel, "Understanding the Historic Divergence Between Productivity and a Typical Worker's Pay," *Economic Policy Institute* (blog), September 2, 2015, http://www.epi.org/publication/understanding-the-historic-divergence-between-productivity-and-a-typical-workers-pay-why-it-matters-and-why-its-real/. Between 1973 and 2014, inflation-adjusted hourly compensation of the median worker rose 8.7 percent. During that same period, net productivity grew 72.2 percent.

35. If the 1968 minimum had kept pace with overall income growth, it would have been $21.16 by 2012. Salvatore Babones, "The Minimum Wage Is Stuck at $7.25; It Should Be $21.16," Institute for Policy Studies, July 24, 2012, http://inequality.org/minimum-wage/. As jobs slowly returned after the 2008 recession they were disproportionately lower waged, paying $13 or less, even though a majority of jobs lost between 2008 and 2010 paid wages between $14 and $30 per hour. National Employment Law Project, "The Low-Wage Recovery: Industry Employment and Wages Four Years into the Recovery." 2014. https://www.nelp.org/wp-content/uploads/2015/03/Low-Wage-Recovery-Industry-Employment-Wages-2014-Report.pdf.

36. Technology-related deindustrialization impacted global and domestic labor. Of the 5.6 million US manufacturing jobs lost between 2000 and 2010, 85% was attributable to technological change rather than factories moving overseas. This trend is poised for a rapid increase. In the United States, human welders make an average of $25 per hour, while over its life a robotic welder costs just $8 per hour. Federica Cocco, "Most US Manufacturing Jobs Lost to Technology, Not Trade," *Financial Times*, December 2, 2016, https://www.ft.com/content/dec677c0-b7e6-11e6-ba85-95d1533d9a62.

37. "Arrested Development," *The Economist*, October 4, 2014, http://www.economist.com/news/special-report/21621158-model-development-through-industrialisation-its-way-out-arrested-development. Ben Bland, "China's Robot Revolution," *Financial Times*, June 6, 2016, https://www.ft.com/content/1dbd8c60-0cc6-11e6-ad80-67655613c2d6.

38. "Wealth Inequality in America: Key Facts & Figures," Federal Reserve Bank of St. Louis, August 14, 2019, https://www.stlouisfed.org/open-vault/2019/august/wealth-inequality-in-america-facts-figures.; Chuck Collins and Josh Hoxie, "Billionaire Bonanza" (Institute for Policy Studies, November 2017), 9. This disparity remains when broken down by race and ethnicity, although dividing a much smaller pool. The wealthiest 1 percent of Black households own 46 percent of all Black-owned wealth, and the wealthiest 1 percent of Latino households own 49% of all wealth owned by Latinos.

39. The net worth of US households and nonprofit organizations was $111.4 trillion in the first quarter of 2019. "Households and Nonprofit Organizations; Net Worth" (Federal Reserve Bank of St. Louis), January 19, 2020, https://fred.stlouisfed.org/graph/?graph_id=369801.

40. "Wealth Inequality in America." Janet Yellen, "Perspectives on Inequality and Opportunity from the Survey of Consumer Finances," Board of Governors of the Federal Reserve System, October 17, 2014, https://www.federalreserve.gov/newsevents/speech/yellen20141017a.htm.

41. Saurav Sarkar and Shailly Gupta Barnes, "The Souls of Poor Folks: Auditing America 50 Years After the Poor People's Campaign Challenged Racism, Poverty, the War Economy/Militarism and Our National Morality" (Washington, D.C.: Institute for Policy Studies, April 2018), 10. And because for many poor families primary residences rather than financial assets are their only form of wealth, they are particularly vulnerable to housing market drops and foreclosure crises. The median nonhome wealth of Black families in 2007 was just $500. Edward Wolff, "Recent Trends in Household Wealth in the United States: Rising Debt and the Middle-Class Squeeze-an Update to 2007" (Annandale-on-Hudson, NY: Levy Economics Institute of Bard College, March 2010), http://www.levyinstitute.org/pubs/wp_589.pdf.

42. Max Lawson and et al., "Public Good or Private Wealth" (Oxfam International, January 2019), https://indepth.oxfam.org.uk/public-good-private-wealth/; Dylan Matthews, "Are 26 Billionaires Worth More than Half the Planet? The Debate, Explained.," *Vox*, January 22, 2019, https://www.vox.com/future-perfect/2019/1/22/18192774/oxfam-inequality-report-2019-davos-wealth; Luisa Kroll, "Forbes Billionaires 2018," *Forbes*, March 6, 2018, https://www.forbes.com/sites/luisakroll/2018/03/06/forbes-billionaires-2018-meet-the-richest-people-on-the-planet/#bd719c06523d. The United Nations uses an international poverty line of US$1.90, calculating that 736 million people live below it. This gives a sense of the scope of extreme global poverty, but as a poverty threshold it falls short of the standards set by the Universal Declaration of Human Rights. It fails to adequately measure global poverty. Furthermore it can be used to argue that poverty is nearly nonexistent within the United States. By establishing the poorest sectors of the global poor as the only true poor, the poor who have more than US$1.90 per day are told they are only "relatively" poor. "Ending Poverty," The United Nations, December 3, 2018, https://www.un.org/en/sections/issues-depth/poverty/. Mark Harrison and Nikolaus Wolf, "The Frequency of Wars," *Economic History Review* `65, no. 3 (July 22, 2011): 1055–76. "Figures at a Glance," United Nations High Commissioner for Refugees, January 19, 2020, https://www.unhcr.org/figures-at-a-glance.html.

43. Martin Luther King Jr., "SCLC Staff Retreat Speech" (Frogmore, SC, November 14, 1966), 20–21, King Speeches, Series 3, Box 13, King Center Archives.

44. The term state violence is inclusive of global and domestic militarism, war, overt and covert police violence, and mass incarceration.

45. Religious leadership is inclusive of ordained clergy, scholars of religious and theological thought, and movement leaders who proceed from their faith and nurture other leaders out of that faith.

46. Vincent Harding, "Introduction," in *Where Do We Go from Here: Chaos or Community?*, by Martin Luther King, Jr. (Boston: Beacon Press, 2010), xii.

Chapter 1

King's Vision for a Campaign of the Poor

When King spoke to the SCLC convention in August 1967, it would be his last address to that assembly. He called the speech, "Where Do We Go from Here?," and he concluded with an answer full of provocative questions.

> "Why are there forty million poor people in America?" And when you begin to ask that question, you are raising a question about the economic system, about a broader distribution of wealth. When you ask that question, you begin to question the capitalistic economy. And I'm simply saying that more and more, we've got to begin to ask questions about the whole society. We are called upon to help the discouraged beggars in life's marketplace. But one day we must come to see that an edifice which produces beggars needs restructuring. It means that questions must be raised. And you see, my friends, when you deal with this you begin to ask the question, "Who owns the oil?" You begin to ask the question, "Who owns the iron ore?" You begin to ask the question, "Why is it that people have to pay water bills in a world that's two-thirds water?"

The persistence of poverty in the midst of plenty had political and theological implications for the direction of the movement. The call to meet the needs of the poor is a call that directs us to discern the source of poverty and change it.

Our own edifice that produces both billionaires and beggars needs restructuring. And so we now ask, why are there 140 million poor people in America? Why are there more empty homes than there are homeless people? Why are Black people incarcerated at a rate five times higher than white people? Why globally do eight people control more wealth than 3.6 billion people?[1] We must echo King's challenge to the inequities of his era, and hear his reply: "As we talk about 'Where do we go from here?'. . .we must honestly face the fact that the movement must address itself to the question of restructuring the whole of American society."[2]

1

As King answered these questions, he insisted that the work ahead was in the realm of human rights. He culled lessons from the past period and argued they needed to shift from mobilizing to sustained organizing. He had some initial plans for how a campaign calling for the right to a job or income could galvanize an even broader "revolution of values." And he had a new idea about who was best positioned to be the leading force of that movement: the dispossessed across racial and ethnic lines, including poor whites who made up the majority of those living in poverty. In the last year of his life King was working tirelessly to organize a Poor People's Campaign to bring thousands of poor people from across the United States to occupy the capital and demand a response to the plight of the poor that would put the nation on a new course socially, economically, and politically. This chapter considers King's strategic vision for how poor people could save the nation.

THE TRIPLE EVILS

King still would have been remembered as a great hero of American history if he had stopped after Montgomery, Selma, and the civil rights bills, Nobel Prize in hand. And yet he was dissatisfied and compelled forward. He took the SCLC to Chicago to attempt to apply their tactics to the entrenched poverty and racism of northern cities. Their campaigns around slum housing met demoralizing defeats, not at the hands of Southern segregationists but Northern Democrats like Mayor Richard J. Daley and his political machine. Against these foes there was no recourse to the Democratic administration of President Lyndon Johnson. The SCLC's ministerial leadership and tactics mobilized smaller numbers of people in the North, and the white backlash to their marches and actions rivaled the brutal abuse of the segregated South. For a growing number of young Black leaders, the Black Power criticism that nonviolence and redemptive suffering were insufficient tactics in a society founded on white supremacy rang true.[3]

King assessed that the urban uprisings in the late 1960s were in response to the painful realization that "the goal of freedom was still distant. . . . All the legislation was designed to remedy Southern conditions, and even these were only partially improved." He told the SCLC staff, "The decade of 1955 to 1965, with its constructive elements, misled us." The uprisings were an expression of a "natural development to a new stage of struggle . . . born of the greater crimes of the white society."[4] He pointed out that the violence of the urban uprisings was directed at property, not persons, and as such was a critique of the distorted values of a racist and materialistic society.

I am aware that there are many who wince at a distinction between property and persons—who hold both sacrosanct. My views are not so rigid. A life is sacred. Property is intended to serve life, and no matter how much we surround it with rights and respect, it has no personal being. . . . The focus on property in the 1967 riots is not accidental. It has a message; it is saying something.[5]

But despite being a message, he argued the uprisings were not a form of protest that would in themselves lead to social change. The expression of anger in spontaneous unrest did not build real power, and could even play into the hands of a right-wing backlash. King struggled to fully comprehend the politicizing and educational role of uprisings as an organizing opportunity in the "new stage of struggle."[6]

King's integrationist nonviolence was a polemical target in the development of Black Power strategy and tactics, but King agreed with much of the criticism of the limits of the organizing strategies of the previous decade.[7] He remained fully committed to nonviolence, but he affirmed that, "Black Power, in its broad and positive meaning, is a call to black people to amass the political and economic strength to achieve their legitimate goals. . . . Power, properly understood, is the ability to achieve purpose. It is the strength required to bring about social, political or economic changes."[8] King's assessment of the strategy of Black Power was that it that did not fully believe change on the scale needed was possible. "Revolution, though born of despair, cannot long be sustained by despair." Despite the language of revolution, if there is not a strategy and tactics for success, it leads to nihilism and disappointment.[9] He was convinced that strategically, "There is no salvation . . . through isolation." He acknowledged that mutual economic support within the Black community was valuable. But he insisted that the depth of Black economic crisis could not be solved on the local level. The "ultimate answer" would require change on a national scale. Even in areas where a Black majority would be possible, they would be limited to changing factors under the control of those isolated areas, leaving few options in an economy with tremendous inequality. And there was no guarantee that Black elected officials could or would make just decisions without deeper systemic change.[10]

King anticipated that the isolation of Black demands, when combined with the threat of violence and urban unrest, would lend support to right-wing leaders as they orchestrated a backlash against the gains of civil rights. And it would further divide the poor across racial lines at the very moment when their unity was needed to build the power necessary to implement larger change. In an interview about why he had taken up the Poor People's Campaign, King said, "Many more riots of the kind we had last summer . . . and we shall be in danger of a right-wing takeover of the fascist type!"[11]

On April 4, 1967, exactly one year before his assassination, King addressed the nation from Riverside Church in New York City. His speech broke his silence around his long-held beliefs about the Vietnam War being immoral and unwarranted.[12] Because the Johnson administration had been instrumental in securing civil rights' legislative victories and had launched the War on Poverty programs, King had remained mostly quiet about his opposition. His decision was not an easy one. Pressure to remain silent came not only from the Johnson administration but also from established civil rights leaders and their liberal allies. In unison they insisted that to take a stance on the war would be detrimental to the cause of civil rights.[13] King confidant Harry Belafonte recalled King's distress when the *New York Times* and *Washington Post* denounced his Riverside speech.[14] Both journals had been important partners in the battle for civil rights, but "so distorted was their critique of him, (King) felt that there was now serious doubt that the responsible platform that (King) thought would be available for open debate and objective examination was now seriously crippled." Yet "the only rage he expressed was at his own naiveté in not clearly understanding that his adversaries would emerge from even the most respected of sources."[15]

For King it was not that he was willing to trade progress on civil rights for a moral stance on the war. It was that he believed racism, militarism, and poverty were knotted together. To pretend that they could address one but not the other was a delusion, perhaps intentionally stoked to secure war support among those who stood to gain little from the war itself. King called the war a, "cruel manipulation of the poor," and when he said poor he meant those in the United States and in Vietnam. There was a "cruel irony" in "watching [Black] and white boys . . . in brutal solidarity burning the huts of a poor village," when they would not be seated together in school or guaranteed the liberties they were purportedly exporting to Vietnam. The poor were disproportionately represented among the military. Their lives were risked, "on the side of the wealthy and the secure while we create a hell for the poor."[16] King later identified US actions in Vietnam as "war crimes."[17]

Not only were poor soldiers endangered by war, but also the poor at home. As with the antagonistic relationship between the war and the gains of civil rights, it was not simply that the war budget deprioritized and defunded Johnson's antipoverty programs (although that was a problem too). The war itself was tied to poverty. War and economic exploitation shared an objectification of human beings and violation of human personhood. King connected that, "If you will treat human beings as a means to an end, you thingify those human beings. And if you will thingify persons, you will exploit them economically. And if you will exploit persons economically, you will abuse your military power to protect your economic investments and your economic exploitations."[18] The spoils of economic exploitation and war required each other to maintain themselves. King pointed to the ability of the poor to rec-ognize this contradiction when, eight months later, he publicly announced the Poor People's Campaign. "Poor people who are treated with derision and abuse by an economic system soon conclude with elementary logic that they have no rational interest in killing people 12,000 miles away in the name of defending that system."[19]

For King the existence of poverty was a critique of the concentration of wealth at the expense of the poor. He interchangeably used the words "poverty," "materialism," and "economic exploitation," as all three terms described the dimensions of his structural economic critique.[20] Just months before his assassination he spoke publicly in terms critical not only of the excesses of capitalism, but of its normal functioning. He drew a line of conti-nuity between the capitalism of the slave economy and the globalizing capi-talism of his own time. "Again we have deluded ourselves into believing the myth that Capitalism grew and prospered out of the protestant ethic of hard work and sacrifice, the fact is that Capitalism was built on the exploitation and suffering of black slaves and continues to thrive on the exploitation of the poor–both black and white, both here and abroad."[21]

King welcomed President Johnson's War on Poverty in 1964. This set of federal programs included Medicare and Medicaid, Head Start, Food Stamps, and various projects under the new Office of Economic Opportunity (OEO). Many of these programs made significant and lasting contributions to reduc-ing poverty, especially in the areas of education, nutrition, and health care. But after an initial drop in the poverty rate from 23 percent to 11 percent, the decades that followed saw increasing numbers of people in poverty and a stagnating or even expanding poverty rate. This is in addition to the increasing insufficiency of that rate in capturing the full extent of poverty and insecurity.[22]

In the midst of the midcentury economic growth, poverty was seen as a problem of exclusion from full participation in the market economy, through racial discrimination, geographic isolation, insufficient education, displace-ment by industry shifts, or by being cultural misfits for employment. The solution therefore was to bring the poor into that system, or at least give them the opportunity to join the system, to share the prosperity through waged employment and higher-skilled jobs. King argued economic opportunity was not the same as the right to employment, decent wages, or a minimum income. King pointed out that many of the poor did work and yet remained poor. At the time of the Poor People's Campaign, the US unemployment rate was 3.3 percent. This was up from the record low 2.5 percent in 1953, but still far below the US average of 5.81 percent.[23] And yet there were 35 million poor people in the United States. The newly created federal poverty threshold used food prices to estimate a minimum family budget, approximately $3,000 for a family of four or $1,500 for an individual. SCLC analysis used a broader definition of poverty than the government criteria. A Poor People's Campaign fact sheet said those who fall below $9,000 for a family of four or $4,000 for an individual, "you are not the poorest but you are poor." Their estimates put 30 million people in that range. In this expanded measure three out of ten people in the United States were poor, despite the low unemployment rate.

The fact sheet talked about poverty not as insufficiencies among the poor or exclusions from the economy but as the result of being "crushed down by economic forces."[24] King argued the fundamental problem was not with the poor but with the concentration of wealth through the exploitation of the poor.

> If [Black people] and poor whites do not participate in the free flow of wealth within our economy, they will forever be poor, giving their energies, their talents and their limited funds to the consumer market but reaping few benefits and services in return. The way to end poverty is to end the exploitation of the poor, ensure them a fair share of the government services and the nation's resources.[25]

Capitalism was designed to extract profit from labor, and because most people depend on wages for the means of survival, they are forced to enter into those relationships with little power to determine the terms. The hard-won gains of the labor movement included the forty-hour workweek, minimum wages, bans on child labor, and collective bargaining rights. But agricultural labor and domestic labor were excluded from many of those protections, and although in total numbers this impacted more white workers, it disproportionately impacted southern Black workers. The failure to secure those rights for all workers contributed to the isolation and weakened position of unions over time.

King perceived that the compromise extended to white industrial labor would be offered to certain sectors of Black leadership and Northern Black laborers. Lower-middle and middle incomes that were enough to pay for a house, car, and children's college tuition, would create a stable middle echelon with enough to lose that they wouldn't agitate for more fundamental change. But King insisted that middle-income Black families were tied to the success of poor Black families.[26] King adviser and later King scholar Vincent Harding reflected that the movement was offered and accepted the interpretation that the problem of poverty was one of exclusion and missed opportunity, not normal operation. In the period that followed King's death, "black folks have decided (consciously or not) to fight racism by seeking 'equal opportunity' or a 'fair share' in the nation's militarism and its materialism. In other words, we have chosen to struggle against one of the 'triple threats' by joining the other two, a destructive choice."[27] King saw the Poor People's Campaign as a response to the interrelatedness of the three oppressions that circumvented some of the maneuverings of elites to play the oppressions against each other. In an interview published posthumously King had said,

> The black revolution is much more than a struggle for the rights of [Black people]. It is forcing America to face all its interrelated flaws—racism, poverty, militarism, and materialism. It is exposing evils that are rooted deeply in the whole structure of our society. It reveals systemic rather than superficial flaws and suggest that radical reconstruction of society itself is the real issue to be faced.[28]

The Civil Rights Movement had exposed the depth of the dysfunction of the US social, economic, and political systems. But the Civil Rights Movement was being isolated and maneuvered away from the structural critique it was revealing.

REFORM TO REVOLUTION

After the Civil Rights Movement's big legislative accomplishments of the mid 1960s, King believed that the greatest battles were ahead of them rather than behind them. The issues they faced would require new strategies, tactics, and leadership. In 1967 King wrote about the limitations of the strategies and forms of organizing of the previous decade. He said the work of that period had taken on "the task of ending conditions that had long outlived their purpose." Because the segregation of public facilities was "overdue for change," legislative victories were obtained and widely applied "where the spotlight illuminated the evil." As a result they "made easy gains" and "built the kind of organizations that expect easy victories, and rest upon them." King acknowledged that it was "curious to speak of easy victories when some have suffered and sacrificed so much." But his assessment was that they had not been compelled by necessity to build "permanent, seasoned and militant organizations" that would build the power necessary for the oppressed to use those laws to transform the material reality.[29]

If they turned to the intertwined evils of poverty, militarism, and racism that were not limited to the legalized forms of Southern segregation, they would be talking social and economic structures that had not yet outlived their purpose and would not be resolved by exposure. The wins of Southern integration and voting rights "didn't cost the nation one penny" and "helped businessmen out." He observed, "We are now making demands that will cost the nation something." Slums could not be ended without taking profit out of slums. Better schools needed the taxes to pay for them. They would be "on dangerous ground" that would interfere with the interests of the "captains of industry."[30] As he continued to develop and share this assessment he wrote,

> We have left the realm of constitutional rights and we are entering the area of human rights. The constitution assured the right to vote, but there is no such assurance of the right to adequate housing, or the right to an adequate income. And yet, in a nation which has a gross national product of 750 billion dollars a year, it is morally right to insist that every person have a decent house, an adequate education and enough money to provide basic necessities for one's family. Achievement of these goals will be a lot more difficult and require much more discipline, understanding, organization and sacrifice.[31]

King had learned from his public opposition to the Vietnam War that this was dangerous ground. Demands that cost businessmen something instead of helping them out would require "candor and self-criticism" about the alignment of forces that had supported their past victories. Many past allies would oppose the work ahead. He knew that "achievement of these goals will be a lot more difficult and require much more discipline, understanding, organization and sacrifice." This candid assessment led King to believe that the next movement required new forms of organization that could make possible the "tortuous job of organizing solidly and simultaneously in thousands of places."[32]

So significant was this shift in strategy and tactics in King's understanding that he said that "with Selma and the voting rights bill one era of our struggle came to a close and a new era came into being."[33] He described it as a movement "from the era of civil rights to the era of human rights"[34] and as a transition from reform to revolution.

> Now, when we see that there must be a radical redistribution of economic and political power, then we see that for the last twelve years we have been in a reform movement. We were seeking to reform certain conditions in the house of our nation because the nation wasn't living up to the very rules of the house that it has prescribed in the Constitution. Then after Selma and the Voting Rights Bill, we moved into a new era, which must be an era of revolution. I think we must see the great distinction between a reform movement and a revolutionary movement.[35]

The Poor People's Campaign was not a prioritizing of one evil over another but a strategy for attacking all three. "We must see now that the evils of racism, economic exploitation and militarism are all tied together. And you really can't get rid of one without getting rid of the others. . . . The whole structure of American life must be changed."[36]

KING'S VISION FOR A CAMPAIGN OF THE POOR

The proposal to bring the poor to Washington came from Senator Robert Kennedy by way of Marian Wright. They had both been shocked and moved by personally witnessing the depth and expansiveness of poverty. Wright was a young lawyer working with the NAACP Legal Defense Fund. The role brought her to Mississippi and into close contact with the extreme poverty of southern black families. In 1967 she invited US senators on a tour of the Delta in an attempt to "capture the imagination and attention of the American public" around the fact that, "even though we had the right to vote" conditions were "getting worse in many ways." Wright succeeded in getting Kennedy to come down "to examine the impact of the poverty program on Mississippi blacks and whites," and he was deeply moved. He suggested to Wright, "Tell (Dr. King) to bring the poor people to Washington." She stopped by the SCLC office with the message and later recollected, "King instinctively felt that that was right and treated me as if I was an emissary of grace here, or something that brought him some light. Out of that, the Poor People's Campaign was born."[37]

King convened his staff in the fall of 1967 to develop a plan around the idea. According to many sources there was very little support from the SCLC staff. William Rutherford, a public relations businessman who had been brought in as the SCLC executive director in 1967, recollected that "almost no one on the staff thought that the next priority, the next major movement, should be focused on poor people or the question of poverty in America." Andrew Young, then executive vice president, said he had felt they did not have the financial resources for the endeavor. He also remembered that "James Bevel wanted to keep us in northern cities in a movement to end slums. Hosea Williams felt as though we should stay in the South and do voter registration. Jesse Jackson was beginning to develop Operation Breadbasket." SCLC board member Marian Logan said she expressed great apprehensions to King: "This bringing of poor people to the seat of government was like throwing it in their faces, and I didn't think too many of the officialdom of Washington was gonna take that with any great grace."[38] But King persisted. His compelling persuasion, combined with a hierarchical leadership structure within the organization, meant that the proposal went forward despite the dissenting opinions and lack of consensus.

In the original plan from Wright and Kennedy, the tactic was that if the decision makers in Washington and, through the national media, the whole nation, could witness the plight of poverty in a dramatic way, they would be moved to fully fund antipoverty programs. This thinking built upon the successes of the Civil Rights Movement in using media to garner sympathy and support outside of the South. The hope was that a dramatic reemphasis of the reality of poverty could secure funding for those programs and the expansion of their provisions.[39] On Dec 4, 1967 the SCLC formally announced plans for the campaign to the press. King spoke in similar terms. They would dramatize the plight of the poor before those who hold "the power to initiate this reform."[40] He similarly said in the Massey lectures that the Poor People's Campaign would show the nation "a sight that will make it stop in its busy tracks and think hard about what it has done."[41] And he mobilized a crowd in Albany, Georgia saying, "We're going to let the whole world know how America is treating its poor citizens"[42]

But King most often used a different language in describing the form and purpose. He was critical of the idea that the scale of change needed could be brought about by illuminating the problem and waiting for those in power to make their decisions differently. He said the dispossessed poor of all races must organize a revolution, and that there were millions of them who could do it. He said the task of that moment was to help them take action together. Only that unsettling force would be powerful enough to change the structures to end poverty. A campaign of the poor was intended to move in that direction and begin helping the poor take action together to claim their revolutionary role.[43]

They were not going to D.C. to secure fuller funding for the Johnson administration's "economic opportunity" projects or new programs that similarly sought to better prepare the poor for the existing economy. In the first announcement of the Poor People's Campaign, King said that the campaign targeted Washington D.C. because for too long the federal government had helped steer the economy to profit the rich and away from the needs of the poor, including through "low minimum wages" and "a degrading system of inadequate welfare." King pointed to the compounding of inequality through "subsidies of the rich and unemployment and underemployment of the poor."[44]

This meant that instead of allies, the Johnson administration and liberal Northern elites would face the demand that would cost them more than the Dixiecrat votes they lost when they supported civil rights legislation.[45] In explaining this difference to the SCLC staff in January 1968 King pointed to the steep and novel challenge, saying,

> When we were struggling in Alabama, it was often the federal government that came to our aid to restrain the brutality, and the recalcitrance of local, state governments. . . . In this instance, we will be confronting the very government, and the very federal machinery that has often come in as our aide. . . . the problem cannot be solved without a radical reordering of national priorities and this is another thing that makes it . . . much more difficult.[46]

In an in-depth interview for the *New York Times Magazine* with King in the SCLC office in the midst of full focus on planning the Poor People's Campaign, Jose Yglesias observed that much of what the national news and congressional committees were riled up about was not actually new. They had mobilized large numbers of people to DC before, leading the 1963 March on Washington. The Kennedy administration had initially tried to get them to call that march off, too, only working with the plans after realizing the planners were not willing to turn back. Yglesias said it was also not new for the SCLC to expect to be jailed or intentionally disrupt a city's normal functioning. Officials in Montgomery, Birmingham, and Selma would surely object to any attempt to say the disruptions to their cities were insignificant. What Yglesias pointed to as the difference between those campaigns and the new campaign was that "in the past they demonstrated, almost without exception, for the implementation in behalf of [Black people] of rights promised to all Americans." But in this new era "they are not going to Washington, as in 1963, to support proposed legislation" with "a line of march benevolently set out for them and protected by a generally approving Administration." He concluded that "the tactics are nonviolent and the tone of the language in S.C.L.C. literature is moral," all familiar features of the Civil Rights Movement. But the significant and striking difference was that "the substance of the demands is revolutionary for America: class demands. . . . They were not speaking for blacks alone but for all poor people."[47]

JOBS OR INCOME

King observed that the findings of the Moynihan Report, the Kerner Commission, and news articles that had brought poverty to national attention were guided by a shared midcentury liberalism: "We have proceeded from a premise that poverty is a consequence of multiple evils: lack of education restricting job opportunities; poor housing which stultified home life and suppressed initiative; fragile family relationships which distorted personality development." These explanations of poverty pointed to there being something wrong with the poor and led to policy proposals that addressed poverty indirectly, seeking, "to solve poverty by first solving something else." Instead King had become "convinced that the simplest approach will prove to be the most effective—the solution to poverty is to abolish it directly by a now widely discussed measure: the guaranteed income." King insisted that "the problem of housing, education, instead of preceding the elimination of poverty, will themselves be affected if poverty is first abolished." This was the analysis that led him to propose that the demand of the Poor People's Campaign would be the right to well-paid employment or income.[48]

King said the call for a guaranteed annual income "doesn't only mean the income for the person, but it means a radical redefinition of work."[49] Too often the poor are "branded as inferior and incompetent," and are blamed for unemployment and poverty. But in reality, "no matter how dynamically the economy develops and expands, it does not eliminate all poverty."[50] The contradiction of three out of ten people being poor or low income while the official unemployment rate was a record low 3.3 percent pointed to the much deeper problem of inequality. The unemployed and underemployed were not only those who lacked the skills but entire sectors of people who had been displaced by new technology in cotton production and coal mining. Automation was just beginning to impact northern industrial jobs, but King understood the implications. "Automation is imperceptibly but inexorably producing dislocations, skimming off unskilled labor from the industrial force. The displaced are flowing into proliferating service occupations." The jobs, King pointed out, were unorganized, paid low wages, and required long hours.[51]

As with the decision to focus on poverty, King's insistence that a campaign of the poor focus on the right to a job or income was as controversial within the SCLC leadership. Speaking to the SCLC staff at a planning retreat in January 1968, King argued that the demand for "jobs or income" is capable of "bringing the whole of society under judgement the way that lunch counters did all of segregation." And in response to arguments for other ideas he said the "simple demand around which you galvanize forces . . . doesn't mean that that's all you are going about . . . and that doesn't mean that's all you're going to get out of it." He reminded the staff that in Birmingham the focus was the integration of lunch counters, "but as a result of that, we so subpoenaed the conscious of the nation to appear before the judgment of morality on the whole question of civil rights, that we got a Civil Rights Bill that had ten titles. Nine of them dealt with things that we weren't even talking about in Birmingham." King believed that at the present moment, the question of jobs or income was one that could rally more people than any other issue and revealed the greater contradictions of the economy, a demand "so possible, so achievable, so pure, so simple that even the backlash can't do much to deny it. And yet something so non-token and so basic to life that even the black nationalist can't disagree with it that much. Now that's jobs or income."[52]

The immorality and instability of poverty brings into judgment the organization of society as a whole. And King saw that because racism was so enmeshed with war, poverty, and materialism, to attack one strategically was to bring all of them under judgment. Because these issues had been siloed from each other, the movements to address them were also siloed, and the analysis of their intransigence was stifled where this depth of understanding did not exist. King worked to persuade those who were convinced that the next step for the movement should be a full attack on the Vietnam War that the demands of the Poor People's Campaign were in effect an insistence that the war be ended. The war in Vietnam could not be waged if the demands of the campaign were met.[53] King said to SCLC staff who argued against the campaign for a more direct response to the war, "Those who believe in peace, and those who are against the war in Vietnam are frustrated, because the more they fight against it, the more we stand up against it, the more you feel that you are running up against a concrete wall."[54] And so they could use the broad public sentiment that poverty is wrong as a strength, whereas directly attacking a still-popular war would have been a harder battle that would leave the question of poverty unresolved.

The emphasis on the right to a job or income as a human right rather than a civil right was an important distinction in King's understanding of the possibilities for social change and understanding of the way that race has operated in history. When Yglesias recounted the inclusion of poor whites, he challenged King, "You can't say you're in civil rights any longer." King responded with a smile, "But you can say I am in human rights."[55]

MULTIRACIAL, MULTIETHNIC DISPOSSESSED

King insisted that the right to a guaranteed income would not be possible for Black people alone.[56] Seeing the "fierce opposition" they would face, King said a cross-racial coalition would be necessary. By "placing economic issues on the highest agenda" they could build a campaign across racial and geographic lines that united Black freedom fighters, the unemployed and underemployed, welfare recipients, and certain sections of labor. This was not a coalition of separate but overlapping interests. The enmeshed crises they faced shared a common root and therefore a common solution in the transformation of the economy and society. Their unity would be "the source of power that reshapes economic relationships," and herald breakthroughs in social change. This source of power would not only realize the total elimination of poverty but through that demand would be the beginning of "the reality of equality in race relations."[57] Their unity around class demands was significant not only in terms of the reform it sought but in its capacity to bring together and unite a leadership and social force capable of gaining revolutionary economic and political power.[58]

In 1968 seven out of ten poor people were white. But the inclusion of poor whites, poor Mexican Americans, poor Puerto Ricans, and poor Native Americans in the Poor People's Campaign not only expanded the pool of people who could be organized around antipoverty demands, it also made a strategic emphasis on the nature of the problem of poverty. The dominant perception of Black poverty followed an integrationist thread; the problem of poor Black people was their exclusion from the economic system parallel to their exclusion from the political system. The existence of millions of poor whites belied that assumption. Their shared economic problems pointed at a different solution entirely, one that was not integrating Black people into a broken economic system. King told a group of confidants gathered at Belafonte's New York apartment, "What deeply troubles me now is that for all the steps we've taken toward integration, I've come to believe that we are integrating into a burning house."[59]

White supremacy was a formidable barrier to this organizing concept. King assessed that the gains of civil rights had revealed racism to be deeper and more systematic than he had hoped, and it remained intransigent after the legal defeat of Jim Crow.[60] But he also insisted that a campaign targeting poverty was a direct targeting of racism. In the South the SCLC had observed that there were class divisions within the white community, but those differences were wielded against the demands of Black equality rather than contributing to class solidarity between poor white and poor Black people. Sometimes the Southern white capitalists would betray the cross-class racial alliance with poor whites by siding with civil rights demands. Abernathy witnessed that in Selma the constituency that showed up behind Sheriff Jim Clark was largely "poor white farmers who particularly feared black advancement, since they believed it would eventually rob them of whatever modicum of dignity they possessed. It was a foolish and fragile illusion, but they clung to it." But the Chamber of Commerce, a small band of businessmen, feared competition with other southern cities for plants and factories if Selma developed a reputation as racially reactionary. Mayor Joseph Smitherman and Commissioner of Public Safety Wilson Baker saw these businessmen as their true constituency. So where Sheriff Clark "moved in with clubs, guns and mobs," Commissioner Baker sought solutions amenable to the Black leadership and local capitalists.[61] Many concluded from this experience and dynamics like it that the real allies of poor Blacks were rich whites (north and south) who could intervene to protect them from poor whites. But King perceived that in the demand for human rights, including the right to a job or income, they would not be able to rely on such alliances. A campaign of the poor would be a step toward finding the right relationships and tactics that would make success possible. To do this they needed to take new risks, study the ways their opponents respond, find their relative strengths, and build campaigns that contribute to a new human rights movement.

King's multiracial strategy was a countertrend amid the growth of anti-integrationist ideas, particularly among young Black organizers developing the ideologies of Black Power. King responded by agreeing with the need to build power but questioning the effectiveness of nationalism. "One unfortunate thing about [the slogan] Black Power is that it gives priority to race precisely at a time when the impact of automation and other forces have made the economic question fundamental for blacks and whites alike. In this context a slogan 'Power for Poor People' would be much more appropriate than the slogan 'Black Power.'"[62] King was not alone even as he faced much resistance for the idea of a multiracial poor joining forces. Grassroots organizers were coming to similar conclusions, like Mississippi organizer Fannie Lou Hamer who said, "Let's face it, man, what's hurtin' the black folks that's without, is hurtin' the white folks that's without. . . . If the white folk fight for theyself and the black folk fight for theyself, we gonna crumble apart. These are kinds of things that we gonna have to fight together."[63] King went looking for those who were interested in just that.

NOTES

1. Sarkar, Sauruv, and Shailly Gupta Barnes, "The Souls of Porr Folks: Auditing America 50 Years After the Poor People's Campaign Challenged Racism, Poverty, the War Economy/Militarism and Our National Morality." Washington D.C.: Institute for Policy Studies, April 2018.☐ Larry Elliott, "World's Eight Richest People Have Same Wealth as Poorest 50 percent," *The Guardian*, January 15, 2017, https://www.theguardian.com/global-development/2017/jan/16/worlds-eight-richest-people-have-same-wealth-as-poorest-50?CMP=twt_a-world_b-gdnworld. See also, Dylan Matthews, "Are 26 Billionaires Worth More than Half the Planet? The Debate, Explained.," *Vox* January 22, 2019, https://www.vox.com/future-perfect/2019/1/22/18192774/oxfam-inequality-report-2019-davos-wealth.

2. Martin Luther King Jr., "'Where Do We Go From Here?,' Address to the 11th Annual SCLC Convention," King Encyclopedia at Stanford, August 16, 1967, https://kinginstitute.stanford.edu/king-papers/documents/where-do-we-go-here-address-delivered-eleventh-annual-sclc-convention.

3. The fight for desegregation in the South was still ongoing. In February 1968 when college students organized to desegregate a bowling alley in Orangeburg, South Carolina, the police murdered three teenagers as they ran away: Sammy Hammond, Delano Middleton, Henry Smith, and injured twenty-seven. None of the state troopers who opened fire on unarmed students were convicted. One of the protesters, SNCC's Cleveland Sellers, was convicted of inciting a riot and served hard labor. (Cleveland Sellers, interview by Blackside, Inc., October 21, 1988, for Eyes on the Prize II: America at the Racial Crossroads 1965 to 1985. Washington University Libraries, Film and Media Archive, Henry Hampton Collection, http://digital.wustl.edu/cgi/t/text/text-idx?c=eop;cc=eop;rgn=main;view=text;idno=sel5427.0215.148.)

4. Martin Luther King Jr., "State of the Movement" (Frogmore, SC, November 28, 1967), 1, King Speeches, Series 3, Box 13, King Center Archives.

5. Martin Luther King Jr., *The Trumpet of Conscience* (New York: Harper & Row, 1968), 56.

6. King earnestly wrestled with these questions. See the interview with Cleveland Sellers on private conversations with King. And one month before he was assassinated, King asked the SCLC field organizers to arrange private meetings for him with the Black nationalists in their area.

7. See Sellers, interview by Blackside, Inc.

8. Martin Luther King Jr., *Where Do We Go from Here: Chaos or Community?* (Boston: Beacon Press, 2010), 37. See also King, "State of the Movement," 9.

9. Martin Luther King Jr., "Why We Must Go to Washington" (Atlanta, GA, January 15, 1968), 7, King Speeches, Series 3, Box 13, King Center Archives.; King, Jr., *Where Do We Go from Here: Chaos or Community?*, 44–46.

10. King, *Where Do We Go from Here: Chaos or Community?*, 48, 49, 50.; Adam Fairclough, *To Redeem the Soul of America: The Southern Christian Leadership Conference and Martin Luther King, Jr* (Athens: University of Georgia Press, 1987), 353. The combination of increasing Black voter registration and the shift of middle-income whites out of urban areas (white flight) meant that majority-Black communities were successful in electing Black officials. In 1972 seventy Black mayors formed a Southern Conference of Black Mayors to share strategies and experiences, but most found few options for responding to "intractable economic problems and poorly funded government bureaucracies" (Timothy J. Minchin, *From Rights to Economics : The Ongoing Struggle for Black Equality in the U.S. South* [Gainesville: University Press of Florida, 2007], 18).

11. Jose Yglesias, "Dr. King's March on Washington, Part II," in *Black Protest in the Sixties*, ed. August Meier, John H. Bracey, and Elliott Rudwick (New York: M. Wiener Pub., 1991), 285. In a *Saturday Evening Post* essay, King explained that division among those who seek "to tackle the social injustices that afflict both of them" will result in "the ascendancy of extreme reaction which exploits all people" (Martin Luther King Jr., "Negroes Are Not Moving Too Fast," *Saturday Evening Post*, November 7, 1964).

12. King had publicly criticized the war during the 1965 SCLC convention, in Los Angeles in February 1967, and elsewhere, but the address at Riverside in 1967 was a clear and full call to end the war.

13. Michael Harrington, interview by Blackside, Inc., October 11, 1988, for Eyes on the Prize II: America at the Racial Crossroads 1965 to 1985. Washington University Libraries, Film and Media Archive, Henry Hampton Collection, http://digital.wustl. edu/cgi/t/text/text-idx?c=eop;cc=eop;rgn=main;view=text;idno=har5427.0719.063. Responding to the tension between the movement work that needs to be done and what foundations and funders are willing to support, King told Urban League's Whitney Young that remaining silent about the Vietnam War because it would deter foundation support was misguided. "Whitney, what you are saying may get you a foundation grant but it will not get you into the kingdom of truth" (James H. Cone, "The Theology of Martin Luther King, Jr," *Union Seminary Quarterly Review* 40, no. 4 [1986]: 34–35).

14. A *New York Times* editorial, "Dr. King's Error" concluded, "This is a fusing of two public problems that are distinct and separate. By drawing them together, Dr. King has done a disservice to both" ("Dr. King's Error," *New York Times*, April 7, 1967). A *Washington Post* editorial similarly argued, "Many who have listened to him with respect will never again accord him the same confidence. He has diminished his usefulness to the cause, to his country and his people" ("A Tragedy," *Washington Post*, April 6, 1967).

15. Henry Hampton, Steve Fayer, and Sarah Flynn, *Voices of Freedom: An Oral History of the Civil Rights Movement from the 1950s through the 1980s* (New York: Bantam Books, 1991), 345–46.

16. Martin Luther King Jr., "A Time to Break the Silence." In *A Testament of Hope: The Essential Writings and Speeches of Martin Luther King, Jr.*, edited by James M. Washington. San Francisco: HarperOne, 1991. This speech was developed from a draft written by Vincent Harding at King's request (Hampton, Fayer, and Flynn, *Voices of Freedom*, 344). The number of Black soldiers in the Vietnam War approximated that general Black population. However 22 percent of soldiers killed in Vietnam were Black, double the proportion of Black soldiers (Pepper, *Orders to Kill*, 453).

17. "Drum Major Instinct," In *A Testament of Hope: The Essential Writings and Speeches of Martin Luther King, Jr.*, ed. James M. Washington. (San Francisco: HarperOne, 1991),181. Kwame Ture, then known as Stokely Carmichael, was head of the SNCC when King invited him and Cleveland Sellers to come to Ebenezer to hear a sermon about the war on April 30, 1967. Ture later reflected, "He used words in that speech that I could never use. I mean, if I were to use those words I would be dismissed as irresponsible. But he said, 'The United States government is one of the greatest purveyors of violence in the world today.' Of course, you must understand the setting. It's made in his church" (Hampton, Fayer, and Flynn, *Voices of Freedom*, 347).

18. Martin Luther King Jr., "Speech at Staff Retreat" (Frogmore, SC, May 1967), 10, King Speeches, Series 3, Box 13, King Center Archives. A similar statement was made in King, "Address to the 11th SCLC Convention: Where Do We Go From Here?" where King roots this pattern of objectification in slavery.

19. Martin Luther King Jr., "Press Conference on Washington Campaign" (Ebenezer Baptist Church, Atlanta, GA, December 4, 1967), 4, King Speeches, Series 3, Box 13, King Center Archives.

20. He used the trio racism, monopoly-capitalism, and militarism in a sermon at Ebenezer in January 1968 (Martin Luther King Jr., "What Are Your New Year's Resolutions?" [January 7, 1968], 10, King Speeches, Series 3, Box 13, King Center Archives).

21. Martin Luther King Jr., "The Three Evils of Society" (National Conference for New Politics, Chicago, IL, August 31, 1967), 7, King Speeches, Series 3, Box 13, King Center Archives.

22. Ajay Chaudry et al., "Poverty in the United States: 50-Year Trends and Safety Net Impacts" (U.S. Department of Health and Human Services, March 2016), 2; Michael K. Honey, *To the Promised Land: Martin Luther King and the Fight for*

Economic Justice (New York: W. W. Norton & Company, 2018), 129. The federal poverty threshold was set by the Social Security Administration in 1964. Estimating that families spend a third of their income on food, the threshold took the Agriculture Department's measurement of an economy food plan and tripled it. This calculation was never based on a full budget that measured the costs of what a family would need to live at a basic level of well-being. The measure adjusts for inflation but has no way of keeping pace with the big changes in the cost of health care and housing (Gordon Fisher, "The Development and History of the Poverty Thresholds," *Social Security Bulletin* 55, no. 4 [1992], https://www.ssa.gov/history/fisheronpoverty.html). The Census' Supplemental Poverty Measure is designed to more accurately calculate cost of living and the impact of government programs.

23. Bureau of Labor Statistics, "Unemployment Rate (1948–2017)," accessed May 14, 2017, https://data.bls.gov/pdq/SurveyOutputServlet.

24. "Poor People in America: Economic Fact Sheet for the Poor People's Campaign" (SCLC, January 1968), Southern Christian Leadership Conference Records, Subseries 10.3, Poor People's Campaign, Box 573, Folder 28, Emory University.

25. King, "The Three Evils of Society," 7.

26. King, *Where Do We Go from Here: Chaos or Community?*, 132. King experienced and witnessed the pressure to become loyal opponents to established powers and systems. He pointed out that the ruling interests "cultivate emerging leaders," from Black communities, encouraging them to take on ruling-class mannerisms, lifestyles, and ideologies. As a result they have a Black representative enforcing ruling-class interests (p. 160).

27. Vincent Harding, *Martin Luther King, the Inconvenient Hero* (Maryknoll, NY: Orbis Books, 2008), 52–53.

28. Martin Luther King Jr., "A Testament of Hope," *Playboy*, April 1969.

29. King, *Where Do We Go from Here: Chaos or Community?*, 166–67.

30. Martin Luther King Jr., "SCLC Staff Retreat Speech" (Frogmore, SC, November 14, 1966), 14, King Speeches, Series 3, Box 13, King Center Archives.

31. Martin Luther King Jr., "Nonviolence: The Only Road to Freedom," in *A Testament of Hope: The Essential Writings and Speeches of Martin Luther King, Jr.*, ed. James M. Washington (San Francisco: HarperOne, 1991), 58.

32. King, *Where Do We Go from Here: Chaos or Community?*, 138–39, 167.

33. Martin Luther King Jr., "All Labor Has Dignity," in *The Radical King*, ed. Cornel West (Boston, Massachusetts: Beacon Press, 2015), 174.

34. Martin Luther King Jr., "To Charter Our Course for the Future" (Address, Frogmore, SC, May 22, 1967), 2, King Speeches, Series 3, Box 13, King Center Archives. That same month SNCC declared itself a "Human Rights Organization" focused on "the liberation struggles against colonialism, racism, and economic exploitation" globally, adding an International Affairs Commission under Jim Forman (Clayborne Carson, In *Struggle: SNCC and the Black Awakening of the 1960s* [Cambridge, MA: Harvard University Press, 1995], 266).

35. King, "Speech at Staff Retreat (May 1967)," 9. Reforms are defined as changes that do not significantly alter existing relationships of power. Concessions to demands

that depend on existing constellations of power, including state power, can actually solidify power by appeasing opposition. Because reforms do not shift power they are dependent on the forces that granted them and can be revoked or diminished (Gary Teeple, *Globalization and the Decline of Social Reform: Into the Twenty-First Century* [Aurora, Ontario: Garamond Press, 2000], 20).

36. King, "Speech at Staff Retreat (May 1967)," 9–10.

37. Hampton, Fayer, and Flynn, *Voices of Freedom*, 451–52, 454.

38. Hampton, Fayer, and Flynn, *Voices of Freedom*, 454, 455.

39. It was not uncommon to perceive that the poor could only be saved by some combination of popular opinion and powerful decision-makers to rescue them. In 1960 the "Harvest of Shame," episode of *CBS Reports* with Dan Rather exposed the conditions of migrant labor and included the assessment, "The migrants have no lobby. Only an enlightened, aroused and perhaps angered public opinion can do anything about the migrants. The people you have seen have the strength to harvest your fruit and vegetables. They do not have the strength to influence legislation. Maybe we do" (Edward Murrow, *Harvest of Shame*, DVD [Docurama, 2005]).

40. King, "Press Conference on Washington Campaign," 4.

41. King, *Trumpet of Conscience*, 61.

42. Martin Luther King Jr., "Address at Mass Meeting" (Albany, GA, March 22, 1968), King Speeches, Series 3, Box 13, King Center Archives.

43. King, *Trumpet of Conscience*, 60.

44. King, "Press Conference on Washington Campaign," 4.

45. This marked the end of the New Deal coalition of Southern Democrats, organized labor, Northern urban political machines, and liberal elites.

46. King, "Why We Must Go to Washington," 17.

47. Yglesias, "Dr. King's March on Washington, Part II," 279–80. King told Yglesias, "We're dealing in a sense with class issues, we're dealing with the problem of the gulf between the haves and the have-nots."

48. King, *Where Do We Go from Here: Chaos or Community?*, 163, 173.

49. King, "SCLC Staff Retreat Speech (November 1966)," 22–23.

50. King, "Address to the 11th SCLC Convention: Where Do We Go From Here?," 8. King pointed out the productive capacity had grown to the extent that poverty was unnecessary. He called for a guaranteed income pegged to the median income, not the federal poverty threshold, and for income to grow with total social income. Alyosha Goldstein points out that many of the midcentury voices suggesting an annual minimum income were interested in securing market allegiance and expanding consumption: "John Kenneth Galbraith advocated the idea of a basic income as a necessary complement to the 'affluent society.' Economist Milton Friedman's scheme for a negative income tax was committed to bolstering consumer-driven market choice. Richard Nixon's Family Assistance Plan introduced the first version of workfare in the guise of guaranteed income" (Alyosha Goldstein, "The Violence of Poverty: A 'Living Memorial' for MLK," *Counterpunch* [blog], April 26, 2012, http://www.counterpunch.org/2012/04/26/the-violence-of-poverty/). New York Governor Nelson Rockefeller convened a 1967 conference on public welfare that drew corporate leaders, politicians, intellectuals, foundation executives, bureaucrats and welfare

practitioners, with a steering committee that included executives from Goldman, Sachs, Ford, Mobil, Pepsico, Xerox, Inland Steel, and the New York Stock Exchange. The steering committee report highlighted, "the present system of public assistance does not work well. It covers only 8-million of the 30-million Americans living in poverty. . . . It should be replaced with an income maintenance system, possibly a negative income tax, which would bring all 10-million Americans up to at least the official poverty line" (Steering Committee of the Arden House Conference on Public Welfare, "Governor's Conference on Public Welfare," in *Welfare: A Documentary History of U.S. Policy and Politics*, ed. Gwendolyn Mink and Rickie Solinger [New York: New York University Press, 2003], 280). But the poverty threshold was already inadequate and over time has become even more so. This is why the leaders from National Welfare Rights Organization specified that their demand was for a guaranteed *adequate* income.

51. King, *Where Do We Go from Here: Chaos or Community?*, 141. King also wrote, "The technological revolution expressed in automation and cybernetics is edging [Black people] and certain poor whites into a socially superfluous role, into permanent uselessness and hopeless impoverishment." (King, "Negroes Are Not Moving Too Fast.")

52. Martin Luther King Jr., "See You in Washington" (SCLC Staff Retreat, Atlanta, GA, January 17, 1968), 6–7, King Speeches, Series 3, Box 13, King Center Archives. King was intervening against arguments from other SCLC leaders for a longer list of demands. He continued, "When you even get the Harris Poll revealing that 68 percent of the people of America feel that this should be done, and 64 percent feel that the slums should be torn down and the communities rebuilt by the people who live in them. When you get that, I believe that we are moving around the right issue—it's a simple thing, jobs or income. . . . We are talking about the right to eat. The right to live. This is what we're going to Washington about." King saw an opening in these trends for making human rights claims and building a human rights movement capable of even deeper social transformation ("See You in Washington," 8).

53. Yglesias, "Dr. King's March on Washington, Part II," 278. Long's study of King's understanding of the state concludes that in the Poor People's Campaign, "By demanding what is due them—basic economic goods—the poor would also be calling upon the state to move its resources from the Vietnam War to the War on Poverty."

54. King, "See You in Washington," 3. In 1968 the Vietnam War was at its height, both in terms of US deployment (541,000) and casualties on both sides, including 16,988 from the United States.

55. Yglesias, "Dr. King's March on Washington, Part II." The longer history of how the Civil Rights Movement of the 1950s and 60s took its particular form is worth studying. Decades of earlier Black freedom struggles organized for expansive economic change alongside social and civil change. Overt and covert anticommunist motions pushed key leaders out and promoted efforts that targeted civil rights objectives. See Carol Anderson, *Eyes Off the Prize: The United Nations and the African American Struggle for Human Rights, 1944–1955* (New York: Cambridge University Press, 2003) and Robin D. G. Kelley, *Hammer and Hoe: Alabama Communists during the Great Depression*, (Chapel Hill: University of North Carolina Press, 2015).

56. SCLC staff Jesse Jackson reflected that King's last organizing work centered around, "this vision we should wipe out poverty, ignorance, and disease, (but) that you couldn't do it on an ethnic basis. That it was never going to be in the plan to wipe out black poverty that would leave the Hispanics in poverty, or whites or women in poverty, or American Indians in poverty, so we had to pull people together" (Hampton, Fayer, and Flynn, *Voices of Freedom*, 463).

57. King, *Where Do We Go from Here: Chaos or Community?*, 142, 165. King believed "the shortage of jobs creates a natural climate of ·competition which tends to divide, not unify. If those who need jobs regard them as bones thrown to hungry animals, a destructive competition would seem inevitable." The Poor People's Campaign's multiracial insistence that unemployment and poverty affected all races prevented being misconstrued by opponents as seeking to take jobs away from white families, a common tactic among racist demagogues. Instead he argued that the "The best course for [Black people] happens to be the best course for whites as well and for the nation as a whole." (King, "Negroes Are Not Moving Too Fast.")

58. King's research committee on political conditions included Michael Harrington, author of influential poverty study *The Other America* (MacMillian, 1962). He recollected that in his last years, in private conversations, King spoke more candidly about the scale of change that would be necessary to end poverty, including "the democratization of investment decisions, and much more democratic allocation of income and wealth and of work." Harrington said part of King's genius was in deciphering how to phrase that insight in order to make it understandable and accessible (Hampton, Fayer, and Flynn, *Voices of Freedom*, 450–51). King hesitated to use the word "socialism" publicly to describe his assessment, saying "People have so many hangups to it, and respond so emotionally and irrationally" (Fairclough, *To Redeem the Soul of America*, 353).

59. Harry Belafonte, interview by Blackside, Inc., May 15, 1989, Henry Hampton Collection, Washington University Libraries, Film and Media Archive, http://digital. wustl.edu/e/eii/eiiweb/bel5427.0417.013harrybelafonte.html. King made this point at other times, including at a November 1967 meeting to plan a ministers training program (Fairclough, *To Redeem the Soul of America*, 360).

60. King, "State of the Movement," 9.

61. Ralph Abernathy, *And the Walls Came Tumbling Down: An Autobiography* (New York: Harper & Row, 1989), 303–4.

62. King, *Where Do We Go from Here: Chaos or Community?*, 51. King argued, "This alliance must consist of the vast majorities of each group. It must have the objective of eradicating social evils which oppress both white and [Black]. The unemployment which afflicts one third of [Black] youth also affects over 12.5 percent of white youth. It is not only more moral for both races to work together but more logical." (King, "Negroes Are Not Moving Too Fast.")

63. *The Movement*, October 1967 (Vol. 3, Issue 10). In the same interview Hamer put this insight in theological frame: "People make fun of me for saying this, but I believe in Christianity. I was just reading yesterday in the Bible what God don't have no respect for a person, and if He made us all and put us on earth together, then there's no need of you trying to get over there by yourself and you wage your little battle.

Because this is something we got to fight in America is for all the people, because you know there's a whole lot of people. There's white that suffer, there's Indian people that suffer, there's Mexican American people that suffer, there's Chinese people that suffer, so as black people, we not the only one that suffer, and I'm perfectly willing to make this country what it have to be. We gonna have to fight these battles together." According to Christopher Ashe, "Her commitment to interracial organizing led some separatists in the organization to dismiss her as 'no longer relevant' and not at their 'level of development'" (Christopher Myers Asch, *The Senator and the Sharecropper: The Freedom Struggles of James O. Eastland and Fannie Lou Hamer* [New York: W.W. Norton, 2008], 231).

Chapter 2

Organizing a New and Unsettling Force

The drive to organize the Poor People's Campaign was moving into full swing by the January SCLC staff retreat in Atlanta. King pitched the significance of their work in biblical language. "It may be true, as Jesus said, that man cannot live by bread alone. But the mere fact that the alone was added means that man cannot live without bread. And we are talking about bread now. We are talking about the right to eat. The right to live. This is what we're going to Washington about."[1] But it was also rights-based language. And it was rights-based language that pushed for understanding rights as not only political and civil rights, but also economic and social rights: food, housing, income, meaningful and dignified work, dignified housing. These were the focus. The question remained as to who would support such a campaign.

It was not simply the righteousness of the claims of the Civil Rights Movement that had brought a diverse coalition to support it. King assessed in 1967, "Our victories in the past decade were won with a broad coalition of organizations representing a wide variety of interests." Key forces, such as the Johnson administration, capitalists, foundations, and sections of the media, supported the movement because it was in their self-interest to do so, even if the movement had to corner them into that position. That broad coalition had included many who would ruthlessly block a movement for the changes in economic and political power that would be necessary to implement the full expanse of human rights. "We deceive ourselves if we envision the same combination backing structural changes in the society. It did not come together for such a program and will not reassemble for it."[2]

Not everyone in that coalition had come willingly, even for civil rights. Many were forced to take sides when Black freedom struggles refused to let the nation continue to condone the conditions of white supremacy in the South. Among that group were powerful forces who joined a coalition for civil rights because they were interested in the domestic stability of democratic capitalism and in its global image in the Cold War as the alternative to communism. It also included those who were interested in the profitability of an integrated (but disunited) Southern labor force where wages were lower than in the North. An alliance of groups around a common interest, doesn't mean those groups have the same self-interest. King argued that studying those differences yielded "keys to political progress."[3] He would experience how quickly alliances can shift a couple months later. When he spoke out publicly against the Vietnam War, many of his past partners denounced him as being out of his lane for bringing war and poverty into his condemnation of racism.

Despite the backlash King persisted in arguing that they needed to think differently about who stood to benefit from a revolutionary movement for human rights. He argued that "millions of underprivileged whites are in the process of considering the contradiction between segregation and economic progress. White supremacy can feed their egos but not their stomachs."[4] Peggy Terry was among the poor whites who took up the Poor People's Campaign. She testified, "I've discovered that kicking black people didn't fill my belly or pay my rent. And it didn't make the cotton I picked weigh a pound more."[5] This was the type of conversion King believed the process of building a multiracial movement would make possible, countering the politics of division that had hindered and circumscribed the long arc of freedom movements across American history.

MINORITY LEADERS GROUP MEETING

SCLC staff started by mapping out who was organizing where. Handwritten staff meeting notes listed key leaders under the headings "Mexican Americans," "Poor Whites," "Farm Workers and Migrants," "Puerto Ricans and Spanish," and "American Indians," along with the National Welfare Rights Organization, and American Friends Service Committee. Under the categories were the names of four to eight activists, often with an organization, and their mailing address.[6]

Bernard Lafayette was the initial lead organizer for this new campaign within SCLC, and two other staff were charged specifically with organizing campaign participants from beyond SCLC's established network: King family chauffer and personal assistant Tom Houck and Kentuckian Ernie Austin, both poor whites.[7] It was Austin who had first pointed out to King that poor whites outnumbered poor Blacks in the United States, to King's surprise. At the time 69 percent of poor families were white.[8] To find leads on community leaders and organizers outside of the usual suspects, Houck recalled reaching out to denominational and ecumenical networks like American Friends Service Committee, United Church of Christ, and National Council of

Churches, as well as through anti-war networks like the Spring Mobilization Committee. He said that social workers and War on Poverty Community Action Projects were sometimes productive sources as well.[9]

The lists turned into telegram invitations to come to Atlanta for the Minority Group Leaders Conference on the Poor People's Campaign in March 1968. Those who convened included more than sixty leaders from across the country, representing a diverse range of communities and issue groups. One third of them were women. Welfare rights organizing was well represented by locals like Chicago Community Welfare (including Dovie Coleman), Brooklyn Welfare Rights, and Rochester Action Welfare Rights. Two community unions that were joint projects between Students for Democratic Socialism and community leaders were there: Chicago's poor white JOIN Community Union (including Doug "Youngblood" Blakey) and the Newark Community Union (represented by Tom Hayden).

Chicano and Puerto Rican organizers joined from groups like Crusade for Justice (CO), Casa Puerto Rico (NY), Mexican American Youth Organization (TX), *Aliauja Federal de Pueblas Libres* (NM), and Latin American Defense Fund (IL). Migrant labor was present in South Florida Migrants Council and Farm Labor Organizing Committee (OH). Ceasar Chavez had hoped to attend, but he had just broken a twenty five day fast. He sent another leader from United Farm Workers. Anti-war organizing was represented by the Fort Hood Three Committee (NY).[10] Among the organizations representing Native American organizing were the Lumbee Indian Citizens Council (NC), Sioux Indian Council (SD), and National Indian Youth Council (represented by Mel Thom).

Of the key civil rights organizations, only SCLC, Student Nonviolent Coordinating Committee, and the Southern Regional Council attended. That group included future US Representative John Lewis. Myles Horton was there from the Highlander Folk School. Poor whites came to the table from organizations like Southern Conference Education Fund (represented by Carl Braden), Poor People's Committee of Hazzard, Kentucky, Appalachian Volunteers, and West Virginia AFL-CIO.

Religious leaders were also present, most from social concerns bodies within larger denominations, including Catholics, Jews, Episcopalians, and Congregationalists. American Friends Service Committee had been partnering with SCLC on the campaign since February, were the connection to several of the new partners, and sent four staff to the meeting.[11]

Many of the people who came together were previously unknown to King, and only a few had been past organizing partners. All of them represented organizations and networks of leaders. They were not social service providers. Many of them were from the ranks of the poor, but they were not symbolic representatives of poverty. They were organizers. Out of the gathering they elected a campaign steering committee that hoped to help the SCLC shape the campaign's demands and strategic and tactical decisions.[12]

The Minority Group Leaders Conference was an attempt to convene an expansive and varied leadership connected to hundreds or thousands of people. This was a historically unprecedented moment in US history, drawing together the organized poor from an expansive geographic reach and broad racial and ethnic diversity around questions of class. And it is a moment that history has largely forgotten. Vincent Harding was among those who joined together at Atlanta and describes, "The room was palpably charged with the tension of uncertainty and the hope of great, though guarded expectations. That was meant to be the vision and the spirit which informed the deepest levels of the Poor People's Campaign of 1968. It was to be the joining of all the causes, all the people."[13] King told those who came together,

> We are assembled here together today with common problems. Bringing together ethnic groups that maybe have not been together in this type of meeting in the past. I know I haven't been in a meeting like this. And it has been one of my dreams that we would come together and realize our common problems. . . . Power for poor people will really mean having the ability, the togetherness, the assertiveness, and the aggressiveness to make the power structure of this nation say yes when they may be desirous to say no.[14]

King knew that "no" would be the answer they would first receive, even in their coming together. The building of "power for poor people" would not be a simple or instinctive coalition of allies. Those gathered discussed how "the established powers of rich America have deliberately exploited poor people by isolating them in ethnic, nationality, religious and racial groups." One of the poor white delegates explained, "It is not really the poor people who are responsible for hatred in our country, but the powerful economic and political managers who want to keep us down. We will no longer permit them to divide us."[15] Taking on a campaign together would be an opportunity to experiment, as King dreamed, with coming together and realizing common problems. Only in struggle together could they begin to build a shared ability, togetherness, assertiveness, and aggressiveness that would make them a force with power.

Already in the Minority Group Leaders Conference, campaign leaders were discovering new challenges in the work of developing a shared strategy. Conflicts arose as leaders worked to find their place in it. They were attempting to build something that was multiracial, multiethnic, multiregional, and multiorganizational. People were coming from the many front lines of poverty, where they organized around the issues that moved their communities to take action. Many of those issues were new to the SCLC, like fishing rights, coal-poisoned water, and theft of treaty-righted land. In part this challenge was rooted in the campaign's strength. They were bringing together existing networks rather than starting from nothing. But how could these diverse issues be understood strategically rather than a joint appeal for a series of isolated demands?

According to Mexican American leader Bert Corona, King showed appreciation for diversity of the historical, cultural, and local conditions represented there in ways that were, "sympathetic and supportive," while also stressing "that we needed to struggle together to correct common abuses." Reies López Tijerina interpreted King's emphasis on the transition from civil rights to human rights as a commitment to all poor people and an openness to the inclusion of land claims, the central focus of Tijerina's organizing.[16] Rodolfo "Corky" Gonzales more pointedly reminded SCLC that incorporating feedback would not be enough. "Conferring is a two-way street. You still lack an understanding of the problems of the Hispanic people. We want to take part in the decision making."

SCLC's James Bevel emphasized that the process of developing policy demands would open up space for their diversity. He said "poverty-stricken people had been walled off from each other in little boxes." And that the campaign "was not a black train they were urged to climb on board, but a train of individual cars made up of all these boxes put together."[17] The train car metaphor was a revealing one, perhaps more so than Bevel intended. He intended to suggest a level of parity and shared authority, with each delegation receiving their own car. But if the tracks had been laid, cars could join only if they followed the same route. And the cars remained distinct from each other, walled off in little boxes, even if coupled together. As the campaign progressed, the steering committee that grew out of the Minority Group Leaders Conference often found that the course had been set.

NATIONAL WELFARE RIGHTS ORGANIZATION

The strong representation of NWRO at the March meeting was significant. Historian Paula Giddings points out,

> The NWRO had actually come up with the idea of a poor people's campaign before King did. And the women in that organization were peeved when King started to beat that drum without even acknowledging their efforts—or their knowledge of the issue. Yet King needed the NWRO, which by 1968 was ten thousand strong and had chapters throughout the country.[18]

Poor women organizing around welfare rights began as community-based responses to shared conditions. Aid for Families with Dependent Children (AFDC) was first established in Social Security Act of 1935 to catch women (and some men) excluded from Social Security programs like unemployment and old-age insurance. But it failed to meet the needs of poor families, was packed with coercive state paternalism, and carried steep bureaucratic barriers for applicants. In response poor women began local organizing efforts to improve their chances of getting the benefits they and their neighbors were entitled to receive, improve how they were treated in welfare offices, and expand benefit programs. This laid the groundwork for the welfare rights movement of the 1960s and beyond, which built upon that local organizing with NWRO's national network in 1966.

Without fully realizing the significance and power of the women's organizing, SCLC arranged to meet with NWRO leaders February 3, 1968. When King shared his plans for the Poor People's Campaign, vice-chairperson Etta Horn asked him to answer questions about newly passed welfare legislation. When he could not, Chairperson Johnnie Tillmon clarified, "She means the Anti-Welfare Bill, H.R. 12080," and offered details that would help him catch up. She continued, 'Where were you . . . when we were down in Washington trying to get support for Senator Kennedy's amendments?" Finally she said, "you know, Dr. King, if you don't know about these questions, you should say you don't know, and then we could go on with the meeting."[19] King capitulated and asked for their help in understanding their policy positions. He promised the SCLC would endorse their policy demands. And he asked for their contributions to the planning of the Poor People's Campaign, including a central role in the Minority Group Leaders Conference the following month. The deep sexism of King and the SCLC leadership was reflected in Young's report of the meeting where he called NWRO leaders, "unbridled horses." His assessment echoed the sexist and racist pathologizing of Black women found in the Moynihan Report, which argued "a system of oppression tends to produce strong women and weak men."[20] Despite King's sexist approach to their intelligence and extensive organizing work, NWRO leaders saw a shared strategy with the Poor People's Campaign and claimed strong leadership roles in it.[21]

The first national gathering of those who would form the NWRO had taken place in Syracuse, New York in January 1966. The multiracial gathering of four hundred people was predominantly composed of poor mothers from major cities, but it also included poor people from agricultural areas, social theorists, and other activists. Together they criticized the inadequacies of welfare and the new War on Poverty programs. And they identified the poor themselves as the key to building a movement to transform the welfare system. They formed a National People's War Council Against Poverty and began organizing an even larger gathering on June 30 of that year where welfare recipients and allies marched from Cleveland to Columbus, Ohio. Coordinated actions in twenty-five cities included six thousand people. By the following August they had established the NWRO with sixty-seven locals and five thousand dues-paying members, with membership limited to welfare recipients. This doubled to ten thousand in 1968, the year King met with them, and reached 22,500 by 1969.[22]

Johnnie Tillmon and Beulah Sanders were the first co-chairs. Tillmon had grown up in Arkansas, picked cotton, worked in laundries, raised six children, and founded welfare rights organization Mothers Anonymous in Los Angeles. She later wrote in *Ms.* magazine,

> I'm a woman. I'm a black woman. I'm a poor woman. I'm a fat woman. I'm a middle-aged woman. And I'm on welfare. In this country, if you're any one of those things—poor, black, fat, female, middle-aged, on welfare—you count less as a human being. If you're all of those things, you don't count at all. Except as a statistic. There are millions of statistics like me. Some on welfare. Some not. . . . Not all of them are black. Not at all. In fact, the majority—about two-thirds—of all the poor families in the country are white.

Tillmon insisted that the welfare rights struggle is a matter of women's liberation, and because women on welfare see, "where this society is really at" and learn how to fight to survive. "Maybe it is we poor welfare recipients who will really liberate women." She called feminists to look critically at welfare policies, culture of poverty myths about of poor women, and the false sense of security that welfare is not their issue.[23]

NWRO was heavily involved in the Poor People's Campaign before and after King's assassination. Out of their leadership at the Minority Group Leaders Conference, Etta Horn chaired the campaign's steering committee. They organized welfare rights leaders to come to Washington, D.C., launched the campaign with a Mother's Day march, lived in Resurrection City, opened a welfare rights desk in its city hall, negotiated many of the campaign's legislative wins, and took part in planning next steps coming out of the campaign.[24]

POOR PEOPLE TO PEOPLE TOUR

After the Minority Group Leaders Conference King continued in a "Poor people to people" organizing tour, an ambitious schedule of back-to-back, cross-country stops to rally support for and participants in the Poor People's Campaign. The original plan stretched nearly every day through mid-April. Field organizers were instructed that King "is not coming to your area to organize it." His job was to "stimulate that which you have already organized." If they hadn't done the groundwork, he "will be of no service or value to your area." A mass meeting at each stop would include a mock trial where King acted as judge, putting "America on trial for robbery and exploitation of the poor" and "for violation of the Declaration of Independence."

The primary directive to field organizers was to "personally give the major part of your time," to "the Grass Root leaders and poor people," as "the most important element of your area." They would meet with King outside of the mass meeting, in a poor area of town, to share complaints, questions, and "demands to take to Washington." Field organizers were instructed to set up shorter meetings with ministers (but only for ministers bringing their congregations and a financial contribution to the mass meeting), community and organizational leaders (like SNCC, CORE, and NAACP), businesses that might make donations, and high school students. Field organizers were also asked to set up a closed meeting with the area's "black nationalists."[25]

If it had gone according to plan, he would have cut across the South over the following weeks, reaching North Carolina on April 4, followed by stops in Cleveland, Detroit, and Chicago. But he was just three days into the itinerary when he got the call from Rev. James Lawson to join Black sanitation workers on strike in Memphis. His staff protested that he was getting distracted from mobilizing the campaign.[26] King insisted that the strike was emblematic of the larger issues the Poor People's Campaign would address, linking a local struggle to the national effort. On March 18 he told the workers, "You are highlighting the economic issue. You are going beyond purely civil rights to questions of human rights. That is a distinction." The civil rights movement

did a great deal to end legal segregation and guarantee the right to vote. With Selma and the voting rights bill. Now our struggle is for genuine equality, which means economic equality. For we know now that it isn't enough to integrate lunch counters. What does it profit a man to be able to eat at an integrated lunch counter if he doesn't earn enough money to buy a hamburger and a cup of coffee?[27]

Between the two sanitation worker marches in Memphis, King did continue the Poor People to People tour, including a trip to Marks, Mississippi. He had stopped there before and been overwhelmed by the poverty he witnessed. This time King was moved to tears by watching several children share a single apple. At the meeting the field organizer set up, mothers testified about being unable to feed their children. One woman pointed out that Johnson had promised to "wipe out poverty, ignorance, and disease. . . . Now where's our money?" King told the group, "It's criminal for people to have to live in these conditions," and "God does not want you to live like you are living."[28]

PLANNING FOR WASHINGTON, D.C.

Before they were derailed by the assassination, SCLC was recruiting, "three thousand of the poorest citizens from ten different urban and rural areas to initiate and lead a sustained, massive, direct-action movement in Washington." Those who joined would undergo three months of training in preparation and would "move on Washington, determined to stay there until the legislative and executive branches of government take serious and adequate action on jobs and income."[29]

The tent city encampment they were planning would facilitate this, but it was not purely spectacle and it was not charity. Those who needed shelter would have shelter. Those who needed health care would see doctors and go to hospitals. All would be fed. But this was not an end in itself. The meeting of needs would both demonstrate the violence of unmet needs and be a base of operations for sustained direct action. King described, "If you are, let's say, from rural Mississippi, and have never had medical attention, and your children are undernourished and unhealthy, you can take those little children into the Washington hospitals and stay with them there until the medical workers cope with their needs."[30] The nation would see that there are children without nourishment and medical care. But the nation would also see the poor demanding health care, making a moral claim for their human rights, and organizing together for significant legislative changes. This is part of why King was insistent that the poor themselves make up the driving force of the campaign and encampment. Worried that the staff was recruiting only college students and middle-income sympathizers, King said, "The much greater thing is for us to get the poor people who will be demanding something because they have been deprived."[31] It was not only a matter of numbers. It mattered who joined them.

King called the SCLC and the new broad leadership to engage in tactics that would build the capacities and confidence of the poor. The maintenance of oppression depended on the cultivation of a sense of incapacity and bewilderment among those who in reality hold the power to transform society. King argued the oppressed were "schooled assiduously to believe in their lack of capacity," blocked from understanding their own "latent strengths." But taking action together would help them, "break out of the fog of self-denigration," study "the science of social change," and "embark on social experimentation with their own strengths to generate the kind of power that shapes basic decisions."[32]

They planned for caravans of people, trained in nonviolence, to travel across the country and join together. They would initially be unknown to each other, having been hidden from one another. They would be revealing themselves to each other as much as they would be revealing themselves to the media, the public, and the decision makers of Washington.

THE LEADERSHIP OF THE POOR

According to Harding, while most approaches to poverty and racism depended on persuading decision makers to enact programmatic solutions, King's "ultimate commitment was to help find the ways by which the full energies and angers of the poor could be challenged, organized and engaged in a revolutionary process that confronted the status quo and opened creative new possibilities for them and for the nation."[33] Against the idea that the poor can only be mobilized but cannot function as organized leadership, King argued that part of the campaign was to reach those who have not had the opportunity to study and "together acquire political sophistication by discussion, practice and reading."[34]

Other organizers had come to see the limits of the dominant civil rights model years before King, and he had long ignored them. Ella Josephine Baker was among them. She argued the poor could play leadership roles and build sustained organization if their organizing models matched that strategy. For Baker it wasn't just that she was personally treated in a sexist manner—she was—but that paternalistic and hierarchical leadership models reinforced poor people's sense of dependency. Poor people didn't need a savior to rescue them. The mobilizing model went hand in hand with SCLC's celebrity leadership model. "When the newspaper people come around, what do they look for? They don't look for the solid organizational drive . . . they look for a miracle performer."[35] Barbara Ransby says this criticism of King is actually a hopeful one. Baker saw that "Martin didn't make the movement. . . . The movement made Martin." If that was true, and they organized knowing that, then an assassination—or the siphoning off of key leaders into lucrative jobs or a FBI defamation campaign—didn't have to kill the movement, too. "The strength and determination of ordinary people and the power of the organizations they build together are the locus of the power that fuels change, power that is bigger than any one individual, no matter how charismatic or committed."[36]

Baker trained organizers to find the "relationships that held communities together" as the "foundation of any sustained local organizing campaign." She knew that in the severe, oppressive conditions in which poor Black families lived, there was a correlating depth of determination and capacity to fight for change. Her organizing model built on her experience of sit-in protests starting local and small and then kicking off through networks like wildfire. Participatory democracy for Baker was not a leaderless "majority rules," but finding the potentially unsettling forces who had been marginalized by both the conditions of oppression and headline-leader mobilizing. The model she used brought the margin to the center.[37]

King worked to convince the SCLC staff and those closest to him that their "responsibility is to lead people into higher levels of fulfillment and into effective strategy that will make change possible."[38] He said that in the era of human rights, the greater alignment of opposition will mean that, "mass non-violent demonstration will not be enough. They must be supplemented by a continuing job of organization." Because the forces opposed to human rights demands would be even more formidable and prepared than those they had confronted before, "when we go into action and confront our adversaries, we must be as armed with knowledge as they. Or policies should have the strength of deep analysis beneath them to be able to challenge the clever sophistries of our opponents." King's critique of the limits of the gains of the Civil Rights Movement were the source of this emphasis on sustained organizing."

> We must frankly acknowledge that in past years our creativity and imagination were not employed in learning how to develop power. We found a method in non-violent protest that worked, and we employed it enthusiastically. . . . When a new dawn reveals a landscape dotted with obstacles, the time has come for sober reflection, for assessment of our methods and for anticipating pitfalls. Stumbling and groping through the wilderness finally must be replaced by a planned, organized and orderly march.

It was these "clever sophistries" of the opposition that would require the inseparable combination of education and action. "Social action without education is a weak expression of pure energy." Without the ability to match opposition, even militant action can be misdirected. And yet education alone is also insufficient. "Deeds uninformed by education can take false directions."[39] Therefore King emphasized education in the development of a nonviolent, organized leadership of the poor capable of responding to powerful ideological, economic, and political forces. The Poor People's Campaign could frame and raise the issue, but it alone would not have the force necessary to solve the problem. The campaign would need to be part of a larger human rights movement to be successful. King said he was "not optimistic about the immediate response of Congress. . . . But you can say that the goal of this campaign will be to expose Congress."[40] The greatest gains would come from effectively using initial losses to better understand the strengths and weaknesses of the opposition. And so in King's vision, the "initial three thousand, this non-violent army, the 'freedom church' of the poor" would need a trained cadre of leaders who could effectively welcome and subsequently train the waves of poor people who would come join them. In order to use the campaign to build toward a larger movement they would need to incorporate training and education that helped direct their tactics and prepared them to draw lessons from both successes and losses. These new insights would help them maneuver subsequent campaigns.

King suggested the content of the education necessary to inform their action was not simply studying programs and proposals, but most immediately they needed to be dedicated to studying relationships of power and the use of power so as to understand what strengths they could leverage in influencing change. In particular he argued they needed to understand "ideological, economic and political" forces. When forces of power within those realms are obscured or indistinct, there is little hope for developing effective strategies for transforming those systems. A deeper understanding of the forces of opposition would be necessary to navigate the landscape of new obstacles.[41]

The theory and tactics of nonviolence would be important aspects of the type of organizing that could bring the poor together as a social force that could win the nation. King was frustrated by those who were critical of the urban uprisings of the mid-1960s. There was a strong hypocrisy to law and order responses from a government that was the "greatest purveyor of violence."[42] He saw the uprisings as evidence that Black people perceived the enormity of the task of freedom, in part because the successful legislative measures of civil rights had been so hard-fought and yet were such partial improvements. Anger at this exposure of the depth of the problems of racism and poverty were a "natural development to a new stage of struggle." Yet King believed that the direction of that frustration into violence as a "tactical theory," while understandable, did not ultimately contribute to materially solving the problems at hand.[43]

> If we say that power is the ability to affect change, or the ability to achieve purpose, then it is not powerful to engage in an act that does not do that . . . no matter how much you sloganize and no matter how much you engage in action. . . . In order for a movement to be effective, it must have the power to pull masses together, and it must have the power to make a dent on that kind of majority that has somehow allowed its conscience to go to sleep.[44]

King sought just such a strategy in the Poor People's Campaign. He believed that the poor themselves, dissatisfied as they were with the conditions of the life of their families and themselves, could be organized toward that ability to achieve purpose. It could have the power to pull masses together.

Educational activities featured prominently in the plans for the campaign. King envisioned that afternoons in the encampment would include "festivals of music and art" and that time would be spent studying W. E. B. Du Bois, political philosophy, heritage, government, and the world.[45] A sketch of the encampment in fundraising materials related to the campaign prominently featured the education tent in the foreground.[46] In addition to the training participants would undergo before arriving in Washington, the encampment was designed to foster education in conjunction with direct action. Planning documents proposed that their task was to equip participants "to deal effectively with the established structures of power." They developed curriculum proposals that would engage people of "greatly varying education backgrounds" (including college students) around "the problem of poverty, both the issue and the tactics for its elimination" through the study of "the corporate establishment to the welfare state." They imagined that a Poor People's University within the encampment would use lectures, films, presentations and discussion groups "to focus and centralize thought" The plans included a broad range of subjects, including economics, history, nonviolence, racism, art and culture in movement building, and foreign policy.[47]

Myles Horton was among those who attended the Minority Group Leaders Conference and believed the emerging constituency and focus of the Poor People's Campaign was groundbreaking. A few weeks later he wrote to Young and Cesar Chavez, "I believe we caught a glimpse of the future . . . the making of a bottom-up coalition." Horton emphasized the importance of a broad and shared leadership in the planning and tactics to overcome the tendency to focus only on SCLC leaders and constituents, even if that shared leadership would be more difficult and time consuming. Together they would "lay the groundwork for something tremendously exciting and significant."[48] King was shot before that letter was mailed. Horton added a postscript saying they now faced a great void and sent it anyway.

KING'S ASSASSINATION

In the end the Poor People's Campaign would be called the Civil Rights Movement's "last gasp," "dissipated dream," and "beloved community gone forever," not by its opponents, but by its top leaders and advisers.[49] But King envisioned the campaign and era not as the conclusion of the past period but as the initiation of the coming one. When King was assassinated this was not a shared understanding. The conflict around the strategy and tactics of the Poor People's Campaign echo in autobiographies, speech transcripts, and FBI memos.[50] Adviser and confidant Belafonte said,

> Dr. King in the Poor People's Campaign . . . was on a thrust here that was going to give a new and a much broader meaning to the movement, which would have

required a more broad based use of people and a more broad based input from leaders on a lot of levels. So that the emerging group that inherited SCLC . . . were caught in a transitional period for which they were ill equipped to do the task. . . . We were just in the process of doing that. Had Dr. King had three more years of refining the leaders and the people who came to be for all these diverse areas, the movement would have been, and the country would have been qualitatively different than where it found itself.[51]

King campaigned to win his closest partners to this new strategic understanding and the tactics he believed would give them some traction, but he had little success. While King was alive there was no consensus, perhaps no deep comprehension, of his strategic vision and the role a Poor People's Campaign might play in it. It was in this moment of disunity that King was assassinated. David Garrow documented the ways in which, "in the last twelve months of his life, King represented a far greater political threat to the reigning American government than he ever had before," supporting Harding's conclusion that his "assassination was surely not the work of some lone and unabetted white racist criminal." King was under constant covert government surveillance, but it wasn't merely for his own safety, despite numerous attempts and threats on his life and his family. Instead the government feared him and his ability to move masses of people.[52] Ramsey Clark, who served as Attorney General under Johnson from 1967–1969, was intimately involved in the Department of Justice and interagency surveillance of King's work and the Poor People's Campaign. Clark later emphasized the importance of "persistent pursuit of the truth" related to government involvement in the assassination as "important to the future of our country."[53]

In his death there was a revival of interest in making King's "last dream" a reality. Donations flowed in, foundations came forward, and the SCLC threw the momentum of their mourning into the task of pulling off the Poor People's Campaign. Abernathy, who followed King as SCLC president, articulated that they "wanted to make the project a living memorial to Martin and what he had dreamed of."[54] Individuals and organizations who had had little interest in the Poor People's Campaign while King was alive rallied to support the effort as a tribute. It is doubtful that the reasons for their initial hesitation were actually resolved, but there was a surge in volunteers and participants. The tent city encampment's name, Resurrection City, was intended to give theological significance to the motion of the new freedom church of the poor. But after King's death it came to represent the resurrection of King himself.[55] A promotional flyer for the June 19th Solidarity Day headlined not "poverty" or "the poor" but "let us continue his work."[56] In the years following his assassination another campaign began. This one quietly replaced King the radical threat with King the successful and celebrated American reformer who demonstrated the perfectibility and essential goodness of the great American capitalist democracy. The poor came to Washington in 1968 to tell a different story.

NOTES

1. Martin Luther King Jr., "See You in Washington" (SCLC Staff Retreat, Atlanta, GA, January 17, 1968), 8, King Speeches, Series 3, Box 13, King Center Archives.

2. Martin Luther King Jr., "Where Do We Go from Here," in *A Testament of Hope: The Essential Writings and Speeches of Martin Luther King, Jr.*, ed. James M. Washington (San Francisco: HarperOne, 1991), 309.

3. Martin Luther King Jr., *Where Do We Go from Here: Chaos or Community?* (New York: Harper & Row, 1967), 151.

4. King Jr., *Where Do We Go from Here: Chaos or Community?*, 153.

5. Gordon Mantler, "Black, Brown and Poor: Martin Luther King Jr., The Poor People's Campaign and Its Legacies" (Dissertation, Duke University, 2008), 321.

6. "Listing of Those to Be Invited to the Minority Group Meeting" (Atlanta, GA, nd), SCLC Papers, Series VIII, 179:11, King Center Archives.

7. Amy Nathan Wright, "Civil Rights 'Unfinished Business': Poverty, Race, and the 1968 Poor People's Campaign" (Dissertation, The University of Texas at Austin, 2007), 181.

8. David J. Garrow, *Bearing the Cross: Martin Luther King, Jr., and the Southern Christian Leadership Conference* (New York: Quill, 1999), 718, note 31.

9. Wright, "Civil Rights 'Unfinished Business,'" 181.

10. In July 1966 three Army privates stationed at Fort Hood, TX—one Black, one white, and one Puerto Rican—refused redeployment (William F. Pepper, *Orders to Kill: The Truth behind the Murder of Martin Luther King* [New York: Carroll & Graf, 1995], 449.).

11. Southern Christian Leadership Conference, "Black and White Together: American Indians, Poor Whites, Spanish-Americans Join Poor People's Washington Campaign," March 15, 1968, 3–4, SCLC Papers, Series VIII, 179:11, King Center Archives.

12. The initial steering committee included Hank Adams of the Indian Committee for Fishing Rights (WA); Corky Gonzales of Crusade for Justice (CO); Robert Fulcher of Mercer County (WV); Grace Mora Newman of Fort Hood Three Committee (NY); Peggy Terry of JOIN Community Union (IL); Reyes Tijerina of the Federal Alliance of New Mexico; Gerena Valentin of the Puerto Rican Committee for Human Rights (NY); and Tillie Walker of United Indian Scholarship Fund (CO). (Southern Christian Leadership Conference, "Black and White Together," 3.)

13. Vincent Harding, *Martin Luther King, the Inconvenient Hero* (Maryknoll, NY: Orbis Books, 2008), 54–55.

14. Sidney Lumet and Joseph L. Mankiewicz, *King: A Filmed Record . . . Montgomery to Memphis*, Documentary, 1970.

15. Southern Christian Leadership Conference, "Black and White Together," 2.

16. Mantler, "Black, Brown and Poor," 111.

17. Barbara Moffett to Eleanor Eaton, "Minority Leaders Conference Washington's Poor People's Campaign," April 2, 1968, 1, CRD Administration 32557, The Archives of the American Friends Service Committee; Brenda Beadenkopf, "Part XVIII: Poor People's Campaign, Assassination of Dr. Martin Luther King," n.d.

18. Paula Giddings, *When and Where I Enter: The Impact of Black Women on Race and Sex in America* (New York: Bantam Books, 1985), 312–13. At first King tried to send his staff to meet with NWRO. They were turned away. NWRO refused to meet with second-tier leadership. When King did come to meet with them, they prearranged the seating in the room with name cards, separating King from his staff and surrounding him with their strongest leaders.

19. Giddings, *When and Where I Enter*, 312–13.

20. Giddings, *When and Where I Enter*, 313–14.; Garrow, *Bearing the Cross*, 595.; Daniel Patrick Moynihan, "The Negro Family: The Case for National Action," in *Welfare: A Documentary History of U.S. Policy and Politics*, ed. Gwendolyn Mink and Rickie Solinger (New York: New York University Press, 2003), 228–29. The report was originally published by the US Department of Labor in 1965.

21. Michael K. Honey, *To the Promised Land: Martin Luther King and the Fight for Economic Justice* (New York: W. W. Norton & Company, 2018), 126–27.

22. Guida West, *The National Welfare Rights Movement: The Social Protest of Poor Women* (New York, N.Y.: Praeger, 1981), 25–26, 50; Marian Kramer, interview by author. Digital audio recording. Telephone, September 15, 2015; Alyosha Goldstein, *Poverty in Common: The Politics of Community Action during the American Century* (Durham: Duke University Press, 2012), 126–28; Premilla Nadasen, *Welfare Warriors: The Welfare Rights Movement in the United States* (New York: Routledge, 2005), 1–2. Coalescing organizations included groups like the Englewood Welfare Rights Organization in New Jersey, Westside Mothers ADC in Detroit, and Aid to Needy Children (ANC) Mothers Anonymous in Los Angeles (by Tillmon). Most local welfare rights groups emerged during the 1960s.

23. Johnnie Tillmon, "Welfare Is a Women's Issue," in *Welfare: A Documentary History of U.S. Policy and Politics*, ed. Gwendolyn Mink and Rickie Solinger (New York: New York University Press, 2003), 373–74, 376, 378–79. Originally printed in *Ms.*, spring 1972, 111–116.; Tillmon called all women to understand how sexism and economic exploitation reinforced each other, asserting that the lies that people believe about women on welfare are believable because they are a "special version of the lies that society tells about all women," and rationalize policies, not just welfare policies, which support and enable male dominance. Tillmon said "Maybe it is we poor welfare recipients who will really liberate women in this country." (376–7).

24. "Meeting Minutes of the Minority Group Steering Committee" (Southern Christian Leadership Conference, April 1968), Southern Christian Leadership Conference Records, Subseries 10.3, Poor People's Campaign, Box 571, Emory University; "Solidarity Day: In Support of the Poor People's Campaign" (Southern Christian Leadership Conference, June 19, 1968), SCLC Papers, Series VIII, King Center Archives.

25. Hosea Williams to Staff of the SCLC, "Memorandum: Weekly Report and Doctor King's People to People Tours," March 8, 1968, 1–4, Southern Christian Leadership Conference Records, Subseries 10.3, Poor People's Campaign, Box 571, Emory University.

26. Stewart Burns, *To the Mountaintop: Martin Luther King's Mission and Its Meaning for America*, 2nd edition (Charleston, SC: CreateSpace, 2018), 521.

27. Martin Luther King Jr., "All Labor Has Dignity," in *The Radical King*, ed. Cornel West (Boston, Massachusetts: Beacon Press, 2015), 173–4.

28. Burns, *To the Mountaintop*, 515; Honey, *To the Promised Land*, 161–62.

29. Martin Luther King Jr., *The Trumpet of Conscience* (New York: Harper & Row, 1968), 60.

30. King, *Trumpet of Conscience*, 60.

31. Mantler, "Black, Brown and Poor," 111.

32. King, *Where Do We Go from Here: Chaos or Community?*, 138.

33. Harding, *Inconvenient Hero*, 67.

34. King, *Where Do We Go from Here: Chaos or Community?*, 155.

35. Barbara Ransby, *Ella Baker and the Black Freedom Movement: A Radical Democratic Vision* (Chapel Hill: University of North Carolina Press, 2003), 190–91.

36. Barbara Ransby, "Ella Baker's Legacy Runs Deep. Know Her Name.," *The New York Times*, January 20, 2020, sec. Opinion, https://www.nytimes.com/2020/01/20/opinion/martin-luther-king-ella-baker.html.

37. Ransby, *Ella Baker and the Black Freedom Movement*, 117, 237–38, 278, 368.

38. Martin Luther King Jr., "Why We Must Go to Washington" (Atlanta, GA, January 15, 1968), 8, King Speeches, Series 3, Box 13, King Center Archives.

39. King, *Where Do We Go from Here: Chaos or Community?*, 131, 147, 155.

40. Jose Yglesias, "Dr. King's March on Washington, Part II," in *Black Protest in the Sixties*, ed. August Meier, John H. Bracey, and Elliott Rudwick (M. Wiener Pub., 1991), 283.

41. King, *Where Do We Go from Here: Chaos or Community?*, 138.

42. Martin Luther King Jr., "Beyond Vietnam: A Time to Break Silence," in *The Radical King*, ed. Cornel West (Boston, Massachusetts: Beacon Press, 2015), 204.

43. Martin Luther King Jr., "State of the Movement" (Frogmore, SC, November 28, 1967), 1, King Speeches, Series 3, Box 13, King Center Archives.; King, Jr., *Trumpet of Conscience*, 56–58.

44. King, "Why We Must Go to Washington," 9–10.

45. Martin Luther King Jr., "Address at Mass Meeting" (Eutaw, AL, March 20, 1968), King Speeches, Series 3, Box # 13, King Center Archives.

46. Untitled drawing of Resurrection City (Southern Christian Leadership Conference, n.d.), SCLC Papers, Series VIII, 177:19, King Center Archives.

47. "A Proposed Plan of Structure of the Poor People's University" (Southern Christian Leadership Conference, n.d.), SCLC Papers, Series VIII, 179:23, King Center Archives. "Poor People's University Proposed Curriculum" (Southern Christian Leadership Conference, n.d.), SCLC Papers, Series VIII, 179:23, King Center Archives. A proposed list of educators included Malcolm X biographer Alex Haley, historian Howard Zinn, anti-war activist Dave Dellinger, Chicano activist

Corky Gonzalez, journalists Chuck Stone and I. F. Stone, and Quaker nonviolence trainers George Lakey and Charley Walker.

48. The letter was dated April 5, 1968 but had been transcribed days earlier. King was assassinated before the letter was mailed, and so Horton added a footnote, "I am too numbed by Martin's death to think clearly and I am sending [the letter] as dictated in the hopes that you who are his heirs may still find these ideas of some value. We now face a great void. The lights are dim in my world today." (Myles Horton to Andrew Young, April 5, 1968, SCLC Papers, Series VIII, 177:20, King Center Archives.)

49. Charles Fager, *Uncertain Resurrection: The Poor People's Washington Campaign* (Grand Rapids, MI: Eerdmans, 1969), 142; Henry Hampton, Steve Fayer, and Sarah Flynn, *Voices of Freedom: An Oral History of the Civil Rights Movement from the 1950s through the 1980s* (New York: Bantam Books, 1991), 477–78, 480.

50. Ralph Abernathy, *And the Walls Came Tumbling Down: An Autobiography* (New York: Harper & Row, 1989), 415. Andrew Young, *An Easy Burden: The Civil Rights Movement and the Transformation of America* (New York: HarperCollins Publishers, 1996), 424.

51. Harry Belafonte, interview by Blackside, Inc., May 15, 1989, Henry Hampton Collection, Washington University Libraries, Film and Media Archive, http://digital. wustl.edu/e/eii/eiiweb/bel5427.0417.013harrybelafonte.html.

52. Harding, *Inconvenient Hero*, 75.

53. Clark's comment was related to the work of William Pepper, the King associate and King family attorney whose work on the civil trial of James Earl Ray extensively documented multilayered government involvement in the events surrounding King's assassination. (William F. Pepper, *An Act of State: The Execution of Martin Luther King* [New York: Verso, 2003], jacket).

54. Honey, *To the Promised Land*, 183; Abernathy, *And the Walls Came Tumbling Down*, 501. At a SCLC staff retreat April 15–17 in Clayton County, Georgia they resolved to move forward.

55. Abernathy, *And the Walls Came Tumbling Down*, 501. McKnight cites similar sentiments from Rev. Billy Kyles (Gerald McKnight, *The Last Crusade : Martin Luther King, Jr., the FBI, and the Poor People's Campaign* [Boulder, CO: Westview Press, 1998], 167, note 1.).

56. "Solidarity Day Program," 1.

Chapter 3

The Poor Come to Washington

New York Poor People's Campaign Coordinator Cornelius "Cornbread" Givens reflected that their tent city occupation of Washington, D.C., Resurrection City "brought people together that had the same thing in common. . . . They came from all of the poor areas of the country, and they were all races, and creeds, and colors of people. If you can gather these folks together, and harness their energies, that is seeds for revolution right there."[1] The breadth of geography echoed and expanded the diversity of those who converged at the nation's capital. They brought culture, religion, family histories, political orientations, and organizing histories. The numbers and proportions varied over the course of the campaign, but over six thousand people lived there at one point or another. At any one moment there was capacity for up to 3,300 residents in Resurrection City and Hawthorne School, a second, indoor location. Northern and southern Black people were the largest delegation, making up nearly two thirds of registered residents, but the other third included Mexican Americans, Puerto Ricans, Natives, and whites.[2] The number of registered occupants doesn't include hundreds of volunteers and staff, participants from the D.C. area who were encouraged to sleep in their own homes, and thousands of people who came in small and large delegations for short visits. Key actions brought even larger numbers. Five thousand joined Coretta Scott King and the National Welfare Rights Organization for the Mother's Day March. Four thousand Puerto Ricans came for a day of action on June 15. And more than fifty thousand surrounded the Lincoln Memorial for Solidarity Day on June 19.

The poor who gathered together came from conditions that were simultaneously unique and shared. The lives and labor of the poor in northern cities looked dissimilar from that of those who came from southern agricultural regions and different again from southwestern Chicanos or Natives from the plains. But they came together under the shared banner that the crises they faced had something to do with poverty and that conditions in which

41

they lived were antagonistic to the right to life, liberty, and the pursuit of happiness.

THE CARAVANS

There were eight official caravans of poor people traveling across the country in May 1968 to convene in the nation's capital. The caravans stopped along the way to join actions in solidarity with ongoing local struggles (such as wrongfully terminated teachers) and commemorate sites of past struggles (like Pettus Bridge in Selma). Rallies at stopover locations drew thousands of people. In the evenings they would convene workshops and trainings to share organizing experiences. On the buses they would exchange books and compare reading notes. The art and cultural exchange that would be an important part of the occupation in D.C. began as they journeyed together, with the exchange of songs and new songs written.[3] Most caravaners experienced hospitality and welcome along the way. They stayed at churches and universities, with congregations organizing food and clothing drives to support the effort. But they also dodged flung cigarette butts, were fed poisoned boxed lunches, and had to wait for their buses to be checked after bomb threats. In Detroit conflict with horse-mounted police left fifteen participants injured and six in the hospital.[4]

The first caravan departed from Memphis on May 1 after a tribute to King at the Lorraine Motel where he had been assassinated less than a month before. Called the "Freedom Train," this caravan of buses was delayed for several days in Marks, Mississippi, before continuing on to Washington, D.C. They were still the first to arrive on May 11 and 12 and were charged with constructing the buildings of Resurrection City.[5] The Southern Caravan traveled from Edwards, Mississippi, stopping at important sites from civil rights campaigns along the way.[6] Caravan leader Albert Turner focused on educational trainings for all participants, including in the theory and practice of nonviolence.[7] The Northeast Caravan traveled along the coast from Maine, growing from fourteen to 625 by the time it reached Resurrection City. The Midwest Caravan started in Milwaukee and gathered large delegations across the industrial North, including Chicago, cities across Ohio, Detroit, Pittsburgh, and Baltimore.[8]

The Western Caravan began at a storefront church in Compton, California with just thirty-four people on May 15, 1968. By the time they reached Washington, D.C., they had grown to two thousand. They wound south to pick up busloads of families in Arizona, New Mexico, and West Texas. A second caravan departed from San Francisco with support from the Black Panther Party. Both lines connected on May 18 in Denver, where at a rally of five thousand people Fred Car testified, "Nobody knows what poor is like the Indian. Nobody has seen horses starving and dead on their own land. The only reason I grew up is because I am mad. We are united with the [Black], Mexican, and white." [9]

Pulling together leadership from existing organizations enabled SCLC-independent recruitment from Native, Chicano, Black, and white communities of California, the Pacific Northwest, and the Southwest, with significant delegations organized by Reies López Tijerina, Corky Gonzales, and Tillie Walker, a member of Mandan-Hidatsa. Tijerina had been an itinerant Pentecostal preacher and organized in New Mexico with the *Alianza Federal de Mercedes* (Federal Alliance of Land Grants) around land rights. [10] Gonzales of Denver-based Crusade for Justice had been active in the Democratic Party and headed Denver's War on Poverty office, but he left both as he moved to bring together increasingly radical Chicano and anti-war activism. [11] Walker was also based in Denver. She organized the participation of over two hundred Native Americans in just two weeks, despite being counter organized by the Bureau of Indian Affairs and the National Congress of American Indians (NCAI). [12]

The Mule Train was a vision of King's. He had been moved by his visits to Marks, Mississippi, where he was overwhelmed by the living conditions of agricultural laborers, many of whom had been rendered superfluous by the mechanization of cotton production. The caravan started from Marks on May 13 but did not arrive until a few days before Resurrection City was shut down. Its antiquated wagons and slow mules recalled the contradiction of poverty in the midst of plenty, while the statements painted in black on the sides offered the solution: "Everybody's Got a Right to Work, Eat, Live," and "Stop the War, Feed the Poor." [13] The 115-person delegation included twenty children as young as one, traveling in seventeen covered wagons. Women played significant roles in the difficult logistics of this mode of transportation. "Queen of the Mule Train" Bertha Burris had six children with her and still managed to coordinate food, shelter, medical care, and the participant roster. [14] SCLC organizer Willie Bolden was responsible for organizing relationships along the route of the Mule Train. "I would solicit help from the local communities at these meetings (along the route). We were received well in almost every community we stopped in. They were poor folks just like us." [15] This way of organizing the caravans drew an even larger body of people into the orbit of the campaign and reminded the caravaners that they were part of and supported by the poor across the country. Their travel was slower than expected, and when they reached Atlanta they disassembled the wagons and loaded them onto trains. When they got to Alexandria, Virginia, they reassembled the mule train to make their final iconic procession into the nation's capital.

Native leadership drawn to the campaign was geographically and tribally diverse, and the issues around which they had been organizing reflected that diversity, although issues like hunger and police brutality were common across many of the reservations. In addition to joining the Western Caravan, an Indian Trail caravan traveled from Seattle and Portland. It included a large delegation of Black leaders from Seattle who had been organizing around education and poverty, with strong leadership from Florestine "Flo" Ware. This contingent was organized by Esther Ross of the Stillaguamish tribe in Washington, her son Frank Allen, and Hank Adams, a member of the Assiniboine Sioux. Many of the Native participants from the area had been involved in the struggle for fishing rights, particularly the Stillaguamish. The Indian Trail caravan grew to twenty-six busloads of participants from Washington, Oregon, Montana, the Dakotas, Alaska, and Wisconsin.[16] It joined the Western Caravan in Chicago on May 22, continuing together to arrive in D.C. on May 24.[17]

The Appalachian Trail caravan was the last to depart. It included partici-pants from West Virginia, Tennessee, and Kentucky. In planning the Minority Group Leaders Conference, King had reached out to Anne and Carl Braden who connected SCLC with Al McSurely and Margaret Herring, a white cou-ple working in Kentucky through the Southern Conference Educational Fund, seeking to contribute to the Black freedom struggles by organizing among their fellow southern whites.[18] They found funding for three school buses to transport their delegation to Washington, D.C., by staging a two-day sit-in at the Council of Southern Mountains in Berea, Kentucky. The FBI, who had been following McSurely and Herring ever since they arrived in Kentucky, checked the identifications of everyone who boarded the buses. McSurely recalled, "I asked why they were asking for everyone's ID as they came on the bus and they said, 'We're looking for Dr. King's assassin,' which I thought was brilliant."[19] Delegations from the region were also organized by the Appalachian Volunteers, Highlander Folk School, and Chicago-based Dovie Coleman of the National Welfare Rights Organization, who had been orga-nizing white welfare moms in Southern Illinois, Kentucky, and Tennessee.[20]

SCLC organizer Ernest Austin observed that in addition to the significance of the introduction of Appalachian poor to the poor from across the country, it was also an opportunity for Appalachian whites who often remained isolated due to geography to meet each other and be bolstered in their confidence that they were not alone in their insistence that more radical change was needed. Even within states and certainly across state lines of Kentucky, West Virginia, and Tennessee there was little knowledge of kindred efforts.[21]

RESURRECTION CITY AND HAWTHORNE SCHOOL

For six weeks the multiracial dispossessed of the Poor People's Campaign occupied fifteen acres of park between the Lincoln Memorial and Washington Monument, just south of the stand of trees that ran along the Reflecting Pool. Resurrection City was a base of operations for its six thousand residents as they were campaigning for a revolution of values. Harry Belafonte recalls, "going to Resurrection City and looking at all the tents and all the people, what I saw there, more than anything else, was a sea of hope and an assumption that we would arrive at the same places with the Poor People's Campaign that we had arrived at with the Civil Rights Movement."[22]

The first nail of Resurrection City was driven by Abernathy on May 13. The city was already being used even as it was built, with the first residents to arrive joining volunteers to build six hundred A-frame tents out of plywood and canvas. They also built a network of amenities. There was a mess hall providing three meals a day, the God's Eye bread bakery, a childcare center named after Coretta Scott King with volunteer Head Start teachers, a city hall, a medical tent staffed by volunteers, a Poor People's University, library, and the Many Races Soul Center for cultural exchange and entertainment. Many of the buildings were painted with messages and images. A collaborative mural, called Hunger's Wall, now hangs in the National Museum of African American History and Culture. The occupation even had its own zip code: 20013. There was no charge for any housing, meals, or services. SCLC pointed out, "There was no jail and there were no landlords."[23] Volunteers and residents joined staff in coordinating the operations of the encampment.[24] Hosea Williams said of the operations of the city, "I never lived in a democracy until I moved to Resurrection City. But looks like the stuff is all right."[25]

The 6,312 registered residents came from forty-eight states, with twenty-two states being home to one hundred or more participants. Sixty-three percent identified as male and 37 percent as female. There was a significant number of teenagers and young adults; about 40 percent were between thirteen and twenty-five years old. There were also lots of families. Forty percent of participants came with one or more family members, and almost one in ten residents was twelve and younger. Among Chicanos and Native Americans more than half of participants came with family. Toward the end of the occupation families were less common, both in terms of who remained and who was newly arriving. Two-thirds of the residents were Black. They were joined by more than three hundred Mexican Americans, twenty-five Puerto Ricans, 110 Native Americans, 1,250 whites, and thirty people grouped by the data as "Asian or multiracial."[26]

Abernathy was disappointed that delegations wanted to live in enclaves. He recalled that a Spanish-speaking Mexican American family was assigned a tent between a Black family and a white family but wanted a tent near other Spanish-speaking families. Abernathy saw this conflict as evidence that the project was doomed to failure. "Resurrection City was flawed from the beginning. It rapidly became a campful of ghettos. . . . I was bitterly disappointed at the beginning."[27] But Abernathy spent little time in Resurrection City. Despite having their own tents and making a public show of moving in with suitcase in hand, many of the top SCLC staff slept and met at a nearby motel.[28] Resident Richard Sidy described less judgmentally that "neighborhoods in Resurrection City formed based on where folks had come from."[29]

Unfortunately, it rained twenty-eight of the forty-two days of the encampment.[30] The dirt paths that traversed the field became thick with mud and some puddles deep and wide enough for kids to use makeshift rafts. Unable to clean or dry clothes, with cold, wet nights, and the stench of the mud, conditions were too much for some. After two nearly back-to-back two-day downpours at the end of May, a large number of people left. The city was down to six hundred residents. But that number built back up, with two thousand new residents arriving in June.[31] Participant-journalist Charlyne Hunter thought the press was more offended by the mud than the residents, who she saw respond with acts of unity, determination, and flexibility. Mrs. Lila Mae Brooks of Sunflower County, Mississippi, said, "We used to mud and us who have commodes are used to no sewers." But the rain did dampen spirits and plans.[32]

Because conditions in Resurrection City had physically deteriorated, some later waves of new participants decided to camp out in local churches and schools. Around one hundred Native Americans stayed at St. Augustine's Episcopal Church, a few blocks from Resurrection City.[33] The largest of the off-site locations was Hawthorne School, a private high school two miles away from Resurrection City, which housed five hundred people from the Western Caravan, largely Mexican Americans and American Indians.[34] A late delegation of 150 Appalachians joined them.[35] Roque Garcia from Santa Fe, who grew up without indoor plumbing, was shocked by the poverty of the Appalachians: "I thought I was poor until I got there and saw some of these people."[36] Corky Gonzales's son Rudy said, "I had never seen poor whites before. I mean dirt poor. Some hardly had shoes." Some of the Mexican Americans responded by gathering their extra shoes and jackets to give to the new white arrivals.[37]

Michael Kline of Appalachian Volunteers was among those who stayed at Hawthorne and reflected,

It was an incredible experience. . . . We just slept on mattresses at the school, and mixed it up with people from the American Indian movement, Reies Tijerina was there, migrant workers from the South West, brown berets and the black panthers were there. Everybody just got along remarkably. Took care of each other. Got involved in prolonged dialogue to change the basic nature of our society. Building coalitions with other groups. It was dynamite.[38]

But this separate location contributed to tensions among the campaign leadership. Hawthorne came to represent a rift between SCLC executive staff and Mexican American leaders. That split, both in leadership and location, was interpreted by the media as evidence that the multiracial aspirations of the campaign had failed. But Appalachian Michael Clark reflected that Hawthorne "was a successful multiethnic community, although the press did not know of it and gave little coverage to the school."[39]

TAKING ACTION

The steering committee that grew out of King's Minority Group Leaders Conference in March helped the SCLC assemble a Committee of 100. This front line of multiracial, multiethnic leaders from among the poor also included religious leaders, civil rights leaders, and a few labor leaders, lawyers, peace activists, and students. They came to Washington, D.C., on April 28 to herald the coming of the poor two weeks later. The group was nearly half women and represented organizing work on a wide breadth of the front lines of poverty. They had drafted the forty-nine page "Statements of Demands for Rights of the Poor Presented to Agencies of the U.S. Government by the Poor People's Campaign." It was a detailed accounting of the enmeshed crises faced by the poor, matched with policy changes to address each issue, directed to the relevant government agency, e.g., wage and employment demands addressed to the Department of Labor and welfare, healthcare, and education demands addressed to the Department of Health, Education and Welfare. Over several days they delivered the demands along with testimonies about the conditions of poverty.

Once the occupation began, campaign leaders and participants regularly ventured beyond Resurrection City and Hawthorne School to engage in actions. Some were conventional legislative visits and meetings with department heads. Others were marches and sit-ins. Some were planned in advance and others spontaneous. Some were amicable and others confrontational. One group protested at the homes of members of Congress. Another kept vigil overnight at the Department of Agriculture. One action brought 160 campaign participants to the Department of Agriculture cafeteria and ceremoniously announced that, as a small portion of what the nation owed the poor, they would not pay for their lunches. After they left the SCLC quietly paid the tab.[40] McSurely described that on a typical day they would go out to a particular target with a large, multiracial protest outside the building and then a smaller delegation would go inside to engage the government officials directly with specific demands.[41]

When a Supreme Court ruling rejected treaty-supported fishing rights of Native Americans in Washington State's Puget Sound, not only did impacted Natives show up, but a multiracial, multiethnic bloc targeted the Court Building on May 29. The action left several windows smashed and the American flag removed. Set off by lewd gesturing from young protesters, D.C. police drove motorcycles through the retreating protesters, nearly hitting children. Twelve of the young men who ran to protect the children were beaten and taken to jail.[42] The *New York Times* headline read, "High Court Stormed in Protest by the Poor."[43]

Leaders from NWRO questioned an undersecretary from the Department of Health, Education, and Welfare on June 17. They asked her if she had a copy of the Constitution, and when she hesitated, one of the leaders added, "I had one in Detroit, but I didn't know I needed to bring it with me. I thought I could find one here." After an aide tracked one down, they had the undersecretary read the preamble, stopping her when after she read, "promote the general Welfare, and secure the Blessings of Liberty to ourselves and our Posterity." One leader asked her if she thought it was a violation of the Constitution that welfare recipients were being pressured to take birth control to get benefits when the Constitution secured the blessings of liberty to their posterity. When she replied, "I hope no welfare department is forcing anybody," they interjected to encourage her to travel around and see what's happening in her own department, and added, "If you keep giving out birth control, you're going to run out of soldiers."[44]

As the logistics of running the campaign became more consuming, the SCLC executive staff increasingly made the majority of decisions concerning the campaign's operations, with declining interest in or capacity to solicit the input of the broader leadership. Tensions about the campaign as a whole played out as conflicts related to decisions about the targets and forms of the actions. But as lines of communication dissolved, non-SCLC leadership was able to plan additional actions independently and without SCLC approval. Buck Maggard, from Appalachia, remembered that the daily demonstrations planned by that broader leadership had a more inclusive strategy and responded to issues raised by the full range of participants.[45]

CULTURAL EXCHANGE AND EDUCATION

Myles Horton recalled, "When the rain started, a shelter was built above the fire where coffee was always boiling and around which good conversation or singing was always taking place. . . . The scheduled sessions soon gave way to an 18-hour round of informal discussions, arguments, music, singing, coffee drinking and eating."[46] These opportunities for multracial cultural, and educational exchanges were an important part of the vision for and reality of the campaign. They were intended to be an important part of how a campaign would develop leaders capable of carrying forward the even larger human rights movement. Much of this exchange was spontaneous, but several committees created cultural and educational opportunities.

The Many Races Soul Center was established to support cultural arts with leadership from Rev. Frederick Kirkpatrick, Jimmy Collier, and Highlander's Anne Romasco. Bernice Reagon, a founding member of SNCC Freedom Singers and later of Sweet Honey in the Rock, said an evening at the Soul Center was a formative experience of multiracial, multiethnic cultural exchange, "I saw musicians relating and shifting their material because they were acknowledging the relationship between who they were and who somebody else was."[47] The genres explored there included work songs, spirituals, gospel, blues, and country. Workshops included the history and significance of folk music. In addition to Reagon, guest lectures and performances included folklorist Alan Lomax, singers from the Georgia Sea Islands, Pete Seeger, and folk guitarist Elizabeth Cotton.[48]

Ernesto Vigil described similar experiences at the at Hawthorne, where a white pianist "starts playing this kick-ass boogie-woogie on the piano, and all of a sudden, these poor white Appalachians were kicking their heels, black folks jump in, and Mexicans sit around tapping their toes. . . . You had an interesting cross-pollination. You can't structure that."[49] SCLC's Richard Sidy remembers "We would all sing the same songs. It kept everybody together. We were connecting through song. Resurrection City was a lot of separate neighborhoods, but when we sang, we were one. It brought us together."[50]

During the campaign Collier and Kirkpatrick wrote new songs like "I Can't Take Care of My Family Thisaway" and campaign versions of existing songs. Kirkpatrick adapted a traditional tune to create "We're Going to Walk the Streets of Washington," which included lyrics like "We're gonna ask for jobs or income," "We're gonna stop police brutality," and "Stop the rats from eatin' our babies." One of the enduring legacies of the music created for the campaign was their song, "Everybody's Got a Right to Live." Its chorus repeated the title three times and added, "And before this campaign fails, we'll all go down to jail, because everybody's got a right to live." Its verses addressing war, poverty, and racism, including verses like, "no more full-time work and part-time pay." Pete Seeger added the verse, "No more some be rich while other dirt poor; All around this world, we say 'poverty no more!'" The refrain of everybody having the right to live followed descriptions of the conditions of poverty and the rights-based campaign demands for their solution. Seeger later said, "Some of the best music I've heard in the last year was not made on any stage or on phonographic record, but down in a very muddy little village in Washington, D.C. called Resurrection City."[51]

Education was such an important part of plans for the campaign that it was subdivided among several committees, each targeting a different set of students and educators. The Poor People's University and library was designed primarily for campaign participants and was intended to "provide the basis for far-reaching and long-lasting ameliorative change." Plans included range of subjects within economics, history, politics, and religion, each designed to contribute to developing racially conscious, class-based, multicultural movement leadership. Courses focused on poverty, peace, the welfare state, ethnic history and literature.[52] Although the plans were more elaborate than what took place, over the course of the occupation there were twenty-five lectures within the encampment—each with as many as two hundred participants— and fifteen lectures at local universities.

There was an intentional effort for the courses for campaign participants to overlap with educational sessions that targeted college students, hoping to build a national collegiate network of young partners who understood poverty's sources and solutions and could support organizing and education work as the campaign built into a larger movement.[53] A Freedom School in Resurrection City focused on school-age children.[54] Calling themselves the "Children of the Universe" and "Soldiers in the Poor People's Army" the children engaged in protests and testimonials before government officials. At the Department of Health, Education and Welfare, Jimmy, last name unknown, of Marks, Mississippi, said, "Some of the things we've learned here have taught us that poor folk ain't the stupid ones, anyway, and besides what could be more stupid than to say somebody deserves to be poor? Well, that's what a lot of people say; but like I said, things are going to be different; we're going to change things."[55]

WOMEN'S LEADERSHIP

The most prominent leadership of the Poor People's Campaign, like the Civil Rights Movement, was dominated by men. This was particularly true in terms of paid organizing positions, resource decisions, and the public spotlight. Ella

Baker, who was foundational to the creation of the SCLC but marginalized as it grew, observed that the SCLC not only privileged men but particularly ordained Christian ministers, so the sexism of the church pervaded the organization.[56] But the historical record and collective memory has excluded many of the contributions women did make. Women were strong organizers and strategic thinkers from the start, and later scholars and activists lifted up the reality of women's leadership across all eras of the Black freedom movement.[57]

This was particularly true of the Poor People's Campaign. While women were blocked from key leadership roles by the SCLC's sexist mode of operation, women did lead the Poor People's Campaign. Among them were Marian Wright, Beulah Sanders, Etta Horn, Annie Chambers, Tillie Walker, Peggy Terry, Dovie Coleman, Grace Moore Newman, Maria Varela, Nita Jo Gonzales, Bertha Burris, Johnnie Tillmon, Coretta King, and all of the women who ran the caravans, Resurrection City, and Hawthorne School residence. Women leaders came from all of the racial and ethnic groups represented in the campaign and were an important part of what made the multiracial, multiethnic character of the campaign possible. They recruited the breadth of participants and reached across lines of difference after they arrived. Many did so with their family in tow.

It was the women of NWRO who led the first march of the Poor People's Campaign on May 12, before the caravans arrived in Washington. The Mother's Day March proceeded for twelve blocks through poor neighborhoods that had been burned out in the post-assassination uprisings. They called attention to the reality that the majority of poor people were women and children. At a post-march rally at Cardozo High School's stadium, Coretta King said that while the nation fixates on urban violence, "the real violence in America is starvation, unemployment, slum housing and poor education."[58] She called "black women, white women, brown women and red women—all the women of this nation—(to join) in a campaign of conscience" that would condemn a "Congress that passes laws which subsidize corporations, farms, oil companies, airlines and houses for suburbia, but when it turns to the poor, it suddenly becomes concerned about balancing the budget."[59]

NWRO used the campaign as an opportunity to make cross-country connections between local welfare rights groups and organize new ones. They distributed flyers in English and Spanish in Resurrection City offering to help residents make sure their welfare payments reached them in D.C. Support for navigating the bureaucratic welfare system was a key organizing tactic in welfare rights.[60]

MARSHALS

King was assassinated while he was in Memphis with striking sanitation workers.[61] A few weeks before he had joined them for a march that broke out in violence, with broken store windows and the police murder of a Black youth named Larry Payne. The media and mayor accused King of negligently fleeing the scene, "like a scared rabbit," and suggested that the Poor People's Campaign would bring even greater violence to Washington, D.C. They were encouraged in this assessment by the FBI's COINTELPRO, who disseminated blind memos to "cooperative media sources" blaming King for the violence and helping them make the connection to the Poor People's Campaign. The Black Organizing Project, better known as the Memphis Invaders, was a politicized Black youth group inspired by SNCC organizing around poverty and racism. They had been pegged as the instigators. When King met privately with their leadership, they insisted that they had been framed and were not the provocateurs. But they also pointed out that they had not be consulted by the leadership in Memphis in the weeks prior to the march. King acknowledged this was a mistake and promised to include them in the future, securing their nonintervention, if not their support and participation.[62]

King turned the lessons from this experience into tactics for the Poor People's Campaign, starting with the intentional inclusion of Black youth. They recruited politically minded groups like the Memphis Invaders to provide internal security during the national caravans to Washington and in Resurrection City, thinking that if they are responsible for the nonviolence, they would take it seriously.[63] Within the plan for marshals was King's observation of the leadership capacities of poor Black youths and their interest in organizing. They turned what had been played as a liability in the Memphis march into an organizing tactic and leadership opportunity. The reviews were mixed. Media reports and many histories of the occupation point to violence within Resurrection City, including theft, stabbings, and sexual assault. Some say the internal security was the root of the criminal activity, with headlines like "Marshals Picked from Gangs." And after violations of camp rules, one of the groups, the Blackstone Rangers of Chicago, were sent home mid-campaign. Others point out that it is unclear to what extent government agents and informants, now well documented as having infiltrated the camp, acted as provocateurs and propagators of rumors.

Participant-journalist Hunter believed the incidents of theft (including one journalist's camera equipment), fights, and stabbings were in part a failure to adequately deal with the diversity of people who came together for the campaign. Unknown to each other and unaccustomed to a political occupation, tension arose not only between racial groups but within them. Hunter pointed out that northern, urban Black youths came into conflict with southern, rural Black youths. She felt the nonviolence training was unevenly applied and many occupation participants had not been churched in the discipline that had kept civil rights actions in line.[64]

Others called attention to the marshals' overall capacity to keep order among a large encampment of strangers. On many occasions they successfully mediated tensions between occupation residents and a hostile police force looming outside their gates. Resurrection City and Hawthorne developed a community policing leadership that was able to maintain order to such an extent that government police forces, except for undercover operatives, were kept outside the boundaries of the camp.[65] This was no small feat in the face of extensive agitation and easily triggered reaction by the police. Andrew Young said the retaliation on the part of the police was "worse than anything I ever saw in Mississippi or Alabama." On one occasion, after a few youths from the campaign threw stones at D.C. police, the officers responded by attacking three hundred residents on their way back to Resurrection City after an action. Campaign marshals intervened swiftly, moving the residents inside the camp boundaries, and evading further conflict. Three nights later the Park Police responded to stones thrown from the camp at passing cars by launching tear gas grenades into the camp itself, violently waking hundreds of sleeping families, some of whom required hospitalization.[66]

EVOLUTION OF THE DEMANDS

When King first proposed a campaign of the poor, he said that "jobs or income" should be the focused demand, one that would tie together a broad set of related issues and diverse constituencies. In "stormy" debates with staff King had argued that the demand for "jobs or income" is capable of "bringing the whole of society under judgement the way that lunch counters did all of segregation." And in response to arguments for other ideas he said the, "simple demand around which you galvanize forces . . . doesn't mean that that's all you are going about . . . and that doesn't mean that' all you're going to get out of it."[67] What seemed like a subverting equally important claims against oppression was actually a strategic emphasis on building a unity that could be, "the source of power that reshapes economic relationships and ushers in a breakthrough to a new level of social reform."[68] In a February 2, 1968, press conference, the SCLC presented three official initial goals: "$30 billion annual appropriation for a real war on poverty, Congressional passage of full employment and guaranteed income legislation, and the construction of 500,000 low-cost housing units per year until slums were eliminated."[69]

King's insistence on the right to a job or income as a unifying class demand came into conflict with the necessity to expand the leadership of and participation in the campaign. Through the Minority Leaders Steering Committee King was bringing together community leaders who were already organizing around issues that galvanized their communities. The fuller breadth of the poor from across the United States meant that they would need to incorporate the ways in which those communities identified the problems of poverty. Although they shared a class position, none of the leaders that answered the call to join the Minority Group Leaders Conference, including King himself, had experience organizing as a class.[70] In his organizing of new constituencies into the campaign, Houck observed that poor whites tended to talk about the problems of poverty in terms very similar to poor Black people, focusing on food and starvation. American Indians identified fishing rights, land rights, and educational autonomy within reservations, responding to gross violations of treaty agreements and the violent history of forced assimilation and abuse in compulsory boarding schools. Mexican American communities had also organized around land issues, including the theft of land from Mexican families following the U.S.-Mexican War of 1848, a primary focus of Tijerina and the *Alianza Federal de Mercedes* (Federal Alliance of Land Grants).[71] Even within SCLC the question of class was controversial, with some preferring demands that would build a stronger black capitalist strata within poor communities. This preference made its way to the short list of demands not long after King's assassination, with the fourth basic demand being "access to capital."[72]

By the end of April, the demands had evolved into forty-nine-page document, "The Statements of Demands for Rights of the Poor Presented to Agencies of the U.S. Government." It expanded five basic demands with specific policy demands directed at relevant administrative agencies. Each petition was presented to that department during the Committee of 100 lobbying effort April 29, 30, and May 1. Each list of policy demands was prefaced with a statement that began with some version of "Mr. Chairman. . . . We come to you as representatives of Black, Indian, Mexican-American, Puerto Rican and White-Americans who are the too long forgotten, hungry and jobless outcasts in this land of plenty." The basic demands started with the right to a "living wage" job or "for all who cannot find jobs or for whom employment is inappropriate" the right to a "secure and adequate income." The right to a job included the demand that the government be, "the employer of first resort," and that they "eliminate programs that try to fit poor people to a system that has systematically excluded them from sharing in America's plenty." Strengthened by the leadership of poor moms from the National Welfare Rights Organization, the details of the jobs or income demand specified that the work of raising children was a reason for which employment would be inappropriate. It called for a full income maintenance program, and in the interim called for the repeal of the work requirement programs that had been added to the AFDC program for mothers in the Social Security Act of 1967. Pending a full repeal, those work requirements should be modified to specify that "no mother be require to work if there is no day care or minimal standards available for her children; if other programs to make her fully employable, including health care, are not available; or if the job to which she is referred does not pay a minimum wage or provide for decent working conditions." The third demand was for "access to land as a means to income and livelihood," calling it a "modernized homestead act" that acknowledged the role of land dispossession in many forms: homesteading and treaty violations, widespread evictions of former sharecroppers displaced by mechanization of cotton production, and corporate resource extraction in Appalachia. The fourth demand was "access to capital" and particularly federal funding for businesses. The fifth principal demand was for "recognition by law of the right of people affected by government programs to play a truly significant role in determining how they are designed and carried out."[73]

The Committee of 100 demands were dismissed as unreasonably expensive and unrealistically expansive, but for the first weeks of the occupation they helped orient the direct actions, each targeting specific offices and departments that had some oversight of components of the demands. But as lines of communication among campaign leaders dissolved, actions were increasingly ad hoc and independent, without a coherent plan for turning the demands into outcomes.

On May 24 Abernathy brought in Bayard Rustin, the organizer of the celebrated 1963 March on Washington, to coordinate the June 19th Solidarity Day. Rustin had been a critic of the Poor People's Campaign when King was formulating it. He was particularly wary of King's opposition to the Vietnam War and overly broad demand for jobs or income, both of which Rustin believed would alienate the Johnson administration and other government allies who would be necessary to achieve the labor focused gains Rustin believed to be in reach. He stipulated that if he took on Solidarity Day, he must be allowed to reformulate the demands, and on June 5 issued, in a solo press conference, a new set of demands under a more conciliatory title, "Call to Americans of Goodwill" and with five narrower and more specific goals tied to expanding or funding existing legislation:

1. Recommit the Federal Government to the Full Employment Act of 1946 and legislate the immediate creation of at least one million socially useful career jobs in public service
2. Adopt the pending housing and urban development act of 1968

3. Repeal the 90th Congress's punitive welfare restrictions in the 1967 Social Security Act
4. Extend to all farm workers the right—guaranteed under the National Labor Relations Act—to organize agricultural labor unions
5. Restore budget cuts for bilingual education, Head Start, summer jobs, Economic Opportunity Act, Elementary and Secondary Education Acts[74]

Chuck Fager recounts that the revised list of demands was "hailed by editors and liberal politicians as an important refinement of the Campaign's sweeping rhetoric into concrete, attainable objectives that could be fitted into conventional political bargaining processes."[75] The *New York Times* called Rustin a "realist" and a "pragmatist."[76] But Rustin's revised demands were issued without the approval of Abernathy or other SCLC staff. Poor People's Campaign leaders objected. Not only were the revised demands smaller than King's vision but they were less diverse that those developed by the multiracial, multiethnic steering committee, leaving out goals like land rights, fishing rights, and opposition to the Vietnam War. Rustin resigned June 7, and the Urban League's Sterling Tucker accepted the position of Solidarity Day coordinator.[77]

In the conflict over demands it remained unclear how to draw a win out of the campaign. In increasing desperation, the SCLC was quietly deemphasizing the class-based, multiracial leadership and relying upon allies from the political establishment. Marian Wright describes the process of negotiation in the last period of the Resurrection City occupation.

> I had a silent, quiet cabinet that would meet every night at 10 or 11 o'clock, people like Lisle Carter who was then an assistant secretary at HEW (the Department of Health, Education and Welfare), Carl Holman who was a deputy director of the Civil Rights Commission, Roger Wilkins who was assistant secretary at the Justice Department, John Schnitker who was the undersecretary of agriculture but someone who cared about hungry people. And there was a network of sympathetic officials. And we would meet and I would draft position papers and they would help me correct them and make sure that I was not off base, and then I would deliver those to Ralph Abernathy over at the motel in the middle of the night, and he would get up and say them the next morning. We were able to function in that way because the poor brought their needs and they brought their eloquence. . .It took the eloquence of the poor but also the technical know-how of those middle class leaders to make it happen.[78]

A week before Solidarity Day, the Poor People's Campaign issued a final set of demands authored by Marian Wright in language that would appeal to legislators and policy experts. It was a joint effort with the Department of Justice's Roger Wilkins and M. Carl Holman. The direction from the attorney general was that their involvement escape public notice but assist the SCLC in finding small victories that could be used to close the campaign. They developed a set of forty-nine demands listed under four categories: food, jobs, housing, and welfare. The goals were actually smaller in scope that Rustin's demands and corresponded closely with the legislative priorities of congressional liberals.[79] As with Rustin's revisions, the press welcomed the tampered and tangible asks, including the *Washington Post*: "The demands of the poor, as now formulated, are neither fanciful nor exorbitant. They reflect, almost without exception, goals already enunciated by the President and seriously contemplated by the Congress. Really, what the poor seek is redemption of promises and an enlargement of opportunity. There is nothing at all unreasonable or un-American about that."[80]

Solidarity Day brought at least fifty thousand people to the capital on June 19 to join the remaining encamped residents in calling for national action on poverty.[81] The day was often compared unfavorably to the 1963 March on Washington for Jobs and Freedom. There were strong contingencies from labor union and religious organizations. Speakers included Johnnie Tillmon, Coretta King, and Peggy Terry. It was not the last action of the Poor People's Campaign, but it marked a point after which the occupation began to dwindle, with fewer than seven hundred people remaining in Resurrection City. And as the occupation thinned it was increasingly possible for the smaller crowds be arrested rather than contained. Most of the 567 arrests over the course of the entire occupation took place after Solidarity Day.[82]

Resurrection City was forcibly shut down and its last occupants arrested on June 24. The remaining occupiers waited for an escalated confrontation, but behind the scenes the SCLC had negotiated with the DC police and Department of Justice for a quietly orchestrated end to the city. The first phase was the distribution of free one-way bus tickets to anywhere for anyone willing to peacefully depart by the next day. Instead of park police, who had a more contentious relationship with the camp, they used D.C. police in riot gear from the Civil Disturbance Unit to arrest the 110 residents who refused to leave. The last occupiers sang freedom songs with Hosea Williams by Resurrection City's city hall while waiting to be carried away to jail. The camp was then swept and demolished. Abernathy had led another delegation of 250 residents to Capitol Hill, where they were arrested.[83] Young admitted at a press conference that afternoon that the eviction was perhaps "a real favor."[84]

One hundred Resurrection City residents who were unsure where they were supposed to be gathered outside the SCLC's D.C. office on 14th Street. A larger crowd of several hundred joined them, followed by a broken window and stolen food. The Resurrection City marshals intervened to keep order, using buses to transport the displaced city residents to a local church for the night. The Civil Disturbance Unit was brought in to deal with the remaining crowd. They responded to tossed bottles and cans with one thousand tear gas grenades and a citywide curfew.[85]

NOTES

1. Amy Nathan Wright, "Civil Rights 'Unfinished Business': Poverty, Race, and the 1968 Poor People's Campaign" (Dissertation, The University of Texas at Austin, 2007), 348.

2. Albert E. Gollin, "The Demography of Protest: A Statistical Profile of Participants in the Poor People's Campaign" (Bureau of Social Science Research, Inc., August 5, 1968), 2, 15.

3. "The Poor People's Campaign: A Photographic Journal" (Southern Christian Leadership Conference, 1968), SCLC Papers, Series VIII, 179:19, King Center Archives; Alex Hing, Remembering Resurrection City, interview by John Alexander, October 2017, University of Virginia, https://eastwindezine.com/remembering-resurrection-city/.

4. Bertha Burris, interview by Colleen Wessel-McCoy et al., May 19, 2008; Hy Thurman, interview by author, July 15, 2015; Alex Hing, Remembering Resurrection City; Michael K. Honey, *To the Promised Land: Martin Luther King and the Fight for Economic Justice* (New York: W. W. Norton & Company, 2018), 184. The three southern caravans were actually less frequently brutalized by law enforcement as they traveled. State troopers escorted the Mule train in both Mississippi and Alabama. Segregationist Georgia Governor Lester Maddox stopped the Mule train at the border but eventually let them through and allowed them to sleep in the Douglasville National Guard Armory.

5. Wright, "Civil Rights 'Unfinished Business,'" 258, 261. Wright's sources on the progress of the caravans include daily reports to the Attorney General Ramsey Clark.

6. The participants in the three caravans that started in the Deep South--Freedom Train, Mule Train and Southern—were predominantly Black, although the Southern Caravan included some poor whites. The Freedom Train included participants from Memphis, but otherwise most of the Southern participants were from smaller cities and agricultural areas. The Southern Caravan started with 120 Mississippians and grew en route to 392 people caravanning in seven buses and ten cars. (Wright, "Civil Rights 'Unfinished Business, 264.)

7. McKnight, *The Last Crusade*, 102. Documentation of these workshops comes from the surveillance memos of the Department of Justice's Community Relations Service Division who traveled with the caravan. The CRS was established by the 1964 Civil Rights Act as a government mediator between civil rights activists and their campaign targets. It moved from the Commerce Department to the Justice Department in 1966. Assistant Attorney General Roger Wilkins became the CRS director in 1968, the highest-ranking Black man in the department. The CRS traveled with the caravans and played a significant role in policing and mediating the entire

campaign, working in coordination with other departments and often playing the "good cop" (p. 99–100).

8. Wright, "Civil Rights 'Unfinished Business,'" 271, 273.

9. Daniel M. Cobb, *Native Activism in Cold War America: The Struggle for Sovereignty* (Lawrence: University Press of Kansas, 2008), 175. Wright, "Civil Rights 'Unfinished Business,'" 282. A third feeder had joined them from South Texas in Kansas City.

10. Robert T. Chase, "Class Resurrection: The Poor People's Campaign of 1968 and Resurrection City," *Essays in History*, Corcoran Department of History at the University of Virginia, 40 (1998): 20.

11. Mantler, *Power to the Poor*, 1, 79–82.

12. Cobb, *Native Activism in Cold War America*, 172. Walker worked for United Scholarship Service in Denver and used the organization to host leaders when in Denver. The work of Walker and other American Indian leaders including Victor Charlo, Bob Dumont, and Hank Adams in organizing the American Indian delegation to the Poor People's Campaign met resistance from some elected tribal leaders and government officials. There was conflict within Native circles over whether to participate in Poor People's Campaign, particularly around the fear the confrontation with the Johnson Administration would jeopardize resources allotted to reservations. President Johnson had just given a special message to Congress on March 6, 1968 called "The Forgotten American" (written by Secretary Udall in 1966) that focused entirely on Indian affairs, the first in the twentieth century. A correlating executive order established the National Council on Indian Opportunity that increased the influence of tribal leadership in the Bureau of Indian Affairs. Counted as a victory, the NCAI leadership including Vine Deloria Jr. rejected the idea that American Indians should join a multiracial confrontation with the federal government. (Cobb, *Native Activism in Cold War America*, 162.)

13. Roland L. Freeman, *The Mule Train: A Journey of Hope Remembered* (Nashville, Tenn: Thomas Nelson, 1998), 124.

14. Bertha Burris, interview by author, May 19, 2008.

15. Wright, "Civil Rights 'Unfinished Business,'" 126.

16. Aaron Scott, "The 'Indian Trail': The Poor People's Campaign of 1968 in the Pacific Northwest," *Kairos: The Center for Religions, Rights and Social Justice* (blog), n.d., 2, http://kairoscenter.org/wp-content/uploads/2014/11/PacNWPPC.pdf.

17. Cobb, *Native Activism in Cold War America*, 173.

18. Al McSurely, interview by author, January 30, 2015. McSurely was also working with Vietnam Summer and the National Conference for New Politics. Having been arrested for sedition the previous August for their anti-racist organizing in Pike County, Kentucky and with a newborn, McSurely and Herring were unable to step into organizing the Appalachian delegation directly and connected SCLC to other Appalachian organizers. As the campaign started, McSurely became more directly involved.

19. Al McSurely, interview by author, January 30, 2015.

20. "The Poor People's Campaign: A Photographic Journal"; Cobb, *Native Activism in Cold War America*, 175; Wright, "Civil Rights 'Unfinished Business,'" 183, 258–59.

21. Wright, "Civil Rights 'Unfinished Business,'" 288.

22. Belafonte, Eyes on the Prize interview.

23. "The Poor People's Campaign: A Photographic Journal."; Cobb, *Native Activism in Cold War America*, 173.; Wright, "Civil Rights 'Unfinished Business,'" 350.

24. The enormous undertaking included planning and operations committees that dealt with transportation, food, medical, sanitation, entertainment, building structures, social services, fundraising, legal services, registration, administration, mass meetings, public relations, and legislative research. ("Poor People's Campaign Committees" (Southern Christian Leadership Conference, n.d.), SCLC Papers, Series VIII, 177:19, King Center Archives.)

25. Charlayne Hunter, "On the Case in Resurrection City," in *The Eyes on the Prize Civil Rights Reader: Documents, Speeches, and Firsthand Accounts from the Black Freedom Struggle, 1954–1990*, ed. Clayborne Carson et al. (New York: Viking, 1991), 434–35.

26. Gollin, "The Demography of Protest: A Statistical Profile of Participants in the Poor People's Campaign," 8, 11–12, 14, 16, 18, 20. The careful and thorough registration process yielded fairly confident demographics for people who stayed in Resurrection City or at Hawthorn School. It misses delegations that stayed elsewhere, including in particular additional Native American participants. As noted above it does not include tens of thousands of participants who didn't stay overnight. The survey did not ask participants about income or class. Golins anecdotally notes that the white delegation included college students, anti-poverty activists, religious leaders, welfare moms, older individuals, and hippies. Late-June arrivals, including the caravan from Appalachia, doubled the number of whites (p. 8).

27. Walls, 517–8

28. "A compound of buildings were built in Resurrection City for Abernathy, a large framed building surrounded by A-frames for his aides, and he made a ceremonial performance of arriving with suitcase in hand, but he never lived in Resurrection City and neither did his top lieutenants" (Hunter, "On the Case of Resurrection City," *Eyes on the Prize*, 433).

29. Richard Sidy, Poor People's Campaign Oral History, interview by John Alexander, August 5, 2015, https://pages.shanti.virginia.edu/ResurrectionCity/oral-histories/richard-sidys-reflections/.

30. Ben W. Gilbert, *Ten Blocks from the White House; Anatomy of the Washington Riots of 1968* (New York: F. A. Praeger, 1968), 209. The total rainfall was almost ten inches. An average for that period would have been about five inches.

31. Gollin, "The Demography of Protest: A Statistical Profile of Participants in the Poor People's Campaign," 15.

32. Charlayne Hunter, "On the Case in Resurrection City," in *Black Experience: The Transformation of Activism.*, ed. August Meier, 2d ed. (New Brunswick, N.J.,: Transaction Books, 1973), 9–11., 431.

33. Cobb, *Native Activism in Cold War America*, 175.

34. Mantler, *Power to the Poor*, 152.

35. Appalachian Caravan leader McSurely remembers that they had been sent to Hawthorne by the SCLC leadership because they had not been properly trained in nonviolence or declined to take an oath of nonviolence, a requirement for entry into Resurrection City. When their buses arrived, a young pastor from SCLC climbed aboard and said, "Welcome to Resurrection City. Now has everybody been trained in nonviolent direct action?" The question was met with silence. McSurely knew that not only had they not been trained, in part his responsibility, but he was certain that Click Johnson had a pearl-handled pistol in his pocket. "He doesn't go anywhere without it." Someone spoke up, "What is nonviolence? Al, what is he talking about?" to which McSurely summarized, "It means is that if a cop or anybody hits you while you're demonstrating, you're not allowed to hit back. You have to just take it." To which he could feel everyone thinking, "Are you kidding me?" The lack of training was true of the American Indian contingent and some of the western caravaners as well, also staying at Hawthorne. The understanding was that they could go through nonviolence training at Hawthorne and then move over to the main encampment. McSurely and the Appalachian delegation stayed at Hawthorne for almost three weeks, spending only the final nights in Resurrection City. (McSurely, interview.)

36. Mantler, "Black, Brown and Poor," 213.

37. Mantler, *Power to the Poor*, 160.

38. Chase, "Class Resurrection," 17–18.

39. Chase, "Class Resurrection," 17, 37 note 80. Mantler documents how Hawthorne in particular offered stability and shelter from the dysfunctionality of the overall campaign. This made it possible for shared living and deeper collaboration between people across race and ethnicity, and in regional networks. Many in the Western Caravan had gone directly to Hawthorne, and SCLS failed to greet them or keep them informed about campaign plans (Mantler, *Power to the Poor*, 156–57).

40. Kathy Lohr, "Poor People's Campaign: A Dream Unfulfilled," NPR.org, June 19, 2008, http://www.npr.org/templates/story/story.php?storyId=91626373.

41. McSurely, interview.

42. Mantler, *Power to the Poor*, 154.

43. Eric Blanchard, "The Poor People and the "White Press,"" *Columbia Journalism Review*, Fall 1968, 64. Blanchard, writing about media coverage of the campaign, points out that the content of the Supreme Court decision was subsumed under coverage of the broken windows, including *the New York Times'* "High Court Stormed in Protest by Poor," on May 30.

44. Associated Press, *Cuts for Story: Wa15023 "Welfare"* (Washington, D.C.: AP Archive, 1968), https://www.youtube.com/watch?time_continue=50&v=IFP4hdp44h0&feature=emb_logo.

45. Chase, "Class Resurrection," 14–15; Southern Christian Leadership Conference, "Statement of Demands for Rights of the Poor Presented to Agencies of the U.S. Government by the Poor People's Campaign and Its Committee of 100," May 29, 1968, SCLC Papers, Series VIII, 177:24, King Center Archives.

46. Mantler, *Power to the Poor*, 140.

47. Mantler, *Power to the Poor*, 140.

48. Wright, "Civil Rights 'Unfinished Business,'" 407–8.

49. Mantler, *Power to the Poor*, 160.

50. Sidy, Interview with John Alexander.

51. Jimmy Collier and Frederick Douglass Kirkpatrick, Everybody's Got a Right to Live, LP (New York: Broadside Records, 1968); Pete Seeger, Frederick Douglass Kirkpatrick, and Jimmy Collier, "Everybody's Got a Right To Live," Pete Seeger Now (Columbia, 1968).

52. "A Proposed Plan of Structure of the Poor People's University", SCLC Papers, Series VIII, 179:23, King Center Archives. "Poor People's University Proposed Curriculum", SCLC Papers, Series VIII, 179:23, King Center Archives.

53. Subjects included "Power and How It Can Be Used Effectively," "Effects of Poverty on Growth and Development," "The Negro in Literature," and "Biblical Bases for Social Action and Human Dignity." Lecturers included campaign leaders and outside guests. (Untitled Report on the Poor People's University [Southern Christian Leadership Conference, n.d.], SCLC Papers, Series VIII, 180:4, King Center Archives., "Newsletter for the Poor People's University" [Southern Christian Leadership Conference, May 31, 1968], SCLC Papers, Series VIII, 179:23, King Center Archives., "Newsletter for the Poor People's University" [Southern Christian Leadership Conference, May 29, 1968], SCLC Papers, Series VIII, 179:23, King Center Archives. Chase, "Class Resurrection," 23.)

54. Kenyon Chan, Poor People's Campaign Oral History, interview by John Alexander, September 16, 2015, https://pages.shanti.virginia.edu/ResurrectionCity/oral-histories/kenyon-chan/. Chan, a student from UCLA, was one of several Asian Americans involved in the campaign. He helped organized the tent city occupation before the caravans arrive and lived in Resurrection City until it was demolished. Reflecting on working with the Freedom School, he said that many of the students had more campaign experience than those assigned as educators, leading some youths to lose interest. "I remember the community, the vigor and the positive spirit the people brought to this. Everyone there was poor. We all grew up poor. I grew up poor, too, but these poor families made my poor family seem rich. My father had a little grocery store, a tiny little one-room store. But at least we had food. Some of these folks were farmers and tenant farmers and laborers. But the spirit of the possibility of change was enormous. I'll always remember the real feeling of power that we thought we could change things."

55. Wright, "Civil Rights 'Unfinished Business,'" 510–11. Presciently, Jimmy articulated environmental concerns as well, "We have to think about changing things, cause if we don't they're going to get worse. Like the air being polluted; you think we want to breathe that? And the water, too—we like to go swimming, and we're going to go swimming. And do you think we want to grow up just so we can go to war—we are going to grow up to live, not to kill and die. I've learned here that there are lots of children in this country that can't go to sleep at night because they're afraid rats are going to eat up their feet. Oh, we gonna change things. Yes, sir. Things are going to be different."

56. Giddings, *When and Where I Enter*, 312. Ella Baker also cited ego among SCLC executive staff as a barrier to women's leadership.

57. See Jeanne Theoharis and Komozi Woodard, eds., *Groundwork: Local Black Freedom Movements in America* (New York: New York University Press, 2005); Guida West and Rhoda Lois Blumberg, "Reconstructing Social Protest from a Feminist Perspective," in *Women and Social Protest*, 1990, 3–36; West, *The National Welfare Rights Movement*; Charles Payne, "'Men Led, But Women Organized': Movement Participation of Women in the Mississippi Delta," in *Women and Social Protest*, ed. Guida West and Rhoda Lois Blumberg, 1990, 156–65; Charles M. Payne, *I've Got the Light of Freedom: The Organizing Tradition and the Mississippi Freedom Struggle* (Berkeley: University of California Press, 1995); Evelyn Brooks Higginbotham, *Righteous Discontent: The Women's Movement in the Black Baptist Church, 1880–1920* (Cambridge, Mass.: Harvard University Press, 1993); Vicki L. Crawford, Jacqueline Anne Rouse, and Barbara Woods, *Women in the Civil Rights Movement: Trailblazers and Torchbearers, 1941–1965* (Indiana University Press, 1990).

58. "The Poor People's Campaign: A Photographic Journal," 3.

59. Wright, "Civil Rights 'Unfinished Business,'" 421–22; Abernathy, *And the Walls Came Tumbling Down*, 511.

60. Hunter, "On the Case in Resurrection City," 1991, 432.

61. McKnight, *The Last Crusade*, 60–61; Burns, *To the Mountaintop*, 526. King had assumed that Lawson and COME had secured the support of these groups in the organizing of the march. McKnight cites the Federal Bureau of Investigation, U.S. Department of Justice, Moore to Sullivan, March 29, 1968, COINTELPRO/"Black Nationalist Hate Groups," Headquarters file, 100–448006–93, and Moore to Sullivan, March 28, 1968, Memphis Sanitation Workers' Strike, Washington Headquarters file, 157–9146-38.

62. This leadership included the Milwaukee Commandos, Louisiana's Deacons of Defense and Justice, and the Memphis Invaders. Some from among these delegations arrived in D.C. early to help build the shelters of Resurrection City. (Wright, "Civil Rights 'Unfinished Business,'" 260.) Individual Black Panthers were involved with the campaign and California and Colorado-based chapters helped organize funding and participants for the campaign. (Mantler, *Power to the Poor*, 125.)

63. Hunter, "On the Case in Resurrection City," 1991, 428.

64. McKnight, *The Last Crusade*, 130.

65. Gilbert, *Ten Blocks from the White House: Anatomy of the Washington Riots of 1968*, 199, 201–2.

66. King, "See You in Washington (January 1968)," 1, 6–7.

67. King, *Where Do We Go from Here: Chaos or Community?*, 1967, 142.

68. Thomas F. Jackson, *From Civil Rights to Human Rights: Martin Luther King, Jr., and the Struggle for Economic Justice* (Philadelphia, Pa: University of Pennsylvania Press, 2007), 343. Jackson notes that these demands would have cost $12 billion more a year than the Freedom Budget for All Americans. The total approximated what was spent on the Vietnam War in 1968.

69. Alyosha Goldstein observes that mid-century liberalism sought to neutralize inequality and racial antagonisms by creating the normative category of poverty as both part of and distinct from liberal society. This categorization circumvented

the persistence of poverty from belying the grand narrative of capitalist liberalism through orchestrated inclusion of the poor under a compatible narrative about who is poor and why they are poor. Along this line the "maximum feasible participation" part of War on Poverty programs circumvented uncontrollable expressions and forms of leadership by creating opportunities for liberal self-expression by the poor in existing structures. Goldstein observes that the Poor People's Campaign defied the containment of the poor as a normative category as well as refusing to be limited to sanctioned avenues of self-expression. "The very heterogeneity of the campaign and the multivalence of the demands that petitioners presented meant that there could be no single spokesman or representative." Goldstein argues the Poor People's Campaign disaggregated "the poor" as a single category and defied the state-sanctioned parameters of political participation. But defying narrow categorization and showing the breadth and depth of poverty was only part of King's vision for a class-based leadership and motion of the poor. Those who came together for the Poor People's Campaign did not successfully move from the disaggregation of the liberal normative categorization of poverty (as anachronistic aberrations from an otherwise healthy system) to re-aggregation as a class on its own terms. This limited their ability to move from an expression of dissent to truly heralding a revolution of values (Goldstein, *Poverty in Common*, 6, 152).

70. Chase, "Class Resurrection," 20.; Mantler, *Power to the Poor*, 69.

71. Black capitalism in the 1960 had roots in Booker T. Washington's leadership and strategy. It was supported by NAACP, Urban League, some leaders within CORE, and others. White elites saw the position as an opportunity for common ground with Black activists and an ideologically acceptable response to Black inequality. Nixon made this position part of his presidential campaign and hired CORE founder James Farmer for his administration.

72. Southern Christian Leadership Conference, "Statement of Demands.," 11, 19, 40–41. For an analysis of the concept of "maximum feasible participation" as a project of liberalism, see Goldstein, *Poverty in Common*.

73. Chase, "Class Resurrection"; Jervis Anderson, *Bayard Rustin: Troubles I've Seen* (New York: Harper Collins, 1997), 347–48; Jerald Podair, *Bayard Rustin: American Dreamer* (Lanham, MD: Rowman & Littlefield, 2009), 85.

74. Fager, *Uncertain Resurrection: The Poor People's Washington Campaign*, 62.

75. Mantler, "Black, Brown and Poor," 331.

76. Chase, "Class Resurrection," 25; McKnight, *The Last Crusade*, 126.

77. Marian Wright Edelman, interview by Henry Hampton, December 21, 1988, Eyes on the Prize II, Washington University Libraries, Film and Media Archive, Henry Hampton Collection, http://digital.wustl.edu/e/eii/eiiweb/ede5427.0676.044m arianwrightedelman.html.

78. McKnight, *The Last Crusade*, 127. Demands included the Clark Emergency Employment Bill, the pending housing bill, and the repeal of the compulsory work requirements of the 1967 Social Security Amendments (a NWRO priority). They asked to "maintain" appropriations for school lunch and breakfast programs and "retain" the Javits Amendment giving $227 million to food programs that year. They

also asked for collective bargaining rights for farm workers, increased appropriations for food stamps and commodity programs.

79. Chase, "Class Resurrection," 27.

80. Juneteenth, now a federal holiday, marks the anniversary of when notice of emancipation finally reached enslaved families in Texas in 1865, two and half years after the Emancipation Proclamation.

81. McKnight, *The Last Crusade*, 130.

82. McKnight, *The Last Crusade*, 136–38.; McSurely, interview.

83. McKnight, *The Last Crusade*, 138. Gilbert, *Ten Blocks from the White House; Anatomy of the Washington Riots of 1968*, 202.

84. Gilbert, *Ten Blocks from the White House; Anatomy of the Washington Riots of 1968*, 206–7.

Chapter 4

Assessing the Campaign

Bertha Burris of Marks, Mississippi, reflected, "We knew that we weren't going to get forty acres and a mule, but we did believe the part about being able to get better jobs and a better education for our children. . . . But most of us came back here to the same old same old." Yet she says she found new courage to address problems in her community. Dora Collins, also of Marks, similarly remembers the disappointment that the problems raised in the campaign remained unaddressed, although she said taking part in the action, "lifted my spirits and changed the way I think forever."[1] When Ethel Mae Matthews came with a two-week welfare rights delegation, she said Resurrection City, "looked like a little chicken coop to me sitting in a mud puddle," but that it also changed her whole life. "Those two weeks was just like going to school."[2]

In assessing whether the campaign was a success, failure, or some mix of both, one's answer depends on how one understands the purpose and possibility of the campaign. Should the demands challenge or align with the Johnson administration? How would the framing of poverty as experienced by Chicanos, Puerto Ricans, Natives, and whites be included in messaging and demands? How could a campaign against poverty respond to racism and war? What was its contribution to a larger movement against the triple evils of racism, poverty, and militarism? These questions deal with how problems become issues, the tension between reforms and revolution, and the relationship of mobilizing to organizing. The Poor People's Campaign was intended to be a living space to interrogate and learn from those questions. What King suggested before his assassination—and what led him to plan the Poor People's Campaign—was that given the conditions of the period, the primary objective was to build strength as a new and unprecedented social force of the poor across racial lines to make moral claims around class demands.

When a people are mired in oppression, they realize deliverance when they have accumulated the power to enforce change. When they have amassed such strength, the writing of a program becomes almost an administrative detail. It is immaterial who presents the program: what is material is the presence of an ability to make events happen. . . . The call to prepare programs distracts us excessively from our basic and primary tasks. . . . We are, in fact, being counseled to put the cart before the horse. . . . Our nettlesome task is to discover how to organize our strength into compelling power so that government cannot elude our demands. We must develop, from strength, a situation in which the government finds it wise and prudent to collaborate with us.[3]

The campaign did prove how nettlesome the task of organizing as a social force with compelling power would be, indeed a thorn in the side. But what made the nettlesome task impossible was that there was not clarity among the leadership about the task itself and how a campaign could be a set of tactics that "organizes our strength into compelling power." King identified that to do that, they would need to consolidate of a new multiracial leadership of poor people who together could figure out how to move forward a human rights movement that strategically attacked the enmeshed evils of racism, poverty, and militarism.

King saw the campaign as an opportunity to assess their strengths and weaknesses relative to the strengths and weaknesses of their opponents. He emphasized that if they were making the right demands, the first answer they would receive in Washington would be no.[4] Their demands would only be achieved by a larger restructuring of society than would be willingly bestowed. But the demands were not supplicants. Initial demands would mirror the aspirations of those who joined the struggle, strengthening organization and deepening commitment among those who are prepared to take action together. Claiming the right to a job or income, to raise your own children, to health care, ancestral lands, education, and housing all galvanized people's imagination around their shared values, the contradiction of poverty in the midst of great productive capacity, and the reality that poverty could be ended. He said they needed demands that Congress could not immediately respond to but that would escalate the campaign in response to that "no." And from that experience they would have new knowledge of their opposition and new, broad relationships. He believed leaders would be compelled forward by wins and learn from losses, both strengthening a new network of leaders for more.[5]

King was killed when he was just beginning to assemble a new leadership around this strategy. In the short weeks before the Poor People's Campaign was launched, SCLC leadership hastily assembled a massive six-week occupation of 6,000 people and a march on Washington of 50,000. The logistics of this type of prolonged action where they were responsible for the well-being of so many people was overwhelming. The multiracial leadership of organizers from across the country that King had assembled in March was critical to the success of the action, but they all struggled to figure out how to work out a shared strategy and then related tactics and demands. In the chaos the SCLC executive staff retreated to what they knew how to do, working independently, hierarchically, and without transparency. And when everyone got rained out and worn out, taking some wins and heading home became very appealing.

And so behind closed doors with the Department of Justice, a small team, including Marian Wright, George Wiley of NWRO and SCLC executives negotiated a set of legislative victories that were, in effect, the terms of surrender. Several of them were pledges from officials that never materialized. Others did meet urgent needs. They added $25 million in funding for Head Start programs in Alabama and Mississippi. The Office of Economic Opportunity added 1,300 new hires. The Department of Agriculture, which had just returned a $200 million surplus to the treasury, agreed to add food programs in all of the one thousand poorest counties and reduced the price of food stamps, which at the time had to be purchased by users. The free and reduced-price school lunch program received an additional $100 million. The Department of Justice pledged to enforce rules prohibiting green card farmworkers from being used to break strikes. (They did not, and this anti-immigrant position among farmworker organizing intensified in subsequent years.)[6] The Department of Interior pledged to accelerate its efforts to develop community-controlled schools for Native American children. Housing and Urban Development pledged to refrain from further evictions without replacement housing in urban renewal projects.[7] (They did not.) The Secretary of State pledged to address Mexican American land disputes. (They did not.) The Labor Secretary pledged to promote policies that would create 100,000 new jobs by the end of the year, although that was already projected by the growth pattern of the first half of 1968.[8] The Department of Health, Education and Welfare streamlined aspects of the welfare application process, a demand from NWRO.[9]

There are three standard assessments of the Poor People's Campaign: failure, failure with some short-term wins, or failure with some long-term contributions. The view that predominated in early histories and media accounts were varying degrees of overall failure. Following the media's lead, some said the poor were hopelessly violent, or pitiful, or in need of saving rather than organizing. Friendlier interpretations pointed to the logistical challenges of a residential occupation, saying leaders were too pulled into mutual aid to work to think clearly on the more political tasks. Some sympathized that in the aftermath of King's death the leadership vacuum would have doomed any undertaking. Indeed, the hierarchical leadership model of the SCLC had made King indispensable. In a variation on this theme, soured and ill-handled relationships with the media were to blame, because no one could handle that aspect of organizing like King. The campaign was also competing for attention in a frantic year, full of domestic and global crises, including the height of the Vietnam War, multiple assassinations, and uprisings in France, Czechoslovakia, and Mexico.[10] And then there was the rain, also to blame.

Speaking personally about the challenge of deciphering what steps would follow the campaign, SCLC Vice President Bill Rutherford reflected, "I think the spirit went out of people. . . . When I say (the Poor People's Campaign) was the Little Bighorn of the Civil Rights Movement, in fact it was the end of the hopes and dreams of many, many people who had come from various parts of the country to participate. It was very sad, depressed, and depressing scene altogether."[11] For many, Chuck Fager's first-person assessment is the standard summary.

> The movement left Congress unmoved and possibly even more hostile to the poor. The inefficiency, waste of resources, and other serious internal shortcomings of the organization became painfully visible, major obstacles to its success. All of these alienated a substantial portion of its previous constituency, black *and* white, very likely set back the prospects for a viable multi-ethnic coalition, and weakened by default the credibility of nonviolent change. None of the objectives Martin Luther King hoped to achieve by the Campaign are much nearer . . . but now we have lost him, his dream has dissipated and the failure of the Poor People's Campaign has left us without an answer to. . . . Where do we go from here?[12]

Michael Harrington, who had worked with King as part of the campaign's research committee to set the initial demands, had a similar assessment after his lecture at the Poor People's University. He said he media reports told him there was violence within the encampment, knowing even going into the experience that "the beloved community was not there by the Washington Monument." But after being so harassed by a resident that he cut the lecture short and ran away, he said, "It dawned on me that this was an end of an entire period of my life . . . and that one of the most marvelous political movements in America . . . had come to an end. And that the beloved community was gone forever."[13]

How one understands the purpose of the campaign correlates with ones assessment of its outcome. From a position of Campaign leadership, Wright saw it as a success.

> The campaign itself and the pressure that was bought to bear on the federal government resulted in major federal investment and at minimum nationwide nutrition programs. Food stamps. School lunches. Did it end poverty? Obviously not. Was it ever going to? No. But did it succeed in bringing attention to poverty in

American and did it result in some federal intervention to alleviate the terrible
conditions that so many were facing in America? Yes, it did.[14]

In Abernathy's telling, "Eventually the Congress enacted virtually everything we wanted," an assessment which gives just as much insight into his
understanding of the campaign's purpose as it does the question of success
or failure.[15]

Social movement theorists Richard Cloward and Frances Fox Piven were
involved in anti-poverty organizing, particularly around welfare rights, and
took part in actions with NWRO during the campaign. Their historical study
of movements argues that the poor only win what, "historical circumstances
[have] already made ready to be conceded."[16] They argue against organizing forms that emphasize leadership development and building sustained
power, which they say dampens the spontaneity and anger that mobilizing
requires. In this strategy organizers must assess the conditions of the period
and find ways to agitate for what a majority of the population will be willing
to concede when the question is forced. In 1968 the nation was engrossed
financially, politically, and emotionally in the Vietnam War, and according
to Cloward and Piven, the public was not interested in responding to the
demands of the poor. A largely conservative Democratic Congress, emboldened by a general fear of urban riots, was ready to rescind, rather than expand,
domestic anti-poverty programs. The policy wins of the campaign came from
finding instances of overlap between campaign demands and the domestic
platform of the Johnson White House and liberal legislators. In this assessment, even if King had lived, even if it hadn't rained, these political conditions would have prevented more substantial gains.

Keri Day brings womanist and Black feminist scholarship to bear on the
pervasive sexism and homophobia and malformed the leadership and strategies of the campaign. It was not simply the exclusion of women from the
central command positions claimed by the SCLC executive staff but also
patriarchal leadership practices, such as the tendency to remain aloof from
campaign participants and seek self-promotion.

Gordon Mantler argues that without strong inner-group racial and ethnic power, the proposal for a multiracial movement was impossible. The
diverse communities that came together in the Poor People's Campaign
lacked equal footing and power that would have enabled them to build the
campaign together on equal terms. As a result, late-1960s attempts of multiracial, class-based organizing like the Poor People's Campaign and original
Rainbow Coalition taught activists that identity, racial pride, and a group's
"unique place in the American psyche" were concepts that "unified people in
a way, at least in the short term, that disparate experiences of poverty often
did not." While this limited the campaign's success in 1968, it was also the

source of its long-term contribution. It helped make connections within ethic groups for regional and national identity-based organizing in the years that followed. Mantler argues it demonstrated the need for the redefining and affirming of identity as an important part of the struggle for political power and as a necessary foundation for class-based organizing.[17]

POLITICAL POLICE

Gerald McKnight argues that more blame for the campaign's failure should be attributed to the interference of surveillance-state provocateurs and agitators. These malicious attacks were not side notes, and they are not limited to that particular administration or moment in history. Washington, D.C., was one of the cities where there had been violence following King's assassination, with eleven deaths, 1,200 injuries, and an estimated $19 million in damages. The plans to bring thousands of poor people to the capital just a few weeks later sparked intense opposition across partisan lines. The SCLC insisted that the campaign was actually the alternative to more rioting, because it used organized nonviolence to respond to the inequalities and stifling existence that gave rise to violent uprisings.[18] It was estimated that there were ten thousand police and military troops on standby for the arrival of the poor in the Capital. Five thousand, four hundred army troops could be there within six hours, and nearly fifteen thousand more within seventy-two hours. D.C. Police, White House Police, Capitol Police, and National Park Service Police each had roles in containing the encampment and daily demonstrations around the city. But the policing of the campaign was not limited to extra police shifts and at the ready military. The Poor People's Campaign was attacked through covert and extrajudicial operations of the US government's extensive surveillance and counterintelligence programs.[19]

In preparation for the encampment, elected officials and the Johnson administration reached to the history and lessons of the Bonus Army, an occupation by World War Iveterans and their families during the Great Depression.[20] This precedent was on the minds of the SCLC as well, a parallel pointed out to them by King adviser Stan Levinson.[21] In the midst of the Great Depression as many as 24,000 poor veterans and their families (totaling 41,000 people) built a multiracial, unsegregated encampment in the Anacostia area of D.C. in the spring and summer of 1932. They were demanding the early payment of earned service "adjusted compensation" that had been granted in the form of bonds that wouldn't mature until 1945.[22] They called their occupation "Hooverville" after then president Herbert Hoover. On July 28 Hoover ordered their removal by military force under the leadership of General Douglas A. MacArthur, Major George S. Patton, Major Dwight D.

Eisenhower, and J. Edgar Hoover. Two veterans were killed, dozens were injured, and the encampment was burned to the ground. This attack on poor veterans was unpopular nationally and contributed to Hoover's reelection loss later that year to Franklin D. Roosevelt. The defeated veterans organized a second occupation in May 1933 and returned to D.C. Although President Roosevelt opposed the early disbursement, he provided the marchers with a campsite in Virginia, three meals a day, and visits from First Lady Eleanor. So while Hoover and Roosevelt held the same position on the bond disbursement, they responded to the occupation differently. One veteran commented, "Hoover sent the army; Roosevelt sent his wife." The veterans eventually won the early full redemption in 1936, overcoming Roosevelt's presidential veto.[23] And so the Johnson administration, also in an election year, eschewed Hoover's mistakes and followed Roosevelt's example. They had no interest in meeting the campaign's demands, but they did grant them the park permit for a legal encampment, along with "an invitation to dialogue, compassionate rhetoric, and, in the words of one staffer, 'some small victories if possible.'"[24]

This outward appeasement and grudging welcome of the Poor People's Campaign, including the park permit for an encampment, was only a small part of the full state response to the campaign, the threat it was imagined to represent, and the threat it actually represented. In the last days of the end of the encampment, the SCLC leadership began to articulate their fears that there were infiltrators and paid agents. Andrew Young said they were, "certain that Resurrection City was infested with undercover agents and agent provocateurs. I believe the National Park Services and other government agencies sent in officers posing as poor people, and it was the infiltrators who kept people stirred up against us inside Resurrection City."[25] But the press dismissed their suspicions as excuses for increasing internal violence and an inability to control those within the city who advocated violent protest.[26] In Al McSurely's experience the FBI were constantly present. "I had an experience with Senator John Cooper, a big shot Republican from Kentucky, who as soon as we came in said, 'Now who of you are from Kentucky?' We raised our hands, including myself; I lived there. And Cooper said, 'Now you're McSurely. You're not from KY.' I don't think he knew me by sight. I think the FBI had told him about me. It was very transparent."[27]

McKnight's study of the role of political police in the campaign concludes that "lawless elements of the American surveillance state, especially the FBI, played a major role in the campaign's bafflement and undoing." The campaign was targeted for disruption, not just surveillance, with a complicit media, legislature and civil society.[28] In all, McKnight has discovered there were at least twenty government agents and symbol (paid) informants within Resurrection City itself, including staffing Resurrection City's lost and found desk.[29] Intelligence gathering, within and outside of Resurrection City, came through agents, operatives, and informants from the following government agencies: U.S. Army Intelligence, FBI's Domestic Intelligence Division, Intelligence Division of the Metropolitan Police Department, the Department of Justice's civil-rights era Community Relations Service Division (CRS) and special task force "RC" (Resurrection City) Squad, National Park Service Police, and Border Patrol.[30]

The FBI's Domestic Intelligence Division used the Counterintelligence Program (COINTELPRO) to monitor, infiltrate, discredit, and disrupt domestic political organizations, including King and the SCLC, across King's career. Paid FBI informant Jim Harrison worked as the SCLC accountant before King's assassination and through the period of the Poor People's Campaign.[31] COINTELPRO's director, William Sullivan, described their work as "rough, tough, dirty business" that aimed to achieve its politically oriented objectives extrajudicially. They created a special unit called POCAM to target the Poor People's Campaign. POCAM records suggest that like in other COINTELPRO operations, the FBI went beyond data collection to engage in disruptive and agitational tactics, including interceding to prevent the campaign from receiving grant funding and spreading rumors among potential recruits that they would be left stranded in Washington.[32] FBI field offices in Alabama and Georgia used their informant network to spread rumors that welfare recipients would lose their benefits if they traveled to Washington, D.C. One POCAM memo recommended the exacerbation of racial tension between a SCLC staffer and white American Friends Service Committee (AFSC) leaders through the dissemination of information about the conflict to "cooperative news media sources." Another planted photos of "militant and aggressive looking" Black youths at a campaign rally in Cleveland with "friendly media sources."[33]

Hoover's directions to agents and their informants asked for the documentation of "immorality, dishonesty, and hypocrisy" among the campaign leadership, a directive he had used extensively in his surveillance of King. The bureau disseminated a heavily filtered narrative of the campaign to the White House, secretary of state, CIA, Defense Intelligence Agency, Army, and Secret Service through teletypes that were further disseminated to a wide range of government agencies, such as the departments of Agriculture, Defense, and Interior. The reports described widespread violence and fixated on interracial sex, including accusations that there were rumors among residents that Abernathy was caught "in bed with a white female."[34] Other rumors focused on "black terrorists" among the camp. Even when these rumors had been proven false, the conclusions drawn from those stories continued to circulate and characterize the Campaign. Rumors within the camp, like that Abernathy had a heart attack, that Stokley Carmichael had been shot, and that there were hidden arsenals of weapons within the camp, contributed to internal agitation, confusion, and demoralization.[35]

The Poor People's Campaign was also the first large-scale application of Attorney General Ramsey Clark's Interdivisional Intelligence Unit (IDIU). The program was developed in the wake of the urban uprisings related to King's assassination. It coordinated intelligence gathering between the DOJ, FBI, and the Army's growing domestic intelligence network, in coordination with local and state governments, to suppress civil disorders. IDIU brought an unprecedented level of monitoring including the unauthorized interception of SCLC radio communications, aerial reconnaissance missions over the city, and a Black major reassigned from Vietnam to participate undercover in the tent city.[36] As noted above, campaign leaders were working closely behind closed doors with the DOJ to developing its demands, tactics, and eventual closure of Resurrection City.[37]

MEDIA

While covered fairly extensively in the media at the time, newspaper sources from the day are remarkably unvaried and generally uninteresting, except in their collective capacity to miss the point. Gordon Mantler observes, "Rather than see the campaign as an attempt to shift from a race-based to a class-based framework and build a new coalition in the process, media frames strongly contributed to one interpretation: that the term poor was just another word for 'Black' and that the Poor People's Campaign was just another civil rights episode. The press pre-empted the class rhetoric and values of the Poor People's Campaign."[38] Black families and young people were two-thirds of Resurrection City residents, but including those who stayed at Hawthorne School and elsewhere, over 1,600 of the participants were not. Yet that historically unprecedented multiracial class character was dismissed, as in *Newsweek*, as a "symbolic smattering of whites, Indians, Puerto Ricans, and Mexican Americans."[39]

The campaign needed supportive media in order to communicate with the public nationally and gain broad pressure for their demands. But sustained conflict with the media limited their effectiveness. Even sympathetic journalists grew frustrated when SCLC executive staff were regularly late to press briefings and shared unclear and incorrect information.[40] The camp marshals, seeking to protect residents from voyeurism, refused unrestricted access to journalists. Accustomed to being courted by civil rights activists eager for coverage, the journalists felt rebuffed by the distancing.[41] As the weeks progressed, sympathetic stories were less frequent. The focus was increasingly on violence, illness, and desertion within Resurrection City. And the assaults of two journalists and theft of an independent photographer's camera were detrimental.[42] Headlines included, "'Oppressed' Adopt Traits of Oppressors" (*Washington Evening Star*), "Threat of Anarchy in Nation's Capital" (*U.S. News & World Report*), "Marshals Picked From Gangs" (*Washington Post*), and "Insurrection City" (*Time*).[43] Abernathy responded saying that while there is no excuse for violence anywhere, violence within Resurrection City is the imitation of a violent society. "There is a greater evil than a few outbreaks in Resurrection City . . . the evil of widespread poverty in America." But his attempt to refocus the message was unsuccessful.[44]

Part of residents' and marshals' refusal to allow unrestricted access to journalists lay in fears that the media would sensationalize and shame what they saw without accurately portraying the ways they were resisting dehumanization, claiming their human dignity, and fighting for social transformation. Distrust increased as that turned out to be true. Eric Blanchard, Information Office Director for the campaign, summarized that the coverage of the Poor People's Campaign was "pedestrian" and "police-blotter superficial."[45] As a trained journalist, he recognized that the communications industry knew little about the subject on which they were to report and therefore could only resort to the immediately observable: march numbers, conflicts, and quotes from recognizable leaders. The campaign and Resurrection City were intended to catch national attention but then draw the nation into a conversation about the substance of the issue. Blanchard reflected, "Unless we can read in our national press about the violence to the poor that comes from starving for a full stomach, equal treatment, and a reasonably secure future, we will remain ignorant and be frightened of their certain and predictable wrath."[46]

A very different role was played by participant journalists Charlyne Hunter and Chuck Fager, and by photographers Roland Freeman, Jill Freedman, and Robert Houston. Aaron Bryant points out that Houston, who was on assignment from *Life* magazine, "created snapshots of dignity and found nobility where it was assumed not to exist." Instead of romanticizing poverty, sentimentalizing residents, or playing to "momentary sensationalism," Houston's images point to a "collective vision."[47] Houston's own experiences within Resurrection City built his commitment to use his skills to amplify their taking action together. At one point a group of police approached him in Resurrection City, but when he stepped back he realized there were hundreds of residents behind him, saying "Don't run. Tell our story." and "We have your back." He said, "You would be surprised . . . when your backs are against the wall, everybody is your brother, everybody is your sister. The misery doesn't respect anything."[48]

Part of the surprise, contradiction, and missed opportunity in the relationship between the Poor People's Campaign and the media was in the failure of campaign leaders to develop new communications tactics instead of relying on what had been effective tactics in the headline campaigns of the Civil Rights Movement. But with an SCLC leadership unconvinced themselves of the significance of the multracial and class character of the anti-poverty campaign, it is not surprising that they were ineffective in communicating that significance to the media or developing actions that catalyzed it. Although this history is more complicated, it is true that northern media coverage of the white supremacy of southern law enforcement, elected officials, and white people's violent repression of Black communities and civil rights activism contributed to the communications needs of the campaigns against segregation and voter suppression.[49] Brutalized yet nonviolent activists galvanized the sympathy of a national audience, forcing the tepid federal government to intervene judicially and militarily. But in the national media southern racism was portrayed as a regionally specific error in conflict with American values. It was a repairable but not fatal democratic flaw.

Thousands of racially and ethnically diverse poor people from across the country converging in the political center of the nation garnered not sympathy but discomfort, fear, and cognitive dissonance. Media often shared more in common with the national response to Black urban uprisings. Perceiving the extent of the critique leveled by the "unsettling force" of the multiracial poor, one journalist candidly observed that the campaign's unspoken limitation was "that eliminating poverty in America is something America does not want to do," because "the problem of structural poverty is the problem of a structure that insures that the poor will be denied access to the means to alleviate their condition."[50] The Civil Rights Movement had forced a country to do what it refused to do, but it did so by winning the eventual support of sections of the nation who were not being asked to give up power or money. As King said, "It didn't cost one penny to integrate lunch counters." But now they were asking the nation to do something that would cost billions of dollars and require shifts in economic and political power.

An approach to media is important for any strategy of social change. It is a miscalculation to think that if the poor can figure out how to make their plight accessible and perceivable, then the media will share that information, some significant portion of the public will be sympathetically moved, and policy makers will respond with solutions. However media coverage can play a significant role in breaking isolation and changing narratives about who is poor and why they are poor.

POST RESURRECTION CITY: CHARLESTON

Abernathy said it was the applause and celebration of his speech on Solidarity Day that gave him hope that "the entire Poor People's Campaign had been justified by that one great rally in which the voice of the poor had last been heard." He continued, "Standing there, listening to the cheers . . . I was prepared to say that we had been successful."[51] Calling the language of the poor "cries and groans" that are then interpreted by campaign leaders, he implies that the only agency of the poor is in an inarticulate expression of powerlessness by which the previously indifferent powerful are moved. The voice of the poor is unintelligible and ready for translation to those with the power to enact change. Even though Abernathy kept the language of King's call for "poor power," and "the poor are no long divided,"[52] the strategy he pursued and tactics he emphasized did not build the forms of multiracial, multiethnic leadership around human rights demands that King suggested when he talked about the nettlesome task of building power for poor people.

The Washington, D.C., encampment has come to represent the entirety of the Poor People's Campaign, but it was intended to be the first of many phases of a campaign of the poor. Under Abernathy's leadership, the SCLC maintained that the events in D.C. were the "Washington Phase" of a continuing Poor People's Campaign. They took the mule train wagons to the 1968 Republican National Convention in Miami and Democratic National Convention in Chicago, without impacting either.[53] But the Poor People's Campaign's post-Washington win came in Charleston, South Carolina, at the hands of four hundred striking hospital workers—the majority of whom were Black women—who took on the Medical University of South Carolina (MUSC). Twelve hospital workers were fired in March 1969 for attempting to form a union. They responded with a walkout that spread to other hospital branches. Their leadership included movement educator Septima Clark and Mary Moultrie, a nurse's aide (even though she was qualified to be a licensed practical nurse) who had been trained at the Highlander Folk School.[54]

The strike was supported by and built on the successes of the New York Local 1199B of the Hospital and Nursing Home Employees Union, also predominantly female, Black, and Puerto Rican. They had just won concessions against nonprofit New York hospitals that were exempt from minimum-wage laws.[55] When the strikers invited the SCLC to join them, the SCLC called it the Charleston Phase of the Poor People's Campaign. After a 113-day strike and more than one thousand arrests, they won a $0.30 raise ($2.27 in 2020 dollars). They didn't win union rights, but they did win a modified collective bargaining process and an employee credit union that made automatic dues possible, forming District 1199B.[56]

Coretta Scott King played a powerful and effective role in the campaign, including leading a Mother's Day march of thirteen thousand people in 1969 that concluded with her speech at Emmanuel AME.[57] This was one year after she had led a Mother's Day march to initiate the Washington phase of the Poor People's Campaign. Despite the effectiveness of her leadership on the campaign's front lines, Coretta was asked by the SCLC executive staff to step away from organizing work and focus on writing a book about being King's wife.[58]

The strike victory was significant for Abernathy. He felt that the failures of the Washington phase of the Poor People's Campaign had been attributed to him, while its successes were attributed to King's legacy. Charleston gave direction and energy to the post-King SCLC. They joined striking sanitation workers in Atlanta, winning raises in 1970.[59] And they organized a "march against oppression," led by a mule-drawn wagon, in the wake of the police shooting of six Black protesters during an uprising in response to the torture and murder of an incarcerated Black sixteen-year-old in Augusta, Georgia, in May 1970.[60] Although they continued to use the language of the Poor People's Campaign into the early 1970s, they didn't try to reconvene the multiracial leadership of the Washington campaign.

The win by the striking hospital workers was also a significant victory for labor and women of color, particularly in the South.[61] Across the 1970s civil rights organizations targeted economic discrimination and exclusions. Although SCLC and others continued to mobilize marches and protests, the organizations whose tactical strengths were litigation, lobbying, and advocacy predominated. The NAACP Legal Defense Fund brought thousands of lawsuits that targeted the enforcement of the 1964 Civil Rights Act's Title VII, which prohibited employment discrimination. The primary targets in the South were textile and paper industry, with nearly all companies in those industries being sued by Black employees in the 1970s.[62] Litigation was increasingly the primary tactic, with less reliance on mobilizing and organizing campaigns.

Not long after the Washington phase of the Poor People's Campaign, Bayard Rustin went on to direct the AFL-CIO-sponsored A. Philip Randolph Institute that registered large number of Black people to vote, claiming credit for one million new Black voters for Carter in 1976, and lobbied for the interests of Black union members. Jesse Jackson went to focus on organizing in Chicago, including Operation Breadbasket, and by 1980 his Operation PUSH had over 70 chapters, negotiating hiring agreements with major corporations like Coca-Cola and General Motors. They played an important role in replacing the Mayor Daley and his political machine with Mayor Harold Washington though a multiracial organizing effort with roots in the original Rainbow Coalition. Andrew Young moved to a successful political career as the mayor of Atlanta, a U.N. ambassador, and even a stint as a spokesperson for Walmart's effort to establish stores in Africa. He was among several civil rights leaders who pursued a strategy of running for elected office, seeking political power hoping that it would lead to greater economic and social power for Black communities.[63]

Belafonte, intimately involved and yet not enmeshed as SCLC staff, witnessed the aftermath. "There was no clarity as to what were the objectives any more . . . and in the confusion . . . a lot of people broke off and did things because they really believe that in light of no real understanding and no great leadership for this, they would do what they could do in their own little environment."[64] He saw the behavior not as power grabs, but a strategic disunity and confusion that made collaborative action impossible. But this strategic disunity predated King's assassination. King disagreed that private-sector programs, even good ones, could solve problems that would actually require the restructuring of the economy and public-sector solutions.[65] Belafonte recalls King being challenged by his SCLC deputies on his accelerating radicalism generally, and the Poor People's Campaign specifically, just a week before he died. Describing King as a "socialist and revolutionary thinker," Belafonte says King clashed with Andrew Young, over not only the Poor People's Campaign, but King's thoroughgoing critique of capitalism.[66] In a later interview, one of King's deputies anonymously told Vincent Harding, "In a way, it was probably best for many of us who worked with Martin that he was killed when he was, because he was moving into some radical directions that very few of us had been prepared for. . . . And I don't think that many of us on the staff would have been ready to take the risks of life, possessions, security, and status that such a move would have involved. . . . I'm pretty sure I wouldn't have been willing."[67] But King was not alone in seeing the task of the era differently.

THE SMALL WINS IN THE BIG LOSS

In Robert Chase's examination of the way that the Poor People's Campaign did and did not contribute to class-based organizing, he observes that while there was "disappointment among the various minority activists concerning the . . . failure to win significant anti-poverty legislation, the participants were still part of a process that formed the beginnings of a 'bottom-up' coalition." He said there was an attempt to "create a democratic, grass-roots system of political representation as an alternative to the traditional politics of Washington, D.C."[68] Leaders from across the country and across lines of division had time together living in Resurrection City and at Hawthorne School to make connections and begin to think about how the struggles they were waging in their own communities related to the whole. Los Angeles Brown Beret Carlos Montes describes going "through a political change, from what I would call a nationalist to more of an international perspective. . . . My rhetoric changed." He began to see class operating among whites, disaggregating white supremacy's cross-class narrative, so he began to more precisely, "criticize the capitalist structure and its most common defenders, *rich* white men." He said this was a valuable lesson for his later work in the Chicano movement and as labor organizer.[69]

Jesse Jackson, who had spent more time on the ground in Resurrection City, was among those who identified objectives beyond legislative demands. "We gained victory in the few concrete programs. . . . But more importantly, our victory was bigger. . . . Victory is the poor of all races coming together. Victory is to be ignored by the political power of the White House but to have the capacity to respond with the soul power of the black house. Victory is the new relationships created and the lessons learned." Jackson put the Poor People's Campaign in the longer arc of social movement building, saying "History is on our side. Resurrection City cannot be seen as a mudhole in Washington, but it is rather an idea unleashed in history." [70]

Al McSurely reflected that perhaps King would have anticipated that, "they're going to run us out of town with guns and free bus tickets," and planned the next step. "But they didn't. There wasn't follow up." He argues that there wasn't a grasp of the potential to build upon the Black leadership that had been developed by the Civil Rights Movement by fostering the development of similar leaders among poor whites, Chicanos, Puerto Ricans, and Natives. "Take the poor whites, we were lucky to have five people who had an all-sided view of what we needed," McSurely said, citing his work in Appalachia. There was a failure in the Poor People's Campaign to develop a "larger view of where that was going to lead."[71]

Among the ideas that grew from the cultural and intellectual exchanges was a Poor People's Coalition and Embassy. The proposal was for a space that would build on the strengths of the campaign's bringing people together. Hank Adams, Reies Tijerina, Mike Clark of Highlander, Dovie Thurman of welfare rights, and SCLC staff were among the fifteen who drafted a grant proposal to support the effort, which said,

(The campaign) has united the poor, the alienated, the disenfranchised from all parts of the country and all races. And it has demonstrated at least for the direct participants and those who observed the process that this kind of experience, apart from its effect upon Congress and the government, can begin to set in motion certain forces, can instill a sense of unity, of leadership, and of solidarity which has a momentum and life of its own.[72]

Many of those who were involved in planning the Coalition had been staying at Hawthorne, and the spirit and intellectual exchange of that space helped foster the vision. They proposed creating, "a national institution by the poor and for the poor," that could freely serve the interests of the poor by remaining independent of corporations and government agencies. The focus would be securing food, basic needs, adequate education, and "honorable jobs."[73] They would create a Poor People's Embassy to serve as a national office. It would be useful as a base for D.C. actions and lobbying, but it was primarily a network center for sharing information, strategic thinking, and campaign tactics among groups seeking to connect their local organizing work with others engaged in class-based multiracial organizing.

McSurely wrote to the Coalition leaders, "We see the dangers in having the timing of a campaign dictated by the liberal establishment, instead of by the people and their proven leaders." He was critical of the ways that the drivers of the Poor People's Campaign directed themselves toward "getting some heads beat on TV." He felt "rich liberals" used their ability to provide funding to push the campaign toward conventional, national political party politics. Instead the work they needed to do was working out a coalition, which, "takes time, planning and mutual experience." He continued, "we must not depend on anyone but ourselves. To meet the needs of the poor in this country, we cannot rely on the consciences of the rich. . . . We can only depend on ourselves—and our organizational strength." But to find funding they applied to foundations. Their appeals met little success, and the project dissolved.[74]

Several other projects grew out of experiences and connections made at Resurrection City and Hawthorne. The Highlander Folk School in Tennessee developed relationships in New Mexico under the name Highlander West. Although it only lasted a few years, while it existed it helped develop leaders in the Southwest and expanded the worldview and connectedness of Highlander's Appalachian base.[75] After leaving Washington, D.C., a contingent led by Hank Adams established Resurrection City 2 in Olympia, Washington, on state capitol grounds. They set up three twenty-foot tee-pees with twenty-nine residents. For three months they occupied the space in protest of fishing limits that violated treaty rights.[76] When members of JOIN Community Union returned home to Chicago, Hy Thurman and others formed the white Young Patriots Organization and partnered with the Illinois Black Panther Party and Puerto Rican Young Lords to become the original Rainbow Coalition.[77] Miguel Barragan, a former Catholic priest from Texas who left the ministry out of frustrations with the church's failure to play a prophetic role on social issues, went on to help found the Southwest Council of La Raza, an organization committed to using the Civil Rights Act of 1964 to expand legal and electoral resources in Mexican American communities.[78] Leaders from Crusade for Justice continued and strengthened their organizing work. In 1969 they hosted the Chicano Youth Liberation Conference, where 1,500 Latinx youths built a nationalist platform and network. This work evolved into *La Raza Unida*, a Colorado political party in 1970.[79]

Having successfully used the Poor People's Campaign to grow their base and expand their media presence, by 1969 NWRO had 250 affiliated welfare rights groups in 46 states.[80] After the national organization was closed in 1975, statewide and local chapters continued to organize. They targeted issues faced by their communities, including utilities, housing, and homelessness. Multiracial, class-based organizing continued to be an important part of the strategy. In the 1980s and 1990s, their organizing expanded to include those who did not qualify for welfare, particularly as changing polices increasingly narrowed who could receive aid.[81]

An important part of assessing the campaign is its capacity to bring poor people together across racial lines in a nation built on white supremacy. King had insisted that they could most directly respond to the racism that persisted among the poor by realizing shared goals across racial lines and beginning to take action together, make sacrifices together, and risk life together.[82] In his attempt to persuade the SCLC staff of the strategy of a campaign of the multiracial dispossessed, King said, "In dangerous moments people begin holding hands that didn't know they could hold them. . . . We'll argue it philosophically, but out there on that line, black folk and white folk get together in a strange way. . . . It's a way to unite forces."[83] If the Poor People's Campaign would really be able to start building the leadership of a new human rights movement, it would need to organize across those lines of division in ways that lead to the abolition of racism. Echoing that assessment after the assassination, Jesse Jackson optimistically argued,

> In Resurrection City the poor whites began to see how they had been used as tools of the economic system to keep other minority groups in check. Perhaps the poor whites were the most tricked of all the poor in that they are in the same economic class as the others. Their problems are basically the same, in fact, as ours: a need for food, jobs, medicine, and schools. However, they were given police rights over 'niggers,' a plan which satisfies their sick egos but does not deal with any of their basic problems. It was our wallowing together in the mud of Resurrection City that we were allowed to hear, to feel and to see each other for the first time in our American experience. This vast task of acculturation, of pulling the poor together as a way of amassing economic, political and labor power, was the great vision of Dr. King.[84]

Similarly, in her Solidarity Day speech, Peggy Terry called to the crowd, "We, the poor whites of the United States, today demand an end to racism, for our own self-interest and well-being, as well as for the well-being of black, brown and red Americans, who, I repeat, are our natural allies in the struggle for real freedom and real democracy in these, our, Unites States of America."[85]

The very act of coming together required addressing those patterns of division that were endemic to US history. Tillie Walker, in a Committee of 100 testimony at the start of the campaign, told Department of the Interior

Secretary Udall, "I want to talk to you a little bit about racism." She described how when she began organizing Native American participation for the campaign, racism was used to dissuade them. At Fort Berthold and Standing Rock, those who had initially signed up for the campaign changed their mind when local Bureau of Indian Affairs officials counter-organized the campaign. They told tribal councils that "Indians don't act like that. Indians don't do things like that." Walker interpreted their implicit threats, "And you know what they mean, Mr. Secretary? They mean that Indians don't work with [Black people] in this country. That is racism, and I am angry."[86] She said she would not be intimidated into stopping organizing the Native contingent to join the campaign. "I'm involved in the Poor People's Campaign because Indian people are poor and the poor know no color. . . . Before your men out there talk to us about 'too much to lose,' have them go out there and live on the 320 acres I own and live off of it—at fifty cents an acre or a dollar an acre—for a year." Organizing farther west, Hank Adams met similar resistance, saying the anti-Black sentiments were "carried to our Indian people by your representatives, and your agents, among others."[87]

In addition to developing new partnerships with Black, white, and brown poor people, the Poor People's Campaign was an opportunity for Native Americans to come together also across the breadth of Native American peoples. Walker and others formed a network called the Coalition of American Indian Citizens. Its steering committee wrote, "the growing revolution of poor people is not an issue of race, class, or culture, but it is a moral issue in the most basic sense—the right of people to live and to live how they choose." The work of the revolution would require, "competent, knowledgeable, and effective," action that didn't just create new programs but, "aimed at breaking apart and dissolving those programs, policies, agencies and traditions," that deny people the right to life and freedom. In place of those old systems new ones would be needed and must be, "founded on that right." Native leaders brought to the campaign the knowledge that colonial dispossession and paternalism of capitalism were at the root of the denial of their right to food, heath care, education, housing, and employment.[88] Freedom was not found in a new social program that channeled dissent and masked control. Freedom could never simply be a larger share of an economy built on neocolonial capitalist globalization.

Many of the factors that limited the success of the campaign were conditions stacked against them. They were raising the question of poverty in a time when unemployment was low and economic ascension was assumed. They were up against strongly entrenched narratives that anyone who really wanted a job could get one and that the poor were to blame for their own poverty due to cultural or moral failings. They were competing for attention in a year of constant social and political crisis around the world. Reeling from the loss of King's leadership and strategic vision, those who stepped forward to put his ideas into motion failed to unite strategically and tactically with the diverse leaders who came forward to be partners in the work. And they didn't know it at the time, but the sophisticated, brutal tactics of covert political policing limited and destabilized the campaign. These complicating factors and leadership failures offer lessons that remain relevant today, because there are always complicated conditions with which to contend.

When King was assessing the work ahead of them after the landmark civil rights victories, he talked about shift to the hard and slow work of sustained organizing, the development of connected leaders, and the building of the power of poor people. He called this form of organizing a necessary but, "nettlesome task," There were glimpses of this kind of relationship building and leadership development within the experience of Resurrection City, even in the midst of its mud and chaos, even if the media missed it. The poor who came together exposed the contradiction of the existence of poverty in the midst of wealth. Residents and volunteers demonstrated that the poor are able to run a tent city, sing together, study together, break bread together, articulate demands, and nonviolently challenge government officials to respond to them. They showed that the poor are capable of understanding economic, social, and political realities and take action in response. They defied the idea that the poor are helpless, that people are poor because their inept, and that charity is the only possible response to poverty. Most importantly they demonstrated these capacities to themselves and each other, so that they could break their isolation, make connections among local struggles, learn from each other, begin to cohere, and form a shared strategy for going forward. But these forms of organizing were not the focus of the campaign. And yet in the possibility of a campaign of the poor, there is the potential for leaders to do the nettlesome work of sustained organizing and emerge as a "non-violent army and freedom church of the poor" that can "take action together" as an "unsettling force."

NOTES

1. Gordon Mantler, *Power to the Poor: Black-Brown Coalition and the Fight for Economic Justice, 1960–1974* (Chapel Hill: University of North Carolina Press, 2013), 210; Bertha Burris, interview by Colleen Wessel-McCoy et al., May 19, 2008.

2. Ethel Mae Matthews and Blackside, Inc., Interview with Ethel Mae Matthews, February 23, 1989, for Eyes on the Prize II: America at the Racial Crossroads 1965 to 1985. Washington University Libraries, Film and Media Archive, Henry Hampton Collection, http://digital.wustl.edu/cgi/t/text/text-idx?c=eop;cc=eop;rgn=main;view=

text;idno=mat5427.0331.105. In addition to her work with NWRO, Matthews went on to be a life-long activist in Atlanta for welfare rights, housing, and jobs.

3. Martin Luther King Jr., *Where Do We Go from Here: Chaos or Community?* (Boston: Beacon Press, 2010), 136–37. Malcolm X said, "The greatest mistake of the movement has been trying to organize a sleeping people around specific goals. You have to wake the people up first, then you'll get action." Malcolm X, *Malcolm X Speaks: Selected Speeches and Statements* (New York: Pathfinder Press, 1965), 198.)

4. Sidney Lumet and Joseph L. Mankiewicz, *King: A Filmed Record . . . Montgomery to Memphis*, Documentary, 1970.

5. Martin Luther King Jr., *Where Do We Go from Here: Chaos or Community?* (New York: Harper & Row, 1967), 136–38.

6. Steven W. Bender, *One Night in America: Robert Kennedy, Cesar Chavez, and the Dream of Dignity* (New York: Routledge, 2015), 109–10. The demands put forward by the Committee of 100 particularly cited immigration from Mexico and the Caribbean as strains on US employment. (p.43)

7. The urban renewal programs, begun in the 1949 Housing Act, often decreased access to affordable housing, as residents in slum housing could not afford the housing that replaced theirs. Despite being billed as an anti-poverty effort, it revealed in almost every case that it was more anti-poor than anti-poverty. (Jennifer Frost, *An Interracial Movement of the Poor: Community Organizing and the New Left in the 1960s* [New York: New York University Press, 2001], 131–32).

8. Bureau of Labor Statistics, "1-Month Net Change, Total Nonfarm Labor, 1968," United States Department of Labor, accessed January 19, 2017, https://data.bls.gov/pdq/SurveyOutputServlet.

9. "Poor People's Campaign Gains" (SCLC, September 1968), Southern Christian Leadership Conference records: Subseries 10.3: Poor People's Campaign records, Box 572, Folder 25, Emory University; Mantler, *Power to the Poor*, 183–84.

10. The Vietnam War was at its height in terms of US deployment (541,000), US casualties (16,988), and anti-war resistance. North Vietnam's Tet Offensive marked the turning point against the South Vietnamese and the United States. In the US elections, Robert Kennedy, one of the Democratic primary candidates, was assassinated. Segregationist-populist George Wallace won several states and 13.5% of the popular vote as a third-party candidate. Richard Nixon defeated Hubert Humphrey with 43% of the popular vote. Freedom struggles continue across a broad range of injustices, including in France (student revolt and general strike), Mexico (student uprising, Tlatelolco Square) and Czechoslovakia (Prague Spring). This was the summer of the Summer Olympics (and Black Power salute by Smith and Carlos). The year included the Orangeburg Massacre (SC bowling alley desegregation), the continuation of the United Farm Workers grape boycott and Chavez's hunger fast, NOW protests at the Miss America Pageant (which selects its first Black Miss America), the American Indian Movement (AIM) founding, original Rainbow Coalition beginning to form in Chicago, and the assassination of MLK followed by urban uprisings in Chicago, Washington, D.C., and Baltimore.

11. Henry Hampton, Steve Fayer, and Sarah Flynn, *Voices of Freedom: An Oral History of the Civil Rights Movement from the 1950s through the 1980s* (New York: Bantam Books, 1991), 480.

12. Charles Fager, *Uncertain Resurrection: The Poor People's Washington Campaign* (Grand Rapids, MI: Eerdmans, 1969), 141–42.

13. Hampton, Fayer, and Flynn, *Voices of Freedom*, 477–78. Harrington said in another interview, "A group of people were sitting on the ground gathered around and a black man among them, I think with emotional problems, decided that I was the incarnation of white racism. And he wanted to know why I, who had been in the process of giving a talk attacking racism . . . was in favor of racism and poverty. . . . And he got very agitated. And I became concerned that he could physically attack me. The meeting sort of came to a very unhappy ending, where my message didn't get across, and it's very hard to concentrate on your talk when you're worried that somebody might be about to jump you . . . I . . . ran away from the meeting. I wanted to get as far away from this place as I could"; Michael Harrington, interview by Blackside, Inc., October 11, 1988, for Eyes on the Prize II: America at the Racial Crossroads 1965 to 1985. Washington University Libraries, Film and Media Archive, Henry Hampton Collection, http://digital.wustl.edu/cgi/t/text/text-idx?c=eop;cc=eop; rgn=main;view=text;idno=har5427.0719.063.

14. Jenée Desmond-Harris, "The Poor People's Campaign: The Little-Known Protest MLK Was Planning When He Died," *Vox*, January 16, 2017, http://www.vox.com/2017/1/16/14271074/the-poor-peoples-campaign-the-little-known-protest-mlk-was-planning-when-he-died.

15. Ralph Abernathy, *And the Walls Came Tumbling Down: An Autobiography* (New York: Harper & Row, 1989), 575.

16. Frances Fox Piven and Richard Cloward, *Poor People's Movements: Why They Succeed, How They Fail* (Vintage, 1978), 36.

17. Mantler, *Power to the Poor*, 209–10. Mantler's close study of the breadth of campaign leaders led him to argue against the idea that the problem is a "white power structure" pitting "racial minorities against each other for economic gain" and circumventing class-based organizing. Instead the, "distinct historical trajectories" of the disparate racial and ethnic groups involved in the campaign meant that their cooperation should not be "held up automatically as the natural and desired outcome." The campaign's greatest contribution was the opportunity to strengthen relationships and organizing within ethnic and racial groups. (p. 7)

18. Amy Nathan Wright, "Civil Rights 'Unfinished Business': Poverty, Race, and the 1968 Poor People's Campaign" (Dissertation, The University of Texas at Austin, 2007), 251.

19. Gerald McKnight, *The Last Crusade: Martin Luther King, Jr., the FBI, and the Poor People's Campaign* (Boulder, CO: Westview Press, 1998), 93, 135. While the FBI's surveillance of King is better documented, military intelligence was also involved in surveillance and counterintelligence operations related to King's organizing. William Pepper argues military intelligence was particularly interested in King's antiwar efforts. After King gave an antiwar speech in Los Angeles on February 25, 1967, focused on the Vietnamese casualties and calling for teaching about the war and

preaching and demonstrating against the war, the army's Assistant Chief of Staff for Intelligence (ACSI) summarized it as "a call to armed aggression by negroes against the American people," and the 111th army military intelligence group (MIG) at Atlanta's Fort McPherson assigned two Black agents to infiltrate the SCLC. In one of the most famous photographs of King's assassination, where King's entourage points in the direction of the gunman, Marrell McCollough is knelt down over King. He was an undercover officer from the Memphis Police Department, and Pepper documents that this assignment was in coordination with the 111th MIG. McCollough went on to work for the CIA (William F. Pepper, *Orders to Kill: The Truth behind the Murder of Martin Luther King* [New York: Carroll & Graf, 1995], 461, 465).

20. McKnight, *The Last Crusade*, 111. In a U.S. Senate Permanent Subcommittee on Investigations "Conference on Problems Involved in the Poor Peoples' (sic) March on Washington" on April 25, 1968, chaired by Senator McClellan, Senator Mundt asked Secretary Udall if the Bonus Army is a "valid analogy" for the types of response this situation required, to which Secretary Udall replied, "It is a close parallel to the Bonus March in 1932. I asked my people, the historians of the Park Service, to dig out the whole history of that incident because I think there are some lessons to be learned from it." United States Congress Senate Committee on Government Operations Permanent Subcommittee on Investigations, *Conference on Problems Involved in the Poor Peoples' March on Washington, D.C. April 25, 1968* (Washington: U.S. Govt. Print. Off, 1968).

21. Adam Fairclough, *To Redeem the Soul of America: The Southern Christian Leadership Conference and Martin Luther King, Jr.* (Athens: University of Georgia Press, 1987), 365. Andrew Young, *An Easy Burden: The Civil Rights Movement and the Transformation of America* (New York: HarperCollins, 1996), 443.

22. Their demand was not for a "bonus." That was the language of detractors, but it stuck. The veterans had earned the compensation because their active-duty military pay had been significantly lower than that of those who remained at home and worked in factories. They also returned home to a tight job market where many positions were already filled by those who had not served.

23. Paul Dickson and Thomas Allen, "Marching on History," *Smithsonian*, February 2003, http://www.smithsonianmag.com/history/marching-on-history-75797769/.

24. McKnight, *The Last Crusade*, 127. At the end, the National Parks Service sent the SCLC a damages bill for over $70,000, the equivalent of over $500,000 in 2020.

25. Andrew Young, *An Easy Burden*, 484.

26. McKnight, *The Last Crusade*, 134.

27. Al McSurely, interview by author, January 30, 2015.

28. McKnight, *The Last Crusade*, 134, 142. We are indebted to the work of those who fought to amend the Freedom of Information Act (FOIA) in 1974 for revealing the scope, scale, and biases of the domestic intelligence activities. See Athan G. Theoharis, *Spying on Americans: Political Surveillance from Hoover to the Huston Plan* (Philadelphia: Temple University Press, 1978). The 1975–6 Church Committee investigation (Senate Select Committee on Intelligence Activities) of the FBI's COINTEL concluded that "the unexpressed major premise of the programs was that a law enforcement agency has the duty to do whatever is necessary to combat perceived

threats to the existing social and political order." The FBI's purpose was not to attack individuals or particular groups, but to "repress all perceived threats to the dominant, status-quo-oriented political culture." Garrow argued the FBI was "not a deviant institution in American society, but actually a most representative and faithful one." (David J. Garrow, *The FBI and Martin Luther King, Jr. : From "Solo" to Memphis* [New York: W.W. Norton, 1981], 209, 211).

29. Symbol informants are paid operatives, as opposed to unpaid "sources," who have passed a probationary period and been given "symbol" code names.

30. McKnight, *The Last Crusade*, 93, 123, 124–25, 134, 135. At one point the Justice Department considered systematically using employees in the War on Poverty programs to gather information about the beneficiaries of the programs for its IDIU network, much as the War on Poverty's model, the Peace Corp, had done internationally. McKnight writes, "Assistant Attorney General John Doar, a noted advocate for civil rights, got swept up in the surveillance mentality. He proposed that War on Poverty workers be tapped to provide the IDIU with information on activists. While Doar recognized the contradictions in exploiting poverty workers for surveillance information, he suggested that the Justice Department could preserve its supposed 'credibility with the people in the ghetto' by preventing exposure of the IDIU" (McKnight, 93–94, 98).

31. McKnight, *The Last Crusade*, 123, 170 n.34.

32. Taylor Branch, *At Canaan's Edge: America in the King Years, 1965–68* (New York: Simon & Schuster, 2007), 709.

33. McKnight, *The Last Crusade*, 26, 27; United States Federal Bureau of Investigation, "Memorandum: Cointerintelligence Program Black Nationalist-Hate Groups Racial Intelligence (Poor People's Campaign)," May 22, 1968, The COINTELPRO Papers, https://en.wikipedia.org/wiki/File:FBI_PPC_1.pdf.

34. McKnight, *The Last Crusade*, 129. Charges of interracial sex against a Black man were particularly loaded, a frequent component of the extrajudicial public ritual of lynching (James H. Cone, *The Cross and the Lynching Tree* [Orbis Books, 2011], 3, 7, 9).

35. McKnight, *The Last Crusade*, 129, 133–34.

36. Attorney General Clark developed the Interdivisional Intelligence Unit (IDIU) in December 1967 after the Newark and Detroit riots. It was tasked with assimilating intelligence from the Justice Department, FBI, and U.S. Army to predict the next uprising, using a working theory that the uprisings were instigated by a small group of Black conspirators/instigators. This massive domestic intelligence apparatus was directed at the Poor People's Campaign in full force (McKnight, *The Last Crusade*, 93).

37. McKnight, *The Last Crusade*, 136.

38. Gordon Mantler, "'The Press Did You in': The Poor People's Campaign and the Mass Media," *The Sixties* 3, no. 1 (June 1, 2010): 46.

39. Wright, "Civil Rights 'Unfinished Business,'" 478.

40. Fager, *Uncertain Resurrection: The Poor People's Washington Campaign*, 46–47.

41. Wright, "Civil Rights 'Unfinished Business,'" 472.

42. Mantler, "'The Press Did You In,'" 42.; Eric Blanchard, "The Poor People and the 'White Press,'" *Columbia Journalism Review*, Fall 1968, 64.

43. Gordon Mantler, "Black, Brown and Poor: Martin Luther King Jr., The Poor People's Campaign and Its Legacies" (Dissertation, Duke University, 2008), 326.; Emilye Crosby, *Civil Rights History from the Ground Up: Local Struggles, a National Movement* (Athens: University of Georgia Press, 2011), 139, note 6; Blanchard, "The Poor People and the 'White Press,'" 61.

44. Wright, "Civil Rights 'Unfinished Business,'" 488.

45. Eric Blanchard, "The Poor People and the 'White Press,'" 61–62; Eric Blanchard, interview with author, July 24, 2015. Blanchard was also an information officer for the Kerner Commission and the Commission on Religion and Race of the National Council of Churches.

46. Blanchard, "The Poor People and the 'White Press,'" 64.

47. Robert Houston and Aaron Bryant, "Most Daring Dream: Robert Houston Photography & the 1968 Poor People's Campaign," *Callaloo* 31, no. 4 (2008): 1273, https://doi.org/128.59.143.41.

48. Angelica Aboulhosn, "'His Camera Is Guided by His Heart': On Robert Houston's Photographs of the Poor People's Campaign," National Museum of African American History & Culture, January 8, 2018, https://nmaahc.si.edu/blog-post/%E2%80%9Chis-camera-guided-his-heart%E2%80%9D-robert-houston%E2%80%99s-photographs-poor-people%E2%80%99s-campaign.

49. See Sasha Torres, *Black, White, and In Color: Television and Black Civil Rights* (Princeton, N.J.: Princeton University Press, 2003).

50. Wright, "Civil Rights 'Unfinished Business,'" 477.

51. Abernathy, *And the Walls Came Tumbling Down*, 528.

52. Alyosha Goldstein, *Poverty in Common: The Politics of Community Action during the American Century* (Durham: Duke University Press, 2012), 141, 152.

53. Fager, *Uncertain Resurrection: The Poor People's Washington Campaign*, 140.

54. Jewell Debnam, "Black Women and the Charleston Hospital Workers' Strike of 1969" (Dissertation, 2016), 1, 31, 52, Michigan State University.

55. Paula Giddings, *When and Where I Enter: The Impact of Black Women on Race and Sex in America* (New York: Bantam Books, 1985), 330–31.

56. Abernathy, *And the Walls Came Tumbling Down*, 570; Giddings, *When and Where I Enter*, 330–31. Among the hospital administrators negotiating the deal was comedian Stephen Colbert's father. Colbert discussed the strike with Andy Young on *The Colbert Report* in 2008 (*The Colbert Report*, January 22, 2008, http://www.cc.com/video-clips/xw3v9i/the-colbert-report-andrew-young).

57. Mother Emmanuel AME was the site of the 2015 Charleston church massacre.

58. Coretta Scott King, *My Life with Martin Luther King, Jr.* (New York: Holt, Rinehart and Winston, 1969).

59. Atlanta's first Black mayor, Maynard Jackson, broke a similar strike in the late 1970s.

60. Timothy J. Minchin, *From Rights to Economics: The Ongoing Struggle for Black Equality in the U.S. South* (Gainesville: University Press of Florida, 2007), 18.

61. Civil and labor rights strategist Jack O'Dell wrote of the strike, "Charleston forged a unity between the community-organizing techniques developed during the civil rights era of the Freedom Movement and the working class organizational techniques of strike action developed by the labor movement" (Jack O'Dell, *Climbin' Jacob's Ladder: The Black Freedom Movement Writings of Jack O'Dell* [University of California Press, 2010], 189).

62. Minchin, *From Rights to Economics*, 5, 23–25. The NAACP suits had some success. Black workers in the textile industries increased from 4.2 to 25 percent between 1960 and 1978. The suits also helped increase mobility within factories, particularly in the paper industry, where Black workers were relegated to lower-paying positions. Black workers used Title VII suits successfully in other industries. Alabama's Black state troopers, under order from a federal judge, increased from none to 20 percent in a decade and growth continued until it was the most integrated department the country in 1992. The tactic sometimes required fighting all-white unions as well as employers, such as in the textile industry, where the union collaborated with companies to protect segregated job progression. Some observant business owners realized breaking segregation enabled them to lower wages for all workers. Fear of competition for higher-paying positions worked in conjunction with white supremacy. Racism and economic fears reinforced each other. As workforces integrated the facilities (social/lunch/restroom) sometimes shut down rather than integrate, some remaining shut down into the 1970s. While there were some intransigent employers who resisted real integration and not all of the Title VII cases were successful, Black people greatly diversified the Southern industrial workforce. Unfortunately these same industries began to be ravaged by a deindustrialization by the mid-1970s, closing plants and shedding jobs in the plants that remained. Black communities in the South were heavily dependent on these jobs and have not found large-scale alternatives. In many areas, both inner city and rural, black economic gains have even declined to preCivil Rights Movement-civil rights levels (Minchin, 7, 24, 31, 32, 33, 35, 51). Other leaders focused on economic development, including Fannie Lou Hamer, who developed a "Freedom Farm" project in the Mississippi Delta that assisted Black people in buying land and marketing produce, complimented by Delta Enterprises in Greenville that ran four manufacturing plants and a farm. (Christopher Myers Asch, *The Senator and the Sharecropper: The Freedom Struggles of James O. Eastland and Fannie Lou Hamer* [New York: W.W. Norton, 2008], x). Floyd McKissick, leader of CORE from 1966–68, founded Soul City in Warren County, North Carolina, in 1973. The residents attempted to build a racially integrated model community with strong black leadership. The project was hindered by the withdrawal of federal funding in 1979, citing the town's failure to attract industry. (Minchin, 59–60, 81)

63. Minchin, *From Rights to Economics*, 25–26.

64. Harry Belafonte, interview by Blackside, Inc., May 15, 1989, Henry Hampton Collection, Washington University Libraries, Film and Media Archive, http://digital.wustl.edu/e/eii/eiiweb/bel5427.0417.013harrybelafonte.html.

65. Fairclough, *To Redeem the Soul of America*, 354.

66. Belafonte, interview by Blackside, Inc.

67. Vincent Harding, *Martin Luther King, the Inconvenient Hero* (Maryknoll, NY: Orbis Books, 2008), 112–13.

68. Robert T. Chase, "Class Resurrection: The Poor People's Campaign of 1968 and Resurrection City," *Essays in History*, Corcoran Department of History at the University of Virginia, 40 (1998): 15.

69. Mantler, *Power to the Poor*, 160.

70. Jesse Jackson, "Resurrection City: The Dream, The Accomplishments," *Ebony*, October 1968.

71. McSurely, interview by author.

72. Brenda Beadenkopf, "Part XVIII: Poor People's Campaign, Assassination of Dr. Martin Luther King."

73. Mantler, "Black, Brown and Poor," 350.

74. Mantler, *Power to the Poor*, 177.

75. Mantler, *Power to the Poor*, 193–94.

76. "Resurrection City, Part 2," *Spokane Daily Chronicle*, June 28, 1968, Final edition, sec. A.

77. Hy Thurman, interview by author, July 15, 2015. See also Hy Thurman, *Revolutionary Hillbilly: Notes from the Struggle on the Edge of the Rainbow* (Berkeley, CA: Regent Press, 2020); Jakobi Williams, *From the Bullet to the Ballot: The Illinois Chapter of the Black Panther Party and Racial Coalition Politics in Chicago* (Chapel Hill: University of North Carolina Press, 2013).

78. Mantler, *Power to the Poor*, 195, 196, note 35.

79. Mantler, *Power to the Poor*, 201–2.

80. National Welfare Rights Organization, "Proposals for a Guaranteed Adequate Income," in *Welfare: A Documentary History of U.S. Policy and Politics*, ed. Gwendolyn Mink and Rickie Solinger (New York: New York University Press, 2003), 373–79. Originally printed in House Committee on Ways and Means, *Social Security and Welfare Proposals*, 91st Congress, 1st sess., October-November 1969, pt. 3, 1018–22.

81. Marian Kramer, interview by author, September 15, 2015.

82. Reflecting on King's vision for the campaign, Vincent Harding drew the assessment that,

> For the first time, American Indians, blacks, Hispanics and poor whites were all beginning to talk about the ways in which we might, together, find a way to speak to the poverty that cuts across all racial lines . . . . King was trying to deal with two things there. He was trying to find a way of organizing folks to deal with poverty through some form of revolutionary nonviolence. But more important for us at this particular moment, this was also King's way of dealing with racism in American society. King said that the way you deal with racism is to find a common vision that will join you together. Find a common task on which those of all races can work together. That is the best way to deal with racism in American society. A thousand conferences will not do what a gathering of people can do when that are convinced that across their racial lines, they have a common goal that they must work for, sacrifice for, and die for. (Danny Duncan Collum, *Black and White Together: The Search for Common Ground* [Maryknoll, N.Y.: Orbis Books, 1996], 72–73., citing Harding speaking in 1983).

83. Martin Luther King Jr., "See You in Washington" (SCLC Staff Retreat, Atlanta, GA, January 17, 1968), 9, King Speeches, Series 3, Box 13, King Center Archives.

84. Jackson, "Resurrection City: The Dream, The Accomplishments," 66.

85. Amy Sonnie and James Tracy, *Hillbilly Nationalists, Urban Race Rebels, and Black Power: Community Organizing in Radical Times* (Brooklyn, NY: Melville House, 2011), 59.

86. Daniel M. Cobb, *Native Activism in Cold War America: The Struggle for Sovereignty* (Lawrence: University Press of Kansas, 2008), 169 note 57.

87. Cobb, *Native Activism in Cold War America*, 169.

88. Cobb, *Native Activism in Cold War America*, 172, note 6, 7.

Chapter 5

Theologies of the Poor People's Campaign

Across his ministry, King had learned that the church was seldom on the right side of social movements. This was particularly true of white churches in the Civil Rights Movement, but it was true of many Black churches as well.[1] At the start of 1968 King preached at his home church Ebenezer Baptist, "we would have a better world," if, "Christians would stop talking so much about religion, and start doing something about it. . . . But the problem is that the church has sanctioned every evil in the world, whether it's racism, or whether it's the evils of monopoly-capitalism, or whether it's the evils of militarism."[2] But King also had learned that those who did answer the call to respond to injustice—joining campaigns that became more than the sum of their parts— were more true to what a church should be than most congregations. The movement was church.[3] He described the poor taking action together as a, "'freedom church' of the poor." In it King is recalling the history of abolition- ist freedom churches and the role of religion and religious leadership in the revolutionary movement to end slavery. The phrase claims the position of the people of God gathered to do the work of Christ. Calling the SCLC staff to understand the significance of the Poor People's Campaign, King said,

> By the thousands we will move. Many will wonder where we are coming from. Our only answer will be that we are coming up out of great trials and tribulation. Some of us will come from Mississippi, some of us will come from Cleveland. But we will all be coming from the same conditions. We will be seeking a city whose Builder and Maker is God and if we will do this we will be able to turn this nation upside down and right side up. We may just be able to speed up the day when man everywhere will respect the dignity and worth of human person- ality and all men will be able to cry out that we are children of God made in His image. This will be a glorious day and that moment the morning stars will shine together and the Son of God will shout for joy.[4]

Their organizing task was to assemble a new freedom church of the poor. Its charge, like the one that preceded it more than a century before, was to save the body and soul of the nation and world by claiming their own human dignity and the human right to the means of life, liberty, and happiness.

DENOMINATIONAL ORGANIZING

King was not alone in thinking theologically and biblically about the Poor People's Campaign. As they were pulling the campaign together, a journalist asked if SCLC was, "getting into radical, working-class politics." Andrew Young replied, "I don't know about that. I am doing what I joined the ministry to do," and cited Jesus' affirmation that his ministry was to bring good news to the poor.[5] One could be forgiven for suspecting this was religious cover for deflecting the question, but it is true that the campaign was developed and carried out by religious leaders and organizations who thought about and talked about their work religiously.

Immediately after the campaign was announced in December 1967, SCLC reached out to American Friends Service Committee (AFSC) to lend staff time, contribute to the logistical planning of the campaign, make connections with their network of community leaders. AFSC agreed. They assigned Tony Henry to the campaign, and four AFSC staff attended the Minority Group Leaders Conference in March. They were joined by representatives from just a few religious organizations: Catholic Bishops Committee on Spanish Speakers, Catholic Interracial Conference, Council of Jewish Federations and Welfare Funds, and Episcopal Peace Fellowship.

Just before King's assassination, the campaign received important endorsements from the D.C. branches of four national bodies: the Council of Churches, Catholic Archdiocese, Jewish Community Council, and Presbytery of Washington City. They were potentially strong contributors to campaign turnout from the D.C. area. This growing institutional religious support alarmed the FBI, triggering a letter from William Sullivan, head of the domestic intelligence division, to deputy director Cartha DeLoach, saying, "Both Protestant and Catholic leadership in Washington give clear signs of being almost totally unaware of the lawlessness and the violence-prone elements who will be involved in this march. . . . I would like to sow the idea that as eminent church leaders they have an enormous responsibility relative to assisting and maintaining law and order."[6] American Friends Service Committee staff involved in the campaign also received a visit from the FBI inviting them to share information about "potential trouble makers." They refused and alerted others.[7] Apart from these examples, the institutional church did not initially bring its resources or leadership to support planning the campaign, and yet the campaign was full of religious and moral leadership.

RELIGION IN RESURRECTION CITY

During the occupation Andrew Young delivered a sermon at the First Congregational United Church of Christ in Washington, D.C. He said the poor, "come here because they see that the system by which God's goods are distributed is not adequate for them."[8] Official campaign documents used moral, civil, and human rights language to say the same. A recruitment flyer included,

> The Poor People's Campaign will address itself to a demand for decent jobs and income for all Americans. The Poor People's Campaign will address itself to the moral and constitutional rights of poor people. The Poor People's Campaign will address itself to those Americans who would oppress and exploit newcomers who are minorities and poor—make them feel unwanted and deny them a share of those resources which they (those Americans) don't own anyway. The Poor People's Campaign will address itself to the dignity and the right of every man to live.[9]

Similar language fills the Statement of the Demands of the Rights of the Poor, presented by the Committee of 100 two weeks before the first caravans would arrive. It describes their unmet human needs as unfulfilled rights, invoking the Declaration of Independence and Bill of Rights, and saying what was at stake went beyond the problems of individual hardship but were questions of society and morality.[10]

Photographic documentation catches hand painted religious interpretations of the campaign. One of the mule trains read, "Don't laugh folks, Jesus was a poor man." The plywood walls of Resurrection City's bakery read, "Bread: Free Forever Give Us This Day," a citation of the Lord's Prayer (Matthew 6:11), "Give us today our daily bread." Here the insistence is that this prayer is about actual bread, not just spiritual nourishment, and that bread should be free for all. One of the A-frame tents was painted with Genesis 37, "And they said one to another, behold, this dreamer cometh. Come now therefore, and let us slay him, and cast him into some pit, and we will say, some evil beast hath devoured him; and we shall see what will become of his dreams," along with "MLK, Jr. 1929–1968"[11]

The registration process for official residents in Resurrection City and the second location at Hawthorne School asked about religious affiliation. This count only catches people who stayed there, but it includes over six thousand people. Sixty percent of residents identified as Protestant, and half of that group specified Baptist. One thousand of the residents identified as Catholics, and black Catholics were present at a rate three times the percentage of black Catholics nationally. They were joined by 115 Jews, fifty-two Muslims, 632 atheists and agnostics, and 102 people who identified as "other."[12]

Less is known about the religious affiliation of the many thousands more came just for a day, stayed somewhere else, volunteered, or took part in the big actions. Local churches and the National Council of Churches played a significant role in the daily life of the campaign, providing meals in particular. African Methodist Episcopal (AME) churches provided hospitality to those whose caravans arrived early to build the encampment, and AME churches convened participants and supporters for mass meetings during the campaign.[13] Photographic records of Solidarity Day include marchers with signs showing that strong religious presence, including Armenian Orthodox Church, The Illinois Conference of the United Methodist Church, Episcopal Diocese of Newark, Brethren Peace Fellowship, American Baptists, Virginia Presbyterians, and Christian Methodist Episcopal Church.[14]

Campaign participant Richard Sidy described that singing, particularly religious songs, was an important element of cohesion. "We would all sing the same songs. It kept everybody together. We were connecting through song. Resurrection City was a lot of separate neighborhoods, but when we sang, we were one. It brought us together."[15] Singing and preaching were part of protests and actions at government agencies and offices, including at the Department of Health, Education, and Welfare, where Assistant Secretary of Education Ralph Huitt said, "I haven't heard preaching and singing like that since I was a boy. Maybe that's what's wrong with me."[16]

Among the religious ideas that echo from the histories of the campaign are a strong identification of the campaign participants with biblical characters. Ralph Abernathy used the story of freedom from slavery in Exodus to describe their tactics, announcing that the poor had come to Washington, D.C., "to plague the Pharaohs of this nation with plague after plague until they agree to give us meaningful jobs and a guaranteed annual income."[17] A fantastic sermon excerpt comes from Chuck Fager's account of a mass meeting held at St. Stephen's Baptist Church during the occupation featuring Rev. C. L. Franklin of Detroit, Aretha Franklin's father. In a sermon titled, "They Wouldn't Bow," he preached on civil disobedience, using the biblical account of Shadrach, Meshach, and Abednego's refusal to worship the pagan gods of Babylon. Franklin pointed out that Nebuchadnezzar solidified Babylon's domination of Judah by forcing its leadership of religious thought, military strategy, and cultural production into the service of Babylon. Shadrach, Meshach, and Abednego recognized that laws requiring the worship of the Babylonian gods were not just about religious belief. They were demands for civil obedience to empire and its exploitation. Given a last chance by the king to prove their loyalty to him and the empire by bowing before his gods, they refused. "They wouldn't bow." Franklin interpreted their disobedience, "There are laws and there are loyalties above patriotic laws, and that loyalty is to God." Franklin said of the United States,

> Our republic is making the mistake of putting law above justice. . . . If the state was as concerned about justice as they are about law and order, there wouldn't be any need for Resurrection City. . . . the power structure will put you in jail . . . they will shoot you down-or have you shot down. . . . They will subject you to indignities and humiliations, and reduce you to poverty circumstances. But I think, all of us should make one firm resolution today: we're not gon' bow.[18]

This biblical and theological interpretation of the campaign and its tactics called those who had joined the campaign to see their actions as a form of loyalty to higher laws, to God, and to the kind of society God commands us to organize. King had preached similarly on the same text at Ebenezer the year before, around the same time they announced the campaign.[19]

The theme of following higher laws over civil laws was echoed in Abernathy's Solidarity Day speech, where he insisted they would not relinquish the ground of the National Mall when their permit expired. "I received my permit a long time ago, and I received it from no government, from no Constitution, but from God Almighty." Quoting the prophets Amos and Isaiah, he described that they would remain until "justices rolls out of the halls of Congress, and righteousness falls from the Administration, and the rough places of the agencies of government are made plain, and the crooked details with the military industrial complex become straightened."[20] The fact that they were soon pushed out of Washington does not separate them from the tradition from which that affirmation of the justness of their cause is derived.

POOR PEOPLE'S CAMPAIGN AS RELIGIOUS LEADERSHIP

Earlier that year King had preached about the campaign during an SCLC staff retreat. It was six weeks after they had publicly announced plans for the Poor People's Campaign, but they remained divided not only on specific tactics for the campaign but also about the strategic focus on poverty. "I'm full of fire about this thing, because I know the nation needs this. . . . And if you get caught up in an idea, you move with that idea. You fire up other folk." King compared the three thousandsouls saved at Pentecost (Acts 2:41) to the three thousand poor people they planned to bring to Washington, D.C., for the Resurrection City occupation, "Aren't we talking about three thousand?" He emphasized the significance of their role as religious leaders and the necessity for them to be clear about the campaign's strategy. Arguing against a controversy over the focus on jobs and income rather than a longer, broader list of specific demands, King said, "I don't know what Jesus had as his demands other than repent, for the kingdom of God is at hand. My demand in Washington is repent America. Now, I'm serious about this. And he just took that simple thing and fired up people." King continues to draw connections between their calling as leaders and the formation of the Jesus movement,

> (Jesus called) a cursing sailor by the name of Peter. And old Peter vacillated. One day Jesus looked at him and said, in substance, 'You are Simon now. Which meant that you are sand, but I'm expecting you to be like a rock.' And it was that pull of expectation that caused Peter, on the day of Pentecost to go out fired up with that something he got from Jesus, and he preached until three thousand souls were converted. Aren't we talking about three thousand? I'm expecting you to be like a rock. Now, we can do that, if we are fired up ourselves.

There was a revivalist spirit to King's call for Pentecost, the birth of a new freedom church of the poor. Like the early church of the early Jesus followers, this church would come from across differences and speak different languages. Like that early church the call to repentance had revolutionary implications for the reordering of society, the kingdom of God at hand. King ended his message to the staff with, "I don't know if I'll see all of you before April. But I send you forth. . . . I'll meet you in Washington."[21] Many would never see him again.

THE FREEDOM CHURCH TRADITION

King was ordained in the Baptist tradition, but his theological ethics wove together several theological and philosophical influences, including abolitionist Black church, social gospel, and personal idealism. King drew all of them into an insistence that Christianity seeks justice within this life, not only in the world to come. He said, "It may be true that Jesus said, 'Man cannot live by bread alone.' But the mere fact that he added the 'alone' means that man cannot live without bread. And anyone that overlooks this is overlooking something basic within our Christian heritage and in our whole struggle for freedom."[22]

While the abolitionist Black church is not the only influence on King's theological ethics, its history and contributions are essential to understanding why King called for a "freedom church of the poor." And while King had learned that the church as we usually think of it was seldom on the right side of social movements, King also learned that in the United States, social movements are simultaneously religious movements. Lewis Baldwin observes that King's study of history revealed that the "activities of black communities in the years before and after the Civil War always paralleled the development and leadership provided by the church."[23]

King's abolitionist Black church social gospel theology was the product of and unfinished business of the abolition of slavery. The white church was an instrument of the enslaving class socially, politically, and theologically. The Black church emerged as a rebellion against it. The independent space created by the Black church helped develop the theological, social, and political capacities of the movement to end slavery.[24] Both AME and AME Zion were openly opposed to slavery, denied church membership to enslavers (there were small-scale enslaving Black people in the border states), and supported campaigns and leaders of the growing abolitionist movement.[25] Mother Bethel AME Church in Philadelphia, founded in 1794, hid people escaping from slavery in its buildings. Its ministers and congregants risked their lives to sabotage slavery as a stop in the Underground Railroad.[26] AME Zion Church was known as the "freedom church" because its members included key abolitionist leaders, including Frederick Douglass, Harriet Tubman, Sojurner Truth, Jermain Louguen, Catherine Harris, Eliza Ann Gardner, and Thomas James.[27]

Black church in North America, as both institutions and practices, began to evolve long before the establishment of independent denominations. While the most common arrangement in the antebellum South was for Black people to attend white congregations, there were independent Black churches and evangelical churches that licensed Black men to preach in the South before 1800.[28] There was actually more independence for Black congregations a century before the Civil War than in the decades immediately before the war. Occasionally before the Revolutionary War there were Black ministers—fewer than ten are known by name—preaching to Black or Black and white congregations. But among the Black congregations that existed, many were officiated and financially supported by whites. Black preachers and white preachers to Black congregants were under constant scrutiny. Enslavers and overseers knew religion's utility as a restraining instrument of control. But they also were attuned to the dangers of religion as a source of rebellion historically. Gayraud Wilmore argues, independent Black churches during and following the Revolutionary War

> must be regarded as the prime expression of resistance to slavery—in every sense, the first black freedom movement. It had the advantage of being carried

on under the cloak of ecclesiastical affairs rather than as an affair of the state or the economy. The movement, therefore, could pass as representing the more or less legitimate desire of the slaves to have "a place of their own in which to worship God." But it was, in fact, a form of rebellion against the most accessible and vulnerable expression of white oppression and institutional racism in the nation: the American churches.[29]

The freedom church theologies and practices were in formation in this spirit, within and beyond official congregations.

The reality that adding the qualification "freedom" to churches was necessary reveals that churches otherwise were "unfreedom" or "anti-freedom." That freedom is sectarian, rather than fundamental, was a crisis for Christianity, whether its leaders acknowledged it or not. Some white theologians, like Jonathan Edwards, condoned slavery by ignoring it.[30] Others directly justified slavery and blessed enslavers, forming a religious leadership that supported the development and maintenance of an economy and society dependent upon enslaved Black labor. These economic forces and theological forces worked in tandem with each other. *Incidents in the Life of a Slave Girl*, fugitive Harriet Jacobs's autobiographical slave narrative, documents a slave hymn that sharply marks the unchristian position of white Christianity and its opposite, God's church of freedom, "Ole Satan's church is here below/Up to God's free church I hope to go."[31]

Following the Revolutionary War, opposition to slavery had emerged among Methodist and Baptist churches in the era's spirit of liberty. The 1784 Christmas Conference voted to expel enslavers from Methodist churches. But in the years that followed, agricultural production changed, and the profitability of enslaved labor increased. The opposition to slavery was rescinded. "When cotton became king, the churches allowed the change in social reality to influence a change in their religious views." By 1816 the Methodist General Conference decided the "evil appears to be past remedy," an equivocation that was in effect full support of slavery.[32]

Unfreedom churches not only spread the gospel of oppression but actively suppressed freedom church motions. Wilmore argued, "Slaveholding Christians knew . . . what they were doing was abhorrent to God. . . . They knew that the argument that God had ordained the enslavement of the African was a lie."[33] King argued people who do wrong seek, "rationalization to clothe their acts in the garments of righteousness." Because slavery was so economically profitable, they needed an ideology to make it morally justifiable. "The attempt to give moral sanction to a profitable system gave birth to the doctrine of white supremacy." As sources of ethics and morality, theology and the Bible were distorted by the white church to make evil a good. Churches sanctified the system of slavery.[34]

Slaveholding Christians knew that "whatever could be done by black preachers to hasten the demise of slavery—whether from the open pulpit or in secret—was a part of their commitment to the ministry." Their interests drove them to "silence the black preacher even when the danger of insurrection was remote."[35] Most of the enslaved Black people who were allowed to worship could only do so in segregated pews in white congregations presided over by white pastors. Other enslavers found the threat of Christianity's freedom narrative too uncontrollable, forbidding all forms of worship among those they enslaved. For some even prayer or song were punishable offenses.[36] But freedom theologies and practices could not be extinguished, and at times withholding the gospel increased the conviction among the enslaved that the message within it was a powerful one.

The three largest slave revolts in US history were led by religious lead-ers who were themselves enslaved--Gabriel Prossser, Denmark Vesey, and Nathaniel Turner. Their rebellions were planned in worship services, prayer meetings, and Bible studies. In these cases the otherworldly, mystic orienta-tion was not in contradiction with action in history. John Brown, a poor white abolitionist, organized an insurrection with whites and free Black people that sought to arm enslaved Black people, a mission they understood biblically and mystically. During the Civil War, Black people left white churches in large numbers. This withdrawal was part of the larger rebellion against the system of slavery, including work stoppages to reduce Confederate supplies and defections to join the US military to defeat the treasonous Confederacy.[37]

Although most abolitionist church leaders did not lead violent insurrec-tions, they were organizing to end slavery by other means. The church was essential ground for the formation of anti-slavery and abolitionist strategies, movement leaders, and the theologies that inspired both. The Convention Movement in particular was the "secular adjunct of the Black church" and contributed to the radicalization of the church's position on abolitionism in the 1840s and 50s.[38] These national gatherings coordinated opposition to slav-ery, forced colonization, and the oppression of free Black people.

As independent black churches and denominations formed in the North, they were able to use independence of finances and governance to openly oppose slavery in previously impossible ways.[39] Eddie Glaude shows how the black churches made space within a racist and exploitative world to "develop a self-consciousness essential for problem-solving," "religious narrative to make sense of the absurdity of their condition" and the ability to "cultivate solidarity."[40] The practice did not automatically lead to a unity of strategy, but there was an opportunity to grapple with a "palpably shared problem."[41] This supported the development of key movement leaders from among those who had been enslaved, including Frederick Douglass, who began his pub-lic career with a preaching license from the AME Zion Church. While the condition of enslavement circumscribed the forms of resistance available to those held in slavery, free Black people could leverage different opportunities. Their commitment to abolition was not as an ally or a "voice of the voiceless." Until freedom was universal, free Black people were not truly free—politically or spiritually—and were always at risk of being stolen into slavery. Speaking in Buffalo at the American Anti-Slavery Society in 1840, Henry Highland Garnet proclaimed, "There is. . .a higher sort of freedom, which no mortal can touch. That freedom, thanks be unto the Most High, is mine. Yet I am not, nay, cannot be entirely free. I feel for my brethren as a man—I am bound with them as a brother. Nothing but emancipating them can set me at liberty."[42]

This "higher freedom," which even the enslaved possessed, was an important part of freedom church theology and practice. Black churches and Black religious leaders, including but not limited to independent churches and preachers, enslaved and free, sustained Black life and contributed to building abolition. King described it as, "we are all free in the sense that freedom is that inner power that drives us to achieve freedom."[43] This holding in tension of God's present and future liberating activity, historical and eschatological, was essential to the Black church and its fight against slavery.[44] The sermon on what to expect in the next life implicitly held God's judgement of this world's exploitation and oppression. It was not only the present reality that mattered. Enslavement was not the entirety of their being.[45] It brought consolation and hope that made survival possible in the midst of the torture of life under slavery.[46]

Preachers navigated their constant surveillance to preach the gospel faithfully. Wilmore points out "It is difficult to know the extent to which the preachers actually conformed to repeated warnings not to stir up discontent, and to what extent they pretended to go along with the system while subverting it."[47] The same is true of our knowledge of how the sermons were received. Enslaved preachers "were not blind to the degradation of themselves and their people" and maneuvered to be loyal to the "demands of the gospel" more than to their enslavers.[48] King preached that "we have much to learn" from the Black preacher who had "no training in philosophical classics," but,

> He knew God. And he knew that the God that he had heard about, and read about, was not a God that would subject some of his children and exalt the others. . .And he'd look out and say, "You ain't no nigger. You ain't no slave, but you're God's children." And something welled up within them, and they could starting singing even though they didn't have any shoes. "I got shoes, you got shoes, all of God's children got shoes. When I get to heaven, going to put on my shoes, and I'm just going to walk all over God's heaven."[49]

Throughout the freedom church tradition there is a synthesis of survival within the conditions of unfreedom and the material achievement of freedom that defies polarization. Albert Raboteau argues, "To decide that religion distracted slaves from concern with this life and persuaded them not to act in the present fails to acknowledge the full story. Slave religion had a this-worldly impact because it helped slaves to experience their own personal value."[50] This distinction is particularly hard to discern as we peer back over centuries and from radically different locations (a challenge we face in reading biblical texts as well).[51] The same sermon in two different contexts would have radically different meanings in relationship to how one responds to social and economic conditions. What is accommodationist in one context might be radical in another. But this deep and ephemeral synthesis means that what was once radical and revolutionary in one context can dissolve into something accommodationist in a new context.

Enslaved and free Black Christians claimed the Bible and shaped an interpretation and set of practices and values. M. Shawn Copeland argues that it came from a "critical reflection on their own condition," and responded to their own existential, psychological, social, and physical needs. Heard from the standpoint of being cast low, Bible texts are clear about God's particular concern for those cast low. Biblical revelation "offered the slaves the 'dangerous' message of freedom, for indeed, Jesus did come to bring 'freedom for the captive and release for those held in economic, social, and political bondage.' It offered them the great and parallel event of Exodus, for indeed, it was for a people's freedom that the Lord God chose, called, and sent Moses."[52] Eddie Glaude says the articulation of faith through the language of Exodus was solidly prominent in the Black tradition by 1840, with Egyptian enslavement and American enslavement drawn in parallel. Later the themes of wilderness and Promised Land would represent the unfinished promise of historical and eschatological freedom.[53] In the crucifixion and resurrection of Jesus Christ they saw "triumph over the principalities and powers of death, triumph over evil in this world."[54] Here too the triumph is both spiritual and historical.

King pointed to the spirituals as resources that disseminated those biblical interpretations. "The slaves, who were our marvelous foreparents, (were called) to add another song to their song on darkness. . . . Darkness came, and they could say, 'Nobody knows the trouble I've seen, nobody knows but Jesus.' But they recognized that there was something, and they could start to sing, 'I'm so glad that trouble don't last always.'"[55] Spirituals became a "resource of resistance" in part because they tied people together and broke isolation. "One woman's, one man's suffering or shout of jubilation became that of a people."[56]

The freedom that enslaved Black people fought for and claimed was both historical and eschatological.[57] King found resonance in and inspiration from the ways in which the church's affirmation of human dignity and Black personhood was a source of hope.[58] Preaching the Sunday following the first public announcement of the Poor People's Campaign, King said the Prophet Jeremiah,

> Noticed good people suffering, and evil people prospering. And he said, 'Is there no balm in Gilead? Is there no physician there?' Centuries later, our foreparents came along, and they noticed the inequalities of life. Nothing to look forward to morning after morning, but the sizzling heat, the rawhide whip of the overseer, long rows of cotton. But they did an amazing thing. They looked back across the centuries, and they took Jeremiah's question mark and straightened it into an exclamation point. And they could sing, 'there is a balm in Gilead to make the wounded whole! There is a balm in Gilead to heal the sin-sick soul.'

Generations later this faith sustained the ongoing, unfinished work of freedom. King's sermons spoke candidly about the discouragement of failed efforts in "in Alabama and Mississippi, and up in Cleveland and Chicago," but that the balm of Gilead his enslaved foreparents affirmed him and soothed his soul as well. "This is the faith that will carry us through the dark days ahead," and it is a faith that believes "ultimately the ground of hope is in the eternality of God."[59]

After emancipation this freedom church theology evolved in response to the political, social, and economic conditions that followed. It is not the entirety of the Black church tradition, and there have been periods of history where the call of the freedom church was faint, although never extinguished. James Cone observes, "Unfortunately, the post-Civil War black church fell into the white trick of interpreting salvation in terms similar to those of the white oppressors. Salvation became white: an objective act of Christ in which God 'washes' away our sins in order to prepare us for a new life in heaven."[60] The long Civil Rights Movement fanned the freedom church flame, both within and beyond conventional church settings. And then in the era of human rights, King called forward a freedom church of the poor to take on racism, poverty, and war.

NOTES

1. James H. Cone, *Martin & Malcom & America: A Dream or a Nightmare* (Orbis Books, 1992), 146–49. Martin Luther King Jr., "Letter from a Birmingham Jail," in *A Testament of Hope: The Essential Writings and Speeches of Martin Luther King, Jr.*, ed. James M. Washington (San Francisco: HarperOne, 1991), 289–302.

2. Martin Luther King Jr., "What Are Your New Year's Resolutions?" (January 7, 1968), 11, King Speeches, Series 3, Box 13, King Center Archives.

3. Cone, *Martin & Malcom & America*, 146–49. Lewis Baldwin, *The Voice of Conscience: The Church in the Mind of Martin Luther King, Jr.* (New York: Oxford University Press, 2010), 52, 102.

4. Martin Luther King Jr., "State of the Movement" (Frogmore, SC, November 28, 1967), 12, King Speeches, Series 3, Box 13, King Center Archives.

5. Jose Yglesias, "Dr. King's March on Washington, Part II," in *Black Protest in the Sixties*, ed. August Meier, John H. Bracey, and Elliott Rudwick (M. Wiener Pub., 1991), 280. This was not the only time Young used that tactic. Responding to charges that the Resurrection City was not going well, Andrew Young answered in theological language, "We move when the spirit says move. Anything outside is God's business. We are incorporated by the Lord and baptized by all this rain" (Hunter, "On the Case in Resurrection City," 1973, 11).

6. Gordon Mantler, "Black, Brown and Poor: Martin Luther King Jr., The Poor People's Campaign and Its Legacies" (Dissertation, Duke University, 2008), 134; Gerald McKnight, *The Last Crusade: Martin Luther King, Jr., the FBI, and the Poor People's Campaign* (Boulder, CO: Westview Press, 1998), 25.

7. Cecil Hinshaw, "FBI Requests for Information of the Poor People's Campaign," May 28, 1968, CRD Administration 32557, The Archives of the American Friends Service Committee.

8. Amy Nathan Wright, "Civil Rights 'Unfinished Business': Poverty, Race, and the 1968 Poor People's Campaign" (Dissertation, The University of Texas at Austin, 2007), 424.

9. "Poor People's Campaign Informational Pamphlet," 1968, document image in Jaid Jilani, "Dr. King Wanted 'Grand Alliance' of Blacks and White to Build Economic Justice," Alternet, August 19, 2015.

10. Southern Christian Leadership Conference, "Poor People's Campaign Declaration," April 28, 1968, 1–2, SCLC Papers, Series VIII, 177:25, King Center Archives.

11. Hunter, "On the Case in Resurrection City," 9.

12. Albert E. Gollin, "The Demography of Protest: A Statistical Profile of Participants in the Poor People's Campaign" (Bureau of Social Science Research, Inc., August 5, 1968), 21.

13. Richard Sidy, Poor People's Campaign Oral History, interview by John Alexander, August 5, 2015, https://pages.shanti.virginia.edu/ResurrectionCity/oral-histories/richard-sidys-reflections/.

14. Oliver F. Atkins, *Atkins_92_cs_20*, 1968, Photograph, 1968, Oliver F. Atkins photograph collection, 1943–1975, George Mason University, Special Collections and Archives, http://sca.gmu.edu/finding_aids/atkins.html., Oliver F. Atkins, *Atkins_92_cs_10*, 1968, Photograph, 1968, Oliver F. Atkins photograph collection, Box 12, Folder 21, George Mason University, Special Collections and Archives, http://sca.gmu.edu/finding_aids/atkins.html.

15. Sidy, Interview with John Alexander. Sidy, of California, described the impact of spontaneous preaching and worship among the campaign participants. "Even youths, 9 years old, telling it like it is. And the response of the congregation, so supportive. And for me, right out of LA, it's like falling into a Southern Baptist church."

16. Charlayne Hunter, "On the Case in Resurrection City," in *The Eyes on the Prize Civil Rights Reader: Documents, Speeches, and Firsthand Accounts from the Black Freedom Struggle, 1954–1990*, ed. Clayborne Carson et al. (New York: Viking, 1991), 435.

17. Ralph Abernathy, *And the Walls Came Tumbling Down: An Autobiography* (New York: Harper & Row, 1989), 512.

18. Charles Fager, *Uncertain Resurrection: The Poor People's Washington Campaign* (Grand Rapids, MI: Eerdmans, 1969), 102–5.

19. James H. Cone, "The Theology of Martin Luther King, Jr," *Union Seminary Quarterly Review* 40, no. 4 (1986): 34.

20. Wright, "Civil Rights 'Unfinished Business,'" 454.

21. Martin Luther King Jr., "See You in Washington" (SCLC Staff Retreat, Atlanta, GA, January 17, 1968), 10, King Speeches, Series 3, Box 13, King Center Archives.

22. Martin Luther King Jr., "Why We Must Go to Washington" (Atlanta, GA, January 15, 1968), 11a, King Speeches, Series 3, Box 13, King Center Archives.

23. Baldwin, *The Voice of Conscience*, 107.

24. C. Eric Lincoln and Lawrence H. Mamiya, *The Black Church in the African American Experience* (Duke University Press, 1990), 47.

25. Gayraud S. Wilmore, *Black Religion and Black Radicalism: An Interpretation of the Religious History of Afro-American People* (Maryknoll, NY: Orbis Books, 1983), 85.

26. The AME church emerged in 1787 with the withdrawal of the Black members of St. George's Methodist Episcopal Church in Philadelphia under the leadership of Absalom Jones and Richard Allen. (Lincoln and Mamiya, *The Black Church in the African American Experience*, 47, 50; Carol V. R George, *Segregated Sabbaths: Richard Allen and the Emergence of Independent Black Churches 1760-1840* (New York: Oxford University Press, 1973), 53–55; Wilmore, *Black Religion and Black Radicalism*, 80.) Even before the split Jones and Allen had formed the Free African Society in 1786 which sought to respond to Black needs unmet by the church, particularly social, political, and economic. These practices became part of the new denomination, which emphasized both worship and Black social welfare, meeting spiritual and material needs (Wilmore 82–83). Allen focused on individual salvation as evidenced by moral reform and social responsibility (George, 126). The AME Zion denomination formed through a similar process in New York City, with its first denominational conference in 1821 (Lincoln and Mamiya, *The Black Church in the African American Experience*, 57). They formally separated from the Methodist Episcopal Church in 1824 and had their first General Conference in 1828.

27. Lincoln and Mamiya, *The Black Church in the African American Experience*, 58, 202. AME Zion also established Underground Railroad stations, particularly in their churches close to the borders of states where slavery was legal.

28. The first known Black congregation was near what is now Mecklenburg, Virginia, organized in 1758 on the plantation of William Byrd under the leadership of white Baptist missionary Shubal Stearns, who evangelized to slaves in North Carolina, South Carolina, and Georgia. Black Baptist churches were founded on agricultural labor camps in South Carolina and Virginia in the early to mid-1770s and

in the Northeast in the first decade of the 1800s, including Abyssinian Baptist in New York City in 1809 (Wilmore, *Black Religion and Black Radicalism*, 79–80.).

29. Wilmore, *Black Religion and Black Radicalism*, 74–75, 77, 78.

30. James H. Cone, *God of the Oppressed* (Maryknoll, NY: Orbis Books, 1997), 44.

31. Cited in M. Shawn Copeland, "Wading through Many Sorrows," in *A Troubling in My Soul: Womanist Perspectives on Evil and Suffering*, ed. Emilie Maureen Townes, The Bishop Henry McNeal Turner Studies in North American Black Religion (Maryknoll, N.Y: Orbis Books, 1993), 119.

32. Cone, *God of the Oppressed*, 45. The Revolutionary War had been billed as a holy war against the oppression of the British Crown, and the spirit of liberty and equality was carried into abolitionist efforts and emancipatory legislation for over a decade, including the Quaker-organized Abolition Society in Philadelphia (1775), abolition of slavery in Vermont (1777), prohibition of the external slave trade in Virginia (1778), and a resolution against slaveholding by the Methodist Church (1784). This period was short lived and gains were rescinded (the Methodist church returned to its sanctification of slavery). But out of this period came the independent Black denominations and independent Black Baptist congregations in the South and Border States (Wilmore 79). The Second Great Awakening (1790–1850) expanded Black conversions to Christianity, aided by a (later rescinded) condemnation of slavery among Baptists and Methodists (Eddie S Glaude, *Exodus!: Religion, Race, and Nation in Early Nineteenth-Century Black America* [Chicago: University of Chicago Press, 2000], 56).

33. Wilmore, *Black Religion and Black Radicalism*, 78.

34. Martin Luther King Jr., *Where Do We Go from Here: Chaos or Community?* (Boston: Beacon Press, 2010), 76–77, 101–2.

35. Wilmore, *Black Religion and Black Radicalism*, 78.

36. Copeland, "Wading through Many Sorrows," 119.

37. Lincoln and Mamiya, *The Black Church in the African American Experience*, 48, 203.

38. Wilmore, *Black Religion and Black Radicalism*, 92.

39. Wilmore, *Black Religion and Black Radicalism*, 96. Some of the most radical Black religious leadership was from predominantly white denominations, including Presbyterian Henry Highland Garnet. And some middle-income northern leaders in the convention movement tended toward reformist anti-slavery positions. Influenced by white William Lloyd Garrison, this became the inclination of the Philadelphia wing of the AME church by 1835. (Wilmore, 93).

40. Glaude, *Exodus!*, 21. This leadership was not limited to northern free blacks. Four days before General William Sherman issued Special Field Order No. 15, which established the Sea Islands and land south of Charleston as a Black settlement, divided into family tracts of forty acres with a loan of mules (the origin of "forty acres and a mule"), Sherman convened twenty leaders from Savannah's Black community, most of whom were Baptist and Methodist ministers and most of whom had been born into slavery. Baptist minister Garrison Frazier, who bought his freedom in 1857 at the age of sixty, defined enslavement as receiving . . . the work of another man, and not by his consent," and freedom as "placing us where we could reap the fruit of our

own labor . . . to have land, and turn it and till it by our own labor." Frazier also told Sherman that freed Black people "would prefer to live by ourselves," as a defense against prejudices against them. Sherman was mostly trying to solve the problem that thousands of Black families had joined his March to the Sea from Atlanta in November 1864, abandoning the plantation labor camps as the US army destroyed the estates (Eric Foner, *Reconstruction: America's Unfinished Revolution, 1863–1877* [New York: History Book Club, 2005], 70–71).

41. Glaude, *Exodus!*, 10–12.

42. Glaude, *Exodus!*, 148.

43. King, "See You in Washington (January 1968)," 11.

44. Reflecting on the relationship between ideology and the ability to take part in the struggle to make freedom from enslavement real, King emphasized "psychological freedom," including Black people claiming dignity and honor, is a "powerful weapon against the long night of physical slavery." (King, Jr., *Where Do We Go from Here: Chaos or Community?*, 44–45.)

45. "Black slaves recognized that human freedom is transcendent—that is a constituent of the future—which made it impossible to identify humanity exclusively with meager attainment in history" (Cone, *God of the Oppressed*, 11).

46. Cone, "The Theology of Martin Luther King, Jr," 26.

47. Wilmore, *Black Religion and Black Radicalism*, 77. Cone points out that, "White slave masters were no brighter than our contemporary white theologians who can see in black religion only what their axiological presupposition permit them to see. And that vision usually extends no further than some notion of black 'otherworldliness' leading to passivity" (Cone, *God of the Oppressed*, 56).

48. Wilmore, *Black Religion and Black Radicalism*, 78.

49. Martin Luther King Jr., "Meaning of Hope" (Dexter Ave. Baptist Church, Montgomery, Alabama, December 10, 1967), 16–17, King Speeches, Series 3, Box 13, King Center Archives.

50. Albert J. Raboteau, *Canaan Land: A Religious History of African Americans* (Oxford; New York: Oxford University Press, 2001), 59.

51. Richard A. Horsley, ed., *Hidden Transcripts and the Arts of Resistance: Applying the Work of James C. Scott to Jesus and Paul*, Semeia Studies, no. 48 (Atlanta: Society of Biblical Literature, 2004).

52. Copeland, "Wading through Many Sorrows," 119–20.

53. Glaude, *Exodus!*, 56.

54. Copeland, "Wading through Many Sorrows," 119–20.

55. King, "See You in Washington (January 1968)," 15.

56. Copeland, "Wading through Many Sorrows," 120. King pointed out that these songs and the theological themes within them were sometimes used to organize resistance in the form of escape, a code system. "They'd start singing, 'I heard of a city called heaven.'" And the white folks thought they were talking about heaven up yonder, but they were talking about Canada, the other end of the Underground Railroad" (King, "Meaning of Hope [December 1967]," 16).

57. James Cone describes the strategy of Black Theology, rooted in this long Black church tradition, as one that asks "in what ways can we best explicate the meaning of

God's liberating activity in the world so that the oppressed will be ready to risk all for earthly freedom?" (James H. Cone, "Black Theology and Black Liberation," in *Black Theology: A Documentary History*, ed. James H. Cone and Gayraud S. Wilmore, 2nd ed., vol. 1 [Maryknoll, N.Y: Orbis Books, 1993], 111). Wilmore writes, "Black theology arose as a 'theology of freedom' in response to crucial events—'events that had the unmistakable sign that God was saying and doing something unprecedented about oppressed minorities and freedom in White America" (Wilmore, *Black Religion and Black Radicalism*, 3).

58. Baldwin, *The Voice of Conscience*, 108. Baldwin observes that "on the level of ideas" King approached the Black church with interest in "its significance as a social institution, and not as a historian or one deeply interested in the details of its development in different time frames." This framing resembled those of the scholars King engaged on the subject, "E. Franklin Frazier, W. E. B. DuBois, Carter G. Woodson, Benjamin E. Mays, and others, all of whom investigated that institution in the context of social-scientific research" (109).

59. King, "Meaning of Hope," 17.

60. James H. Cone, *A Black Theology of Liberation* (Maryknoll, NY: Orbis Books, 1986), 225–26.

Chapter 6

King's Theological Ethics

In an interview during the planning of the Poor People's Campaign, King resisted the suggestion that because they were bringing the poor together around the right to eat, the right to income, and the right to live, they had moved away from the appropriate domain of the church. "In a sense, you could say we are engaged in the class struggle, yes. . . . It will be a long and difficult struggle, for our program calls for a redistribution of economic power. Yet this isn't a purely materialistic or class concern." Underscoring his belief that human dignity is central to his theology, he continued, "I feel that this movement on behalf of the poor is the most moral thing—it is saying that every man is an heir to a legacy of dignity and worth."[1] King often turned to his theological ethics to find language to articulate the significance and purpose of a movement of the poor. But those theological ideas were not only rhetorical. They impacted his political vision for organizing a campaign of the poor in the era of human rights. The central themes are ones that span his ministry—human dignity, the kingdom of God, beloved community, and the interrelatedness of justice, love, and power.

HUMAN DIGNITY

King believed and preached a personal God and the infinite value of human personality. When he talked about every person being "an heir to a legacy of dignity and worth," King was drawing from his graduate training in Boston personalist theology. This study gave philosophical buttressing to his life experiences and theological upbringing.[2] King identified that personal idealism was his "basic philosophical position," and said personalism "strengthened me in two convictions: it gave me metaphysical and philosophical grounding for the idea of a personal God, and it gave me a metaphysical basis for the dignity and worth of all human personality."[3] The personal God of love and reason with no limitation was the source of the infinite dignity, the ultimate value in life.[4] For King the Bible's "image of God" means "every human being has etched in his personality the indelible stamp of the Creator." This is the source for assertion that every person must be respected. It is theological and political.[5] Theologian Garth Baker-Fletcher describes King's personalist theology as "somebodyness," created in the image of God, and inherently full of dignity as children of God.[6]

From there King draws the assertion that human dignity is both the source of society and society's objective. The application of personalism to racism and segregation exposes the full evil of white supremacy as a system that degrades and humiliates personality, denying personhood and life to Black people. It is an assault on the divine spirit within the oppressed.[7] And the application of personalism to poverty exposes the evil of economic exploitation, denying personhood and life to poor people. King argued we must "outlaw poverty" for both material reasons and concerns of "our mind and spirit." The "profound moral fact" that all human beings are "souls of infinite metaphysical value," is "deeply woven into the fiber of our religious tradition." Because we are all made in the image of God, "we cannot be content to see men hungry, to see men victimized with ill-health," when ending poverty is materially possible.[8] But instead of being organized around human "somebodyness," society is organized around the "thingification" of human beings. King traced this to the patterns that established and justified slavery in the formation of the United States. "A nation that will keep people in slavery for 244 years will "thingify" them and make them things. And therefore, they will exploit them and poor people generally economically." The pattern of exploitation and degradation within the United States is practiced globally. "A nation that will exploit economically will have to have foreign investments and everything else, and it will have to use its military might to protect them. All of these problems are tied together."[9]

The corollary to thingifying human beings was sanctifying property. King said, "There are many who wince at a distinction between property and persons—who hold both sacrosanct. My views are not so rigid. A life is sacred. Property is intended to serve life, and no matter how much we surround it with rights and respect, it has no personal being. It is part of the earth man walks on; it is not man."[10] But the sanctification of property and denigration of human beings was pervasive and deep. It came with a selfish materialism that blocked change. King said the "radical reordering of our national priorities" will be resisted by those who may not say so directly, but their "real motivations are that the fact that they cherish that second colorvision set, and that sports car, and that extra country home so much, that the comforts have caught up with their lives, and they don't want to make the sacrifices necessary to make sharing a greater reality."[11]

The theological foundation of human dignity and rejection of the sanctification of property contributed to King's belief that the means of life were
rights—politically and morally. While this was based in King's Black church
and social gospel personalism, King found affinities with American civil and
human rights traditions that framed personhood as endowed with rights. He
talked about the campaign as demanding "the right to eat" and "the right to
live." He framed the call for a guaranteed annual income as "taking seriously"
the Declaration of Independence: "We hold these truths to be self-evident
that all men are created equal, that they are endowed by their Creator with
certain inalienable rights, and among these are life, liberty and the pursuit of
happiness." He said society currently believed a person is owed a job only
"if he can get it." Morally that violated human dignity. Practically, he argued,
that way of organizing the economy was detrimental to national productivity,
family stability, and heath. But a guaranteed income would mean a "radical
redefinition of work," where one's livelihood and vocation are not subservi-
ent to market forces.[12]

King saw that the economy was changing. He and others saw that the manufacturing sector was being forever changed by automation and new technology, pushing increasing numbers of people into low-waged and un-unionized
service sector jobs. Economists and politicians were calling for studies of the
trend, but King argued that from a "moral point of view" the response to the
trend should be a guaranteed income that makes possible the pursuit of contributions to society that "fulfill your own nature" rather than serving the directions of capitalist markets. Criticizing federal programs that attempt to better
prepare people for the existing labor market, like War on Poverty programs,
he argued that the right to income combined with a redefinition of labor is the
"only way ultimately to solve the problem of poverty."[13] Wages limited the
search for human dignity because society's "measure of value revolved about
money." And it's orientation towards using capitalist markets to distribute the
means of life put the responsibility on individuals and families. "If society
changes its concepts by placing the responsibility on its system, not on the
individual, and guarantees secure employment or a minimum income, dignity
will come within reach of all."[14]

Along with this commitment to a systemic solution to human needs as
rights, King was critical of charity responses to poverty. He saw that charity
solutions in the private sector and stop-gap programs in the public sector,
were incompatible with human dignity because they did not change the distorted structures and social values that created poverty. Therefore charity was
incapable of solving the problem of poverty or respecting the human dignity
of the poor. King acknowledged we must "help the discouraged beggars in
life's marketplace. But one day we must come to see that an edifice which
produces beggars needs restructuring." King often used the parable of the

Good Samaritan to make this point. Caring for those left for dead on the road-side would be only an "initial act" that supports the transformation of "the whole Jericho Road . . . so that men and women will not be beaten and robbed as they make their journey through life." Whereas much of the way poverty is responded to, even in terms of policy, is like "flinging a coin to a beggar," the real solution is "that an edifice which produced beggars needs restructur-ing." Charity does not address the "glaring contrast of poverty and wealth."[15]

King pointed out that charity responses to the problems of society rely on pity. "Pity is feeling sorry for somebody. Empathy is feeling with them. Ultimately people don't want you to do something for them, they want you to do something with them." A "paternalistic bind" lets people think they are "helping a particular group that's oppressed," when "deep down within there is still a subconscious feeling of superiority, because they want to do something for them rather than to do it with them." Empathy is when you act with people, not for people. Empathy is when you see the single garment of destiny covers you as well.[16] Charity is impotent economically, socially, and theologically. It fails to solve poverty or respect of human dignity.

The belief that humans are endowed with the divine spirit not only makes the abolition of social evils necessary; it also makes it possible. For King the image of God with which we are endowed is freedom, and so our personality in God's image is also freedom. We have God's "indelible imprint of dignity and freedom." The denial of freedom by social, political, and economic evils is a sin against God. Because we are marked by God with freedom, when freedom is denied by oppression and exploitation, God' imprint becomes a "throbbing desire for freedom." It is the very endowment by God of our inner freedom that drives those, "robbed of their external freedom fight to regain it"[17] King specifies that he is talking about the freedom of the whole person, "not the freedom of a function called the will,"[18] which can be used theologi-cally in ways that separate spiritual freedom from material freedom and con-tribute to otherworldly religiosities. In the "Letter from a Birmingham Jail" he had criticized, "a strange, un-Biblical distinction between body and soul," that coincided with the defense of segregation.[19] We are inheritors of dignity that must be wrestled into reality. But that very wresting with reality is made possible by our endowment with personality that cannot be fully taken away, no matter how degrading the conditions of life.

In describing the theological significance of what they would attempt in the Poor People's Campaign, King said, "what we hope for as we go to Washington is freedom. And I would hope that . . . we'd know that we are not free—overtly, externally, but we are all free in the sense that freedom is that inner power that drives us to achieve freedom."[20] Our human dignity, our "somebodyness," is inherently free, and so there is a drive for that freedom to be matched by external freedom. The oppressed have to fight for overt, external freedom, and so that inner power that drives the pursuit of external freedom is the potential force to drive the transformation of society. This is why King said "The only real revolutionary, people say, is a man who has nothing to lose." If the millions of poor people, Black, brown, and white could, "take action together, they will do so with a freedom and a power that will be a new and unsettling force in our complacent national life."[21] This freedom and power is political and theological.

This is why the idea that charity will fix the poor is politically and theologically misguided. The "throbbing desire for freedom" does not automatically translate into effective action, but King said, if they can be organized together, the poor become the force of transformation, unsettling the complacent middle to join a fight against those who actively maintain the status quo for their own benefit.

Knowing that the freedom and dignity they seek cannot be realized apart from power, King says the organizing of the poor in a campaign to go to Washington would not meet immediate success, but would be part of the poor becoming a force that, "may just be able to speed up the day when man everywhere will respect the dignity and worth of human personality and all men will be able to cry out that we are children of God made in His image." King described their mission as, "seeking a city whose Builder and Maker is God." And said, "If we will do this we will be able to turn this nation upside down and right side up."[22]

KINGDOM OF GOD

When King says the poor will go to Washington seeking the city of God that reverses the order of the existing world, he is using theological language to describe the world's social and economic disorder and the role of the poor in its reordering. This interpretation of the biblical, "kingdom of God" draws from the Social Gospel movement, prominent in the late nineteenth and first half of the twentieth century, including Walter Rauschenbusch's emphasis on the state as a guarantor of the means of life—economic, social, and political.[23] God's commandments were not only directed to the individual. Social Gospel thinkers emphasized the application of biblical principles to the transformation of society, including state, economic, institutional, and family systems and cultures. The Bible was full of imperatives for how society should be in God's kingdom: prisoners and slaves are set free, the hungry are fed, immigrants are welcomed, and the poor have what they need to survive. The Bible was also full of condemnations of empires, kingdoms, kings, and caesars who did not follow God's instructions for social order. King said, "America, too, is going to hell if she doesn't use her . . . vast resources of wealth to end poverty and make it possible for all of God's children to have the basic necessities of life."[24]

King didn't accept liberal optimism about inevitable social progress found in some liberal theologies, but he had strong political and theological ideas about social progress coming from the agency of the oppressed. King agreed the kingdom of God could not be perfected in history, a tenet of Christian realism.[25] But King believed a greater resonance between the Kingdom of God and human society than realists thought possible.[26] The state was a trustee of the resources of creation, and people were entitled to demand basic economic goods alongside the demands of political rights.[27] One need not be a Christian to hold this view, but for King they were central Christian beliefs. He articulated them as such.

> God has left enough and to spare in this world for all of his children to have the basic necessities of life, and God never intended for some of his children to live in inordinate superfluous wealth while others live in abject, deadening poverty. . . . I believe firmly that the earth is the Lord's and the fullness thereof. I don't think it belongs to Mr. Rockefeller. I don't think it belongs to Mr. Ford. I think the earth is the Lord's, and since we didn't make these things by ourselves, we must share them with each other. And I think this is the only way we are going to solve the basic problems and the restructuring of our society which I think is so desperately needed.[28]

Racism, political exclusion, and state violence could not be resolved while vast inequalities of wealth and power persist.[29] True freedom cannot be known when the basic necessities of life are not rights and wage employment determines ones relationship to them. Poverty was not new, but what was new was the material and technological ability to resolve it. The gains of productivity and technology were rapidly expanding, and yet those gains were channeled towards the benefit of the few. The concept of the kingdom of God influences and strengthens the political and theological position that a movement for human rights would need strategies that could move the poor and dispossessed from a position of unfreedom and powerlessness into an organized force with the power to transform society.[30]

BELOVED COMMUNITY

For King the beloved community is both political and theological, realized and realizable in history as the kingdom of God. Beloved community depends upon the divine indwelling that characterizes all human beings and makes possible a regenerated society where the spirit and value of every person is cherished.[31] Self and other are cared for and care for one another, with no one valued more than another. Where the beloved community is realized, exploitation and the false divisions of society are no longer the determinants in social relationships. Instead our lives are organized by our shared human-ness and shared abundance. The use of capitalist markets to distribute basic necessities and organize labor, racist conceptions of belonging and differ-ence, state violence, and nationalist exploitation and war cannot coexist with beloved community.

There is a temptation to interpret, "beloved community" as reformist integrationism, the kind that King warned was "integrating into a burning house."[32] Too often King's phrases like "'whiteness' and 'blackness' pass away as determinants in a relationship," are taken as an invitation to avert the work of the abolition of racism with "color blindness." There is also a temptation to interpret "beloved community" as a romanticized localism, where justice and care are possible only interpersonally and communally, rather than as a whole nation or world. But King uses the term "beloved com-munity" neither in the sense that justice is possible only in local communities nor that racial justice is merely colorblindness in an otherwise dysfunctional, dehumanizing and poverty-producing system.

Beloved community also is not charity responses to poverty. Because char-ity depends on inequality—with the giver having power over the receiver—charity distorts human relationships. A philanthropist, "may be self-centered in his self-denial and self-righteous in his self-sacrifice. His generosity may feed his ego, and his piety may feed his pride." Generosity that comes from real love is not marred by pride and ego, but real love also demands that human dignity be respected materially by making charity unnecessary through the structural meeting of needs.[33]

The demands of beloved community necessitate dealing with questions of the state. It is not enough to change how we interact with one another inter-personally—to have better behavior within existing structures. We cannot be who God calls us to be or follow God's imperatives in the existing society. And at the same time we cannot transform society without changing how we interact with each other. This holding together of both the change we seek in the world and the process by which we make that change real is expressed by King as beloved community. It describes the character and content of the social movement to transform society as directly related to the character and content of the society transformed.

It was here that nonviolence was both an organizing tactic and a deeply held theological position about how we respond to God and the other. In rela-tionship to the dismantling of legalized segregation, King reflected, "We shall not in the process relinquish our privilege and our obligation to love. While abhorring segregation, we shall love the segregationist. This is the only way to create the beloved community."[34] The poor would forward a "revolution not against the lives of the persons" but "against the structures through which the society is refusing" to address poverty."[35] And in a sermon on the lessons from anti-colonial movement in India, King preached, "Gandhi followed the way of love and nonviolence, refusing to hate and refusing to follow the way of violence. . . . The aftermath of violence is always bitterness; the aftermath of nonviolence is the creation of the beloved community."[36] In all of these examples King is thinking about both how change really happens and what the changed society looks like. It is an assessment of existing inequalities of power and the redistribution of economic and political power. This mattered to King because beloved community was not an abstract ideal. It was a means and a destination. It transformed the individuals who took action and the larger society who witnessed. It responded to social evil with love, to violence with nonviolence. Despite the seemingly insurmountable barriers to its accomplishment, King believed we could achieve greater approximation of the kingdom of God within history.

LOVE, JUSTICE, AND POWER

King wrestled new meaning into the Christian ethic of love. He contended with the practices of segregation and traditions of white supremacy, not by deciding that love was inapplicable to a world structured by evil, but by finding love's revolutionary power.

> When (Jesus) says (love) he means it. Love is not meekness, without muscle. Love is not sentimentality without spine. Love is not a tender heart without a tough mind. While it is none of that, it does mean caring. Love means going to any length to restore the broken community. Love means going the second mile to restore the broken community. Love means turning the other cheek to restore the broken community. And this is all the cross means to me. . . . This is what we are called to do.[37]

Love's partner in the transformation of society is justice, and justice cannot be realized apart from power. At every turn the Civil Rights Movement had met the chorus of "wait and see" in response to the demands of citizenship, but knowing they would see no progress, they organized campaigns that refused to wait.

Appeals to the morals of love and justice were important aspects of movement building. They developed the leaders who engaged in nonviolent action, those who were transformed and recommitted by the experience. But ethical appeals alone would yield no more than, "wait and see." Strategies of social change that rely only on the moral upper-hand, persuasion, and suffering, "underestimated the structures of evil" and left the violence of white supremacy unchecked. King observed, "Southerners are making the Marxist analysis of history more accurate than the Christian hope that men can be persuaded through teaching and preaching. . . . Businessmen act much more quickly from economic considerations than do churchmen from moral considerations." A strategy for social change needed to fully account for the strengths and weaknesses of ones opponents. This was confirmed by the successes and failures of the long history of the Black freedom struggle. The genius of the leadership of the movement was the combination of, "ethical appeals . . . undergirded by some form of constructive coercive power."[38] The redemptive suffering of nonviolent resistance to evil was not a shying away from power but a consciousness and creative response to how power operates, particularly state power. Nonviolence was a politically effective and theologically potent means for the relatively powerless to outmaneuver those with more power, including in its capacity to gain power by winning middle sections of society to its side.[39]

Against the many religious leaders who have problems with power, King argues power used correctly is not the problem. Too often in the history of Christianity love and power were considered opposites, with love interpreted as "resignation of power," and power identified as "denial of love." King countered, "power at its best is love implementing the demands of justice, and justice at its best is love correcting everything that stands against love."[40] Too often it is those who possess power who propagate moralities that equate power with sinfulness, encouraging the powerless to seek change through strategies of moral suasion devoid of power. Michael Long points out that King knew the state "would never effect the revolution of values that King sought." It would have to be compelled to do so. In the campaigns of the Civil Rights Movement, it was only when strategically employed tactics compelled the federal government to take sides against southern state and local governments that the federal government was willing to use its power against legalized segregation and voter disenfranchisement.[41]

As King reassessed the accomplishments of the civil rights campaigns of the 1950s and 1960s, King asserted that they had not effectively built sustained power or fundamentally changed the structure of political and economic power. In the coming period, in order to shift from a civil rights movement to a human rights movement, the "basic challenge is to discover how to organize our strength into economic and political power." Solutions to the triple evils had a shared opponent in the existing inequality of economic and political power. Their interrelatedness made clear that the nation required new structures and institutions rather than the expansion of existing ones.

This would require, "confrontation between the forces of power demanding change and the forces of power dedicated to preserving the status quo."[42]

The transformation would be so significant that King described it using the theological language of the nation being "born again" and becoming "new life." And King saw that, "this new life will not emerge until our nation undergoes a radical revolution of values."[43]

> A true revolution of values will soon look uneasily on the glaring contrast of poverty and wealth. With righteous indignation, it will look at thousands of working people displaced from their jobs with reduced incomes as a result of automation while the profits of the employers remain intact, and say: ""This is not just." It will look across the oceans and see individual capitalists of the West investing huge sums of money in Asia, Africa and South America, only to take the profits out with no concern for the social betterment of the countries, and say: "This is not just." It will look at our alliance with the landed gentry of Latin America and say: "This is not just."[44]

This revolution of values is something very different from moral appeals to power, and yet it is at the heart of the relationship of justice, love, and power. It is the relationship of values to the very real grappling with evil structures, building the power of the poor, and forcing the "radical redistribution of political and economic power."[45] King knew that a transition to a new order of justice would not be tensionless.[46] This is why the Poor People's Campaign was a national campaign that drew together leaders form local struggles to build "power for poor people."[47] It took a deep faith in human dignity to lead a movement for this scale of social transformation. It also required a political strategy for realizing a redistribution of political and economic power that was consistent with that faith in human dignity. And in the campaign of the poor, he had a theory about who could be that force of change.

NOTES

1. Jose Yglesias, "Dr. King's March on Washington, Part II," in *Black Protest in the Sixties*, ed. August Meier, John H. Bracey, and Elliott Rudwick (New York: M. Wiener Pub., 1991), 280–81.

2. King's doctoral studies at Boston University trained him in the school of personalism, particularly under the guidance of L. Harold DeWolf, part of personalism's third generation of scholars. DeWolf blended philosophy and evangelical theology, a combination that resonated with King's own sense of the two. Personalism was a neo-Kantian idealism developed in the late nineteenth and early twentieth centuries by philosopher Borden Parker Browne. The central argument was that personality is a reality that cannot be explained by anything else. The self is the center of conscious

experience and cannot be fully attributed to matter. Gary Dorrien demonstrates that on central doctrinal issues King very much follows in the tradition of social gospel personalism. For example, against objectivist atonement theories he takes up and applies the position of Bowne and Knudson where Christ's crucifixion reveals, in the words of King, "the sacrificial love of God intended to awaken an answering love in the hearts of men" (Gary Dorrien, *Breaking White Supremacy: Martin Luther King Jr. and the Black Social Gospel* [New Haven: Yale University Press, 2017], 275).

3. James H. Cone, "The Theology of Martin Luther King, Jr," *Union Seminary Quarterly Review* 40, no. 4 (1986): 23.; Dorrien, *Breaking White Supremacy*, 280.

4. Dorrien, *Breaking White Supremacy*, 21.

5. Martin Luther King Jr., *Where Do We Go from Here: Chaos or Community?* (New York: Harper & Row, 1967), 97.

6. Garth Baker-Fletcher, "Somebodyness and Self-Respect: Themes of Dignity in Martin Luther King and Malcolm X," *Union Seminary Quarterly Review* 48, no. 1–2 (1994): 8.

7. Gary Dorrien, *The Making of American Liberal Theology: Crisis, Irony, and Postmodernity 1950–2005* (Louisville: Westminster John Knox Press, 2006), 154.; Gary Dorrien, *Social Ethics in the Making: Interpreting an American Tradition* (Chichester, U.K.; Malden, MA: Wiley-Blackwell, 2008), 394.

8. King, *Where Do We Go from Here: Chaos or Community?*, 191.

9. Martin Luther King Jr., "'Where Do We Go from Here?,' Address to the 11th Annual SCLC Convention," King Encyclopedia at Stanford, August 16, 1967, https://kinginstitute.stanford.edu/king-papers/documents/where-do-we-go-here-address-delivered-eleventh-annual-sclc-convention.

10. Martin Luther King Jr., *The Trumpet of Conscience* (New York: Harper & Row, 1968), 56.

11. Martin Luther King Jr., "Why We Must Go to Washington" (Atlanta, GA, January 15, 1968), 16–17, King Speeches, Series 3, Box 13, King Center Archives.

12. Martin Luther King Jr., "SCLC Staff Retreat Speech" (Frogmore, SC, November 14, 1966), 22–23, King Speeches, Series 3, Box 13, King Center Archives.

13. King, "SCLC Staff Retreat Speech (November 1966)," 21–23.

14. King, *Where Do We Go from Here: Chaos or Community?*, 87.

15. Martin Luther King Jr., "A Time to Break Silence," in *A Testament of Hope: The Essential Writings and Speeches of Martin Luther King, Jr.*, ed. James M. Washington (San Francisco: HarperOne, 1991), 241. Gary Dorrien points out that this interpretation drew from preacher George Buttrick (Dorrien, *Breaking White Supremacy*, 430.) In addition to "A Time to Break Silence," cited above, King's uses the Good Samaritan parable in *Where Do We Go from Here?* (his final book), "Where Do We Go from Here?" (his final SCLC Convention speech, August 1967), "To Minister to the Valley" (a speech at the Ministers Training Program held in Miami, FL, February 1968), and "I See the Promised Land," (his final speech the night before his assassination).

16. Martin Luther King Jr., "Who Is My Neighbor?" (Ebenezer Baptist Church, Atlanta, GA, February 18, 1968), 6, King Speeches, Series 3, Box 13, King Center Archives.

17. Baker-Fletcher, "Somebodyness and Self-Respect," 8.

18. King, *Where Do We Go from Here: Chaos or Community?*, 97.

19. Martin Luther King Jr., "Letter from a Birmingham Jail," in *A Testament of Hope: The Essential Writings and Speeches of Martin Luther King, Jr.*, ed. James M. Washington (San Francisco: HarperOne, 1991), 289–302.

20. Martin Luther King Jr., "See You in Washington" (SCLC Staff Retreat, Atlanta, GA, January 17, 1968), 11, King Speeches, Series 3, Box 13, King Center Archives.

21. King, *Trumpet of Conscience*, 60.

22. Martin Luther King Jr., "State of the Movement" (Frogmore, SC, November 28, 1967), 12, King Speeches, Series 3, Box 13, King Center Archives.

23. Michael G. Long, *Against Us, But for Us: Martin Luther King, Jr. and the State* (Mercer University Press, 2002), 54, 111. Long argues that academic study with sociologist Walter Chivers, with whom King took seven courses at Morehouse, gave King an assessment that the poor must force the state to fill this proper function, against the idea that the progress of humanity would move in that direction naturally (p. 38, 210).

24. Martin Luther King Jr., "All Labor Has Dignity," in *The Radical King*, ed. Cornel West (Boston, Massachusetts: Beacon Press, 2015), 174.

25. Dorrien, *The Making of American Liberal Theology*, 145–46.; Lewis Baldwin, *The Voice of Conscience: The Church in the Mind of Martin Luther King, Jr.* (New York: Oxford University Press, 2010), 53–54, 65, 71.

26. See for example, King, "Who Is My Neighbor? (February 1968)," 13–14; King, "State of the Movement," 11.

27. Long, *Against Us, But for Us*, 208, 211. When King spoke of "a nation which hath foundation, whose builder and maker is God," (King, "Who Is My Neighbor? [February 1968]," 13–14), it was not an argument for a convergence of the church as an institution with the state. He knew well that the, "ecclesiastical power structure" was not more ethical or moral than the "economic and political power structure." But he did believe the state should be a steward of resources and protector of human rights and human dignity. (Baldwin, *The Voice of Conscience*, 86.)

28. King, "SCLC Staff Retreat Speech (November 1966)," 21.

29. Martin Luther King Jr., "The Other America: Address at Local 1199" (Hunter College, New York, NY, March 10, 1968), King Speeches, Series 3, Box 15, King Center Archives.; Martin Luther King, Jr., "Speech at Staff Retreat" (Frogmore, SC, May 1967), King Speeches, Series 3, Box 13, King Center Archives.; King, "Why We Must Go to Washington."

30. Dorrien articulates this well, "Freedom has no reality apart from power. Power is integral to hope and liberation. Integration requires equal access to political and economic power. Freedom is participation in power. For King, the goal of the civil rights movement was precisely to transform the lack of power of black Americans into creative, vital, interpersonal, organized power. All could be free, but only if all were empowered to participate" (Dorrien, *Breaking White Supremacy*, 441).

31. King was introduced to this phrase at Boston University by his personalist teachers. It was originated with American philosopher Josiah Royce (Dorrien, *Social Ethics in the Making*, 395).

32. Harry Belafonte and Michael Shnayerson, *My Song: A Memoir* (Alfred A. Knopf, 2011), 329.

33. Martin Luther King Jr., "'Where Do We Go From Here?,' Address to the 11th Annual SCLC Convention." This is similar to King's sermon, "Paul's Letter to American Christians" (Dexter Avenue Baptist Church, Montgomery, AL, November 4, 1956)

34. Martin Luther King Jr., "Loving Your Enemies," in *The Radical King*, ed. Cornel West (Boston, Massachusetts: Beacon Press, 2015), 55–64.

35. King, *Trumpet of Conscience*, 59–60.

36. Martin Luther King Jr., "Palm Sunday Sermon on Mohandas K. Gandhi (March 22, 1959)," in *The Radical King*, ed. Cornel West (Boston, Massachusetts: Beacon Press, 2015), 23–38.

37. King, "Speech at Staff Retreat (May 1967)," 27–28.

38. King, *Where Do We Go from Here: Chaos or Community?*, 129.

39. Larry L. Rasmussen, "Life Worthy of Life: The Social Ecologies of Bonhoeffer and King," in *Bonhoeffer and King: Their Legacies and Import for Christian Social Thought*, ed. Willis Jenkins and Jennifer M. McBride (Minneapolis: Fortress Press, 2010), 67. After King's study in India he said he was, "more convinced than ever before that nonviolent resistance is the most potent weapon available to oppressed people in their struggle for freedom." Dorrien points out that although King identified that he integrated a Gandhian understanding of nonviolence and its relationship to social change when introduced to it by Mordecai Johnson while at Crozer, it was a synthesis of this academic introduction and on-the-job training in Montgomery with Bayard Rustin and Glenn Smiley, a Fellowship of Reconciliation activist. King did not use Gandhi's jargon or argue for absolute pacifism. Jesus was always an important model of nonviolence, with King using biblical language more than Gandhian religious language (Dorrien, *Breaking White Supremacy*, 266).

40. King, *Where Do We Go from Here: Chaos or Community?*, 137–38.

41. Long, *Against Us, But for Us*, 205. Long points out that "King continued to rely heavily upon the power and coercion of the state in order to carry out his nonviolent protests. King's reliance was not passive, either. As he carefully planned his nonviolent marches, he also carefully engineered the presence of armed troops that would allow his nonviolent marches to move forward. Thus, King continued to emphasize the importance of the political value of justice as armed protection." Demonstrators were often surrounded by police or military, e.g., Chicago, Meredith March.

42. King, *Where Do We Go from Here: Chaos or Community?*, 36–37.

43. Martin Luther King Jr., "The Three Evils of Society" (National Conference for New Politics, Chicago, IL, August 31, 1967), 10, King Speeches, Series 3, Box 13, King Center Archives.

44. Martin Luther King Jr., "The Three Evils of Society" (National Conference for New Politics, Chicago, IL, August 31, 1967), King Speeches, Series 3, Box 13, King Center Archives.

45. Yglesias, "Dr. King's March on Washington, Part II," 280–81.

46. King, *Where Do We Go from Here: Chaos or Community?*, 90.

47. Sidney Lumet and Joseph L. Mankiewicz, *King: A Filmed Record . . . Montgomery to Memphis*, Documentary, 1970.

Chapter 7

Movement as Church

When Vincent Harding wrote, *Martin Luther King Jr: An Inconvenient Hero*, he picked a subtitle that reminded us King's leadership is a costly, unfinished challenge to the status quo. King's "great danger" was that, "the poor and oppressed wherever they were . . . became like a fire in his bones . . . and . . .to recall him is to recall them." But where the ruling ideas of today attempt to make King the singular, inimitable, safely-dead martyr, Harding describes King's heroism as akin to John the Baptist, the biblical figure that proclaims the coming of Jesus. Whose coming does King herald? The poor, uniting and rising up. Just before his assassination King "announced, like some well-dressed John the Baptist, that in a few weeks some folks would be coming to Washington (in the Poor People's Campaign) to see if the will was still alive in this nation." It was not King who would save the nation, but King announced and baptized those who would.[1] When he called the nation to rebirth, King knew that the "new and unsettling force" would be propelled by necessity—the millions of poor people "who had little or nothing to lose." But their anger would not be enough. King saw his pastoral role included, "the supreme task . . . to organize and unite people so that their anger becomes a transforming force."[2]

King felt called to be a pastor and remained a pastor. While at Crozier Theological Seminary he wrote that as an "advocator of the social gospel," he believed that, "On the one hand I must attempt to change the souls of individuals so that their societies may be changed. On the other I must attempt to change societies so that the individual soul will have a change. Therefore, I must be concerned about unemployment, slums, and economic insecurity."[3] The transformation of society and the transformation of the individual were reciprocal, and a social gospel pastoral ministry was an opportunity to attend to both. Gary Dorrien traces how the Black social gospel spread and nurtured (spiritually and intellectually) the leadership of the long Civil Rights Movement, including King, who in turn made his own significant contributions to it. The tradition was passed to him by pastor-scholars Benjamin E.

Mays and Mordecai Johnson, along with Baptist ministers who shared their political ideas with the congregations they led, like Martin Luther King, Sr., and J. Pius Barbour. He drew deeply from the leadership model and writings of Howard Thurman, including *Jesus and the Disinherited* (1949).[4]

King knew deeply and personally the failures of the church, across history, to protect life and human dignity. Established religion and its leadership rarely stood up against the forces of evil. Christian practice was too often un-christlike, easily acquiescing to the status quo. King repeatedly heard criticisms from other ministers that the work of the Civil Rights Movement addressed "social issues, with which the gospel has no real concern."[5] And he experienced that yet again as even churches that had supported the Civil Rights Movement turned away from a campaign for universal jobs or income. King soberly told 150 Black clergy gathered for Ministers Training Program in 1968, "Let us acknowledge that even the black church has often been a tail-light rather than a head-light."[6]

King rejected the distinction between the gospel and social issues. In his "Letter from a Birmingham Jail," he traced the failure of the church to respond to white supremacy to "watching many churches commit themselves to a completely other worldly religion which makes a strange, un-Biblical distinction between body and soul, between the sacred and the secular." This practice of Christianity promoted religiosities that encouraged self-preoccupation and a personal salvation that ignored the social character of the gospel. But this critique of churches as supporters of the status quo was not only a theological conflict. It was also a material conflict. Churches were tied to social, economic, and political interests. "Far from being disturbed by the presence of the church, the power structure of the average community is consoled by the church's silent—and often even vocal—sanction of things as they are."[7] Those who preached individual salvation apart from the social gospel had positions on segregation, war, and poverty—a position of acceptance and acquiescence, or support and sanctification. "The church has often been on the side of the rich, powerful, and prejudiced."[8]

For King the movement was church. Where the majority of churches were silent on social and economic issues, King said, "We are no better than strangers even though we sing the same hymns in worship of the same God."[9] But when King invited the mass meeting gathered Eutaw, Alabama to join him in Washington D.C. for the Poor People's Campaign, he described it as an invitation to join "a great camp meeting in the Promised Land," a revival that would prepare them to do the work of the Lord.[10] They would be coming together in the belief that to defeat poverty, racism, and war was to be faithful to the gospel. This new "freedom church of the poor" would win its own freedom and lead the nation to rebirth and new life.

THE INNER CHURCH

In the midst of the Birmingham campaign eight prominent white clergy wrote a public, "Call for Unity," that said segregation laws should be changed gradually by courts and peacefully obeyed until then.[11] Their unity was of oppression, suffering, and exploitation under the leadership of the powerful, sanctified by the church. "Letter from a Birmingham Jail" was King's reply. He said, "Perhaps I must turn my faith to the inner spiritual church, the church within the church, as the true ekklesia and the hope of the world. But again I am thankful to God that some noble souls from the ranks of organized religion have broken loose from the paralyzing chains of conformity and joined us as active partners in the struggle for freedom." Those who had done so met censure, lost jobs, and some lost their lives. "But they have acted in the faith that right defeated is stronger than evil triumphant. Their witness has been the spiritual salt that has preserved the true meaning of the gospel in these troubled times."[12] Dorrien points out that King drew the distinction between the spiritual and organized church from L. Harold DeWolf, his theology professor at Boston University, when King wrote, "The true Church is the spiritual Church. If there are any claims to infallibility it is here. It is in the spiritual church that we witness the kingdom of God on earth."[13]

Many of the people who contributed leadership to the movement were not clergy. Not all were even churchgoers. But Baldwin observes that those "who launched street demonstrations, boycotts, sit-ins, freedom rides, prayer vigils, mass meetings, and other acts of nonviolent protest . . . represented the very best elements of the spirit and character of the African American church tradition."[14] King knew from history that "There has always been and always will be that section of the church that joins in the struggle of the disadvantaged and disinherited peoples of the world." Although this section was small, it was actually truer to the genesis of the church. "It recognizes as Jesus did, that it must preach the gospel to the poor and deliver those who are captives."[15]

Important to this understanding of church as movement was King's biblical interpretation that the mission of Jesus and the early church were ones that battled the powers and principalities for change within history and was considered dangerous by the state for doing so. Looking at the elites of the Roman Empire--the opponents of Jesus and the early Jesus followers—King saw exploitation, violence, and arrogance that echoed that of the United States. He preached that Jesus and the early Christians stood up to Caesar and his elites who charged that they were "disturbers of the peace," and that we must do the same.[16] King said it was Jesus who, "initiated the first sit-in movement. The greatest revolutionary that history has ever known."[17]

Even if this revolutionary thread was a quiet stream within much of church history, King knew that a small vanguard can grow into a movement. He believed that a section of the church within the church—clergy, parishioners, and nonchurchgoers—could seed a movement much larger than the sum of its parts, as it had in the Civil Rights Movement. His hope was that world translate to the poor across race. In the ways that Black people were "superbly equipped" by "the flames of suffering" to "call our beloved nation to a higher destiny . . . to a more noble expression of humanness," King hoped the experiences of poverty and economic exploitation would, lead them to give "ultimate allegiance to the empire of eternity," like the early Jesus followers did when being crushed by the Roman Empire.[18]

SUFFERING AND SALVATION

The relationship between suffering and social movement activism is closely related to King's understanding of the theological significance of the crucifixion of Jesus by the Roman Empire. King said Jesus was "the child of a poor peasant woman," in an "obscure village," and yet, "They called him a rabble-rouser. They called him a troublemaker. They called him an agitator. He practiced civil disobedience; he broke injunctions. And so he was turned over to his enemies."[19] Their attempt to break the Jesus movement with crucifixion was defeated in the resurrection.

James Cone discerns that one of King's distinctive theological contributions is his interpretation the suffering of Jesus in the crucifixion as redemptive because it was selfless resistance to further suffering. This idea is easier to understand when it is held together with King's insight that church is social movement, because it makes clear that suffering itself is not redemptive. Cone argues, "Structural injustice is never redemptive . . . it is the suffering that comes from fighting injustice that is redemptive."[20] Bus boycotts, sit-ins, and marches "taught King to see the christic image of embodied self-offering in suffering resistance"[21] To respond to suffering with nonviolent love is participate in God's work of reconciling a broken world, bearing the cross as Jesus did.[22] Suffering in nonviolent resistance to oppression is a response that turns suffering into an opportunity to transform the conditions of suffering. In that experience King says he had been personally transformed, growing closer to God and better understanding God's salvation as both personal and social.[23] Raphael Warnock discerns that by "acknowledging the random violence and suffering which encroaches daily upon individual black lives as well as that of black people in general," as Black faith has always done, King moved the communities in which he organized "to suffer in a creative and organized way in the hope of redemption."[24]

One must take seriously the theological interventions of Delores Williams who challenges any correlation between suffering and redemption. She points to the long and deep history of Christianity placing the suffering servant of the cross at the theological center of social and economic systems that force Black women into positions of surrogacy, suffering, and death. And she rejects the idea that Jesus' own suffering was salvific or God's desire. This critique endures and calls us to hold King's theology in tension.[25]

King understood the Civil Rights Movement along the lines of redemptive suffering. When suffering that is already a reality is responded to in ways that "transform the suffering into a creative force," there is redemption.[26] Suffering is not inherently redemptive. Resistance to suffering with nonviolence does not automatically end the violence. But where suffering is a lived reality, responding to suffering with nonviolence and love, can be tactically effective. And this practice points to the theological and historical significance of the crucifixion, which was followed by resurrection. This theological understanding cannot be separated from the political reality that nonviolent suffering in response to oppressive violence was an effective tactic within the strategy of the movement. The individual and the movement are strengthened rather that defeated. Against certain defeat at the hands of the powerful, the church, as movement, as the body of God, is risen.[27]

King challenged interpretations of the crucifixion that suggest Christ reconciles us only as individuals and apart from our suffering. King preached about how when asked by Nicodemus, "What shall I do to be saved?" Jesus didn't talk about individual morality.

> He didn't say now Nicodemus you must not drink liquor. He didn't say Nicodemus you must not commit adultery. He didn't say Nicodemus you must not lie. He didn't say Nicodemus you must not steal. He said, Nicodemus you must be born again. In other words Nicodemus, the whole structure of your life must be changed. . .America must be told today is that she must be born again. The whole structure of American life must be changed.[28]

Salvation is both individual and the social, and because the evils of racism, poverty, and war were so deeply structured into the nation, only a transformation of the whole, a rebirth, is capable of dealing with problems that cannot be solved in isolation from one another.

UNITY AND SALVATION

Speaking to the Ministers Training Program, King said, "what we see going on in our nation and world" is the "sin of separation," citing a concept from

Paul Tillich. "We are separated from ourselves, separated from our neighbors, and finally, separated from God." And so King calls them to organize their congregations to join him for the Poor People's Campaign, where they would "try to deal with some of those problems."[29] That same month King preached at Ebenezer,

> I must be a neighbor to my neighbor because I can never be what I ought to be until my neighbor is what he ought to be. And you can never be what you ought to be until I am what I ought to be. . . . So long as people are poverty stricken, nobody can be totally secure . . . we are all caught in an inescapable network of mutuality tied in a single garment of destiny. . . . America will never be totally secure so long as she has forty or fifty million people poverty stricken, even though she has a national gross product of eight hundred billion dollars. No we are tied together. We are neighbors whether we want to be or not.[30]

King understood unity between self and other both politically and theologically, with important implications for understanding church as movement. He said a self-focused principle has guided most of history to our own detriment. "From time immemorial men have lived by the principle that 'self-preservation is the first law of life.' But this is a false assumption. I would say that other-preservation is the first law of life. It is the first law of precisely because we cannot preserve self without being concerned about preserving other selves."[31] King explained that "The cross is the revelation of the extent to which God was willing to go to restore broken humanity."[32] Human beings are reconciled and united with Jesus and with each other as children of God.

Speaking to the sanitation workers in Memphis, King proclaimed, "We are determined to gain our rightful place in God's world. And that's all this whole thing is about. . . . We are saying that we are God's children. And that we don't have to live like we are forced to live. Now, what does all of this mean in this great period of history? It means that we've got to stay together. We've got to stay together and maintain unity." Theologically he argued all are God's children. Politically he was arguing that the church as movement must anticipate that the forces of opposition would do whatever they could to disrupt that unity. Recalling the process of leadership development that made Exodus possible, King continued saying Pharaoh had a "favorite formula" for securing the system of slavery in Egypt: "He kept the slaves fighting among themselves. But whenever the slaves get together, something happens in Pharaoh's court, and he cannot hold the slaves in slavery." The end of slavery begins with the unity of the enslaved.[33]

Similar themes emerge in King's assessment of the Vietnam War, where he pointed out that Black people and white people were united by the military only in the mission to kill poor Vietnamese. Poor whites, poor Black people, and poor Vietnamese are divided against each other to their own detriment, materially and spiritually. It is a "cruel manipulation of the poor" when "[Black] and white boys" are in "brutal solidarity burning the huts of a poor village, but we realize that they would never live on the same block in Detroit." King foresaw that US soldiers will realize that they have been sent into a struggle in which "we are on the side of the wealthy and the secure while we create a hell for the poor." This was a "madness" that violated their shared position as children of God. "I speak as a child of God and a brother to the suffering poor of Vietnam. . . . I speak for the poor of America who are paying the double price of smashed hopes at home and death and corruption in Vietnam."[34]

The Civil Rights Movement demonstrated that those most affected by the problem must be the social force to find its solutions and make them real. King wrestled to bring groups together around human rights demands. In this era King anticipated there would be a shift in those who compose that group, with important implications for who are thought to be self and those who are thought to be other. Poor people across race lines had been steeped in their differences and poor whites raised on white supremacy. This overcoming of self-preservation with other-preservation is more than a simple regard for other. It is the realization that the other is not really other, against all efforts by society to reinforce the opposite. We are created by God, as the children of God, to be for others. While this was not practiced in churches preoccupied with individual salvation, it was a defining characteristic of the inner church as movement. That unity, with its origins in God, could change the conditions of society, understood theologically as the overcoming of the sin of separation and understood politically as an essential strategy for social change.

FREEDOM CHURCH OF THE POOR

When King described the campaign of the poor as a "non-violent army" and "freedom church of the poor," he was talking about the three thousand poor people who would engage in "sustained, massive, direct action." They were not the whole of the dispossessed of the nation. But like the church within the church, they would be the initial leadership. Like the first freedom churches, that first leadership, with direction, training, and unity, could unsettle the nation, grow its "congregation" by drawing forward an entire movement of poor people from among the dispossessed, across race, who had little to lose. Even if three thousand could be told no, the freedom church was only part of the whole that would grow into a force that could transom the whole.[35]

Freedom church is a term that ties together theology, biblical interpretation, history, and social theory, making claims within each. God desires freedom for God's people and is the source of that freedom. The Bible is full of stories of the poor claiming their freedom. Freedom has been achieved in history and is therefore possible in the future. And it is those who are committed to those principles, in partnership with each other and with God, who strive to make that freedom reality. The people of God gathered to do the work of Christ.

While freedom church is, as a whole, a form of leadership for the direction of society, there is also a leadership within the freedom church. These are those who take responsibility for the "supreme task" King laid out of organizing and uniting the inner church so that it can accomplish what it is commissioned to do. King called for movement leaders who could develop a "dangerous unselfishness," a "dangerous altruism," and bear "that cross until it leaves the very marks of Jesus Christ on your body and your soul."[36] King's own leadership was developed and incubated by Thurman, Barbour, Mays, and other Black clergy who practiced committed empathy and dangerous altruism. But King went even farther, forever changing the boundaries of the pastoral role in relationship to social movements.

He said the vocation of Christian leadership was not "alms or religious salve for the souls of the poor," but a convening role in the campaigns that build movements. The night before he was assassinated King lifted up the strong representation of clergy among the crowd gathered with the striking sanitation workers, "Somehow the preacher must be an Amos, and say, 'Let justice roll down like waters and righteousness like a mighty stream.' Somehow, the preacher must say with Jesus, 'The spirit of the Lord is upon me, because he hath anointed me to deal with the problems of the poor.'"[37] It was important to King that he was a pastor at Ebenezer, that he preached two Sundays a month, and that the SCLC was an organization that forwarded religious leadership. This leadership included organizing campaigns, mobilizing for actions, negotiating with elected officials and prophetic public speaking. It was also a leadership of theological reflection, biblical interpretation and, in conversation with other disciplines, political strategy.

As religious leaders it was also within their vocation to provide opportunities for the cultivation of hope in the midst of despair. Again trying to win the staff to the Poor People's Campaign he said, "I would hope that we at SCLC are the custodians of hope. And I'm talking about a kind of realistic hope now. I'm not talking about some kind of superficial optimism which is little more than magic. I'm talking about that kind of hope that has an 'in spite of' quality . . . the final refusal to give up." King elaborated this dialectical process,

Genuine hope involves the recognition . . . that what is hoped for is already here. It is already present in the sense that it is a power which drives us to fulfill that that we hope for. . . . That hope involves hoping for something that is not here and yet it is here in the sense that it is a power within you that drives you to fulfill the hope. . . . You've got to realize that the kingdom of God is in you, it's right now as an inner power within you that drives you to fulfill the hope of a universal kingdom.[38]

Because the kingdom of God is within us, if we can realize it is within is, it becomes an inner power driving the work of justice forward. The task of religious leadership is to nurture consciousness of one's own human dignity, of the kingdom of God within us, and of the righteousness of the drive to make the kingdom of God real. This task is shared by both individual leaders and the freedom church of the poor as a whole—movement as church leading by example and calling others into the fold through a hopeful refusal to give up.

King didn't just move from theory to practice, as if ideas lived in one space and organizing in another. King's organizing experiences changed his understanding of history, theology, and political strategy. He synthesized these ways of knowing. He drew theoretical lessons and developed ethical principles from the movement. And the movement led him to revisit history and theology with new questions. His conclusions about the necessity of multiracial leadership of the poor and dispossessed was not only politically strategic but also theologically and ethically potent.

King's theological genius was in the integration of theologies from a range of sources. King was driven to cross those boundaries and disciplines because his ministry was one of solving the problems his congregation faced. He wasn't trying to develop a discreet theology or ideology, but to bring intellectual resources that helped him most effectively lead the church towards renewal and society towards transformation. King wove together a unique set of sources and influences—religious and secular—to craft a theology that was not separate from the political task of his era but also not reducible to that political task or that particular era.

When King asked from the Birmingham jail, "Is organized religion too inextricably bound to the status quo to save our nation and the world?," he found that indeed, though individual clergy might be leaven in the freedom struggles, it was ultimately "the church within the church," that would be "the true ekklesia and the hope of the world."[39] And as the victories and defeats of the Civil Rights Movement gave way to his call for a human rights movement, King saw potential for a "freedom church of the poor" as the hope of the world, theologically and politically.

NOTES

1. Vincent Harding, *Martin Luther King, the Inconvenient Hero* (Maryknoll, NY: Orbis Books, 2008), 9, 123, 125.
2. Martin Luther King Jr., "Honoring Dr. DuBois," *Freedomways* 8, no. 2 (Spring 1968): 109.
3. Lewis Baldwin, *The Voice of Conscience: The Church in the Mind of Martin Luther King, Jr.* (New York: Oxford University Press, 2010), 63.
4. Gary Dorrien, *The New Abolition: W. E. B. Du Bois and the Black Social Gospel* (New Haven: Yale University Press, 2015), 1–2; Gary Dorrien, *Breaking White Supremacy: Martin Luther King Jr. and the Black Social Gospel* (New Haven: Yale University Press, 2017), 2–3. The white Social Gospel tradition arose during the Progressive Era, with its greatest prominence from 1900 to 1917. The Black social gospel tradition of which King was a part and to which King contributed significantly shared key assumptions with the white Social Gospel movement, including a focus on ameliorating economic exploitation and inequality and seeing the state, particularly the federal government, as an important force for curbing the excesses of capitalism that generated economic inequality. They also shared similar responses to cultural and ideological shifts towards modernism by engaging modern ideas (even if not always accommodating them) rather than doubling down with neo-orthodoxies. Unlike white Social Gospel, Black Social Gospel recognized the centrality of white supremacy as inseparable from understanding the economy, society, and politics.
5. Martin Luther King Jr., "Letter from a Birmingham Jail," in *A Testament of Hope: The Essential Writings and Speeches of Martin Luther King, Jr.*, ed. James M. Washington (San Francisco: HarperOne, 1991), 299.
6. Martin Luther King Jr., "To Minister to the Valley" (Ministers Leadership Training Program, Miami, FL, February 23, 1968), 4, King Speeches, Series 3, Box 15, King Center Archives. This was the commitment he sought when he convened Black pastors for a Ministers Training Program in Miami, imploring them to join the Poor People's Campaign and orient their own social gospel towards building a movement for human rights. FBI reports, to the extent that they can be taken as accurate representations, said most Black ministers in Miami remained noncommittal about the Poor People's Campaign (Michael K. Honey, *Going Down Jericho Road: The Memphis Strike, Martin Luther King's Last Campaign* [New York: W.W. Norton & Co, 2007]). Separate Black institutions did not always ensure true independence. A study of churches in Birmingham, Alabama in the early years of the civil rights movement revealed how the theology, ministry, and practices of independent Black churches could be controlled through financial support, forestalling confrontation with social and economic arrangements. Gary Selby points out that, "Industrialists had kept black preachers on their payrolls, constructed churches for mill village employees, and promoted a fundamentalist view of individual salvation with its concomitant belief in social Darwinian damnation" (Gary S. Selby, *Martin Luther King and the Rhetoric of Freedom: The Exodus Narrative in America's Struggle for Civil Rights* [Waco: Baylor University Press, 2008], 4).
7. King, "Letter from a Birmingham Jail," 299, 300.

8. Martin Luther King Jr. "Advice for Living," *Ebony*, April 1958.

9. Martin Luther King Jr. *Where Do We Go from Here: Chaos or Community?* (New York: Harper & Row, 1967), 151.

10. Martin Luther King Jr., "Address at Mass Meeting" (Eutaw, AL, March 20, 1968), 6, King Speeches, Series 3, Box # 13, King Center Archives.

11. The authors included Episcopal, Catholic, and Methodist bishops, a Presbyterian moderator, a rabbi, and a Baptist pastor. In a twist of theological irony, they published the letter on Good Friday.

12. King, "Letter from a Birmingham Jail," 300.

13. Gary Dorrien, *Breaking White Supremacy: Martin Luther King Jr. and the Black Social Gospel* (New Haven: Yale University Press, 2017), 276.

14. Baldwin, *The Voice of Conscience*, 8.

15. "Advice for Living" *Ebony*, April 1958, p. 104. Willis Jenkins called them the, "radical minority even among dissenters—of those willing to risk themselves for the sake of others" (Willis Jenkins, "Conclusion: Christian Social Ethics After Bonhoeffer and King," in *Bonhoeffer and King: Their Legacies and Import for Christian Social Thought*, ed. Willis Jenkins and Jennifer M. McBride [Minneapolis: Fortress Press, 2010], 256).

16. Martin Luther King Jr., "What Are Your New Year's Resolutions?" (January 7, 1968), 10, King Speeches, Series 3, Box 13, King Center Archives. See also Martin Luther King Jr., "The Drum Major Instinct," in *A Testament of Hope: The Essential Writings and Speeches of Martin Luther King, Jr.*, ed. James M. Washington (San Francisco: HarperOne, 1991); King, "Letter from a Birmingham Jail."

17. King, "To Minister to the Valley (Ministers Training Program, February 1968)," 5.

18. Martin Luther King Jr., "State of the Movement" (Frogmore, SC, November 28, 1967), 9, King Speeches, Series 3, Box 13, King Center Archives.

19. King, "The Drum Major Instinct," 266.

20. James H. Cone, "Systematic Theology 393: Malcolm and Martin" (Lecture, Union Theological Seminary, New York, NY, March 28, 2006).

21. Jenkins, "Conclusion: Christian Social Ethics After Bonhoeffer and King," 253.

22. James H. Cone, *The Cross and the Lynching Tree* (Orbis Books, 2011), 70–71. Cone exegetes both the cross and the lynching tree, showing "While the cross symbolized God's supreme love for human life, the lynching tree was the most terrifying symbol of hate in America. King held these symbols together in a Hegelian dialectic, a contradiction of thesis and antithesis, yielding to a creative synthesis."

23. Martin Luther King Jr., "Suffering and Faith," *Christian Century*, April 27, 1960, The Martin Luther King Jr. Research and Education Institute.

24. Raphael Gamaliel Warnock, *Churchmen, Church Martyrs: The Activist Ecclesiologies of Dietrich Bonhoeffer and Martin Luther King, Jr* (New York: Union Seminary, 1994), 22. See also, Raphael Gamaliel Warnock, "Preaching and Prophetic Witness," in *Bonhoeffer and King: Their Legacies and Import for Christian Social Thought*, ed. Willis Jenkins and Jennifer M. McBride (Minneapolis: Fortress Press, 2010).

25. Delores S. Williams, *Sisters in the Wilderness: The Challenge of Womanist God-Talk* (Maryknoll, N.Y.: Orbis Books, 1993), 174–75. Instead of suffering being redemptive, Williams argues Jesus's life and ministry righted relationships. Jesus Christ then becomes a source for Black women's rejection of surrogacy.

26. King, "Suffering and Faith," 510.

27. Dorothee Solle talks about the relationship between suffering and salvation in terms of Christ freeing the oppressed for action and suffering, where we were once just victims: "Human dignity is being insulted. . . . Christ restores the insulted dignity of men and women and makes them again capable of action and suffering, where they were previously only the passive victims of what was done to them" (Dorothee Solle, *Choosing Life* [Philadelphia, PA: Fortress Press, 1981], 65).

28. Martin Luther King Jr., "Speech at Staff Retreat" (Frogmore, SC, May 1967), 9–10, King Speeches, Series 3, Box 13, King Center Archives.

29. King, "To Minister to the Valley (Ministers Training Program, February 1968)," 14.

30. Martin Luther King Jr., "Who Is My Neighbor?" (Ebenezer Baptist Church, Atlanta, GA, February 18, 1968), 13–14, King Speeches, Series 3, Box 13, King Center Archives.

31. Martin Luther King Jr., *The Radical King*, ed. Cornel West (Boston, Massachusetts: Beacon Press, 2015), 86.

32. King, "Speech at Staff Retreat (May 1967)," 28.

33. Martin Luther King Jr., "I See the Promised Land," in *A Testament of Hope: The Essential Writings and Speeches of Martin Luther King, Jr.*, ed. James M. Washington (San Francisco: HarperOne, 1991), 280–81.

34. Martin Luther King Jr., "A Time to Break Silence," in *A Testament of Hope: The Essential Writings and Speeches of Martin Luther King, Jr.*, ed. James M. Washington (San Francisco: HarperOne, 1991), 233.

35. Martin Luther King Jr., *The Trumpet of Conscience* (New York: Harper & Row, 1968), 59–60.

36. King, "To Minister to the Valley (Ministers Training Program, February 1968)," 15; King, "I See the Promised Land," 284. At the May 1967 staff retreat King said, "The cross is something that you bear and ultimately that you die on. The cross may mean the death of your popularity. It may mean the death of your bridge to the White House. It may mean the death of a foundation grant. It may cut your budget down a little, but take up your cross and bear it. And that is the way I have decided to go" (King, "Speech at Staff Retreat [May 1967]," 31–32).

37. King, "I See the Promised Land," 282.

38. Martin Luther King Jr., "See You in Washington" (SCLC Staff Retreat, Atlanta, GA, January 17, 1968), 10–11, King Speeches, Series 3, Box 13, King Center Archives.

39. King, "Letter from a Birmingham Jail," 300.

Chapter 8

Freedom Church of the Poor Today

Facing pervasive and deepening crisis, we are called to become the unsettling force that King prophesied. Although he is most celebrated for his moral witness and martyrdom, what is most valuable for the task before us is his theological and political vision. His legacy is not that he took a principled stand in the face of power and died a martyr's death. King worked diligently to build a revolution of values and died believing there was even harder work ahead. He organized among the dispossessed, sought leaders from their ranks, and began to tie them together as a united force. His theology and its application lead to his death, because the force he was organizing was an actual threat to power.

King heralded the "church within the church," the "freedom church of the poor." This movement congregation developed new theologies together, interpreted the Bible together, and made gospel claims about society together. King made significant contributions to the longer history of those liberating theologies and ethics. But just as the freedom church of the poor has yet to be realized, the theology and ethics that church will create together is still growing. Pastors, activists, and scholars –poor, not poor, and not yet poor alike—are discerning Christian ethics for this task. Among them are Womanist ethicist Keri Day, Chaplains on the Harbor's Sarah Monroe and Aaron Scott, and the Poor People's Campaign: A National Call for Moral Revival's William J. Barber II and Liz Theoharis. These moral leaders have turned to the 1968 Poor People's Campaign as a source of historical, theological, and ethical knowledge. They each assert that Christian ethics cannot be abstracted from the organizing poor of today. And each of these voices is from and for what King called the freedom church of the poor.

KERI DAY

Womanist ethicist Keri Day criticizes neoliberal ideology as a vision of society where the dominant value is competition for wealth. Unregulated but state-backed markets determine not only socioeconomic decisions but interpersonal and communal relationships. The result is the cultivation of market-oriented social values and practices: alienated individualism, the worship of material acquisition, meritocracy, selfishness, fear of the other, narcissism, and profit maximization. There is no structural support for the values of human dignity, mutual respect, personal worth, love, trust, community, and generosity.[1] And so Day brings the resources of Black liberationist, Black feminist, and womanist traditions to articulate an alternative capable of displacing neoliberal principals of market competition as the organizing ideology of all of social life. She identifies the task of ethics as one of reorienting human meaning beyond "things" so that we can envision and pursue human flourishing. Those who are compelled by necessity and survival to practice those new values, lead the way forward toward their broader adoption.[2]

Day's *Unfinished Business: Black Women, the Black Church, and the Struggle to Thrive in America*, was one of the first substantial scholarly treatments of the Poor People's Campaign from the perspective of Christian social ethics. She contributes an analysis of the ways in which attention to "gender and sexuality could have strengthened its class-based efforts to address the growing economic inequities." The hegemonic Black masculinities of the leadership of the campaign failed not only the immediate safety of participants but the overall mission of the campaign. They relied upon Black women for logistical and tactical successes without acknowledgment. They denied Black women the opportunity to take leadership roles in which they would have flourished. But amid these failures, the idea of the Poor People's Campaign introduced churches to a "class-based, multiethnic movement for economic justice" where prosperity is both personal and structural, individual and communal. The lesson for today remains: challenging the "individualistic market understanding of prosperity" which not only predominates in society but is theologically sanctified in our churches. It steers antipoverty work toward "faith-based initiatives" that target the poor as the sources of their own poverty rather than exploitative economic institutions. Too often "prosperity gospel theology that reinforces neoliberal free-market values," ignoring that in market capitalism, wealth negatively impacts the poor.[3]

In *Unfinished Business,* Day brings the message "class does matter" to Black churches and communities, calling for their leadership in more effectively creating a more just future for Black women and Black families.[4] Within the United States, poor Black people, and particularly poor Black women, have been intentionally constructed as the "face" of American poverty. Although capitalist systems and practices are the cause of poverty, there is a perverse "mythological narrative of poor black women as the cause of poverty." Economic elites create and use this narrative for the dual purpose of, "persuading the masses that the poor are morally culpable," for their own poverty and simultaneously blaming poor Black people—and again poor Black women in particular—as consuming more than their share of scarce resources. This isolates and further endangers poor Black families. Economic elites use free-market values of fairness, parity, and individualism in conjunction with these narratives to "maintain the immutability and inviolability of these economic arrangements."[5]

Against tendencies of Black religious leaders to subordinate arguments about class and even follow dominant narratives about poverty being sinful, she says Black churches must better understand political economy. They must look critically at how race, class, and gender intersect in the lives of poor Black women, including how their poverty cannot be adequately addressed apart from that of poor people across race. "Black women's opportunity to thrive is really about the thriving of all poor persons." Antipoverty approaches that focus on personal improvement without accounting for the disappearance of work cannot succeed.

In imagining how Black churches and leaders can take the structural barriers to Black women's flourishing seriously, Day cites the Poor People's Campaign as a model of religious leadership in developing class-based visions of economic justice. She says, "This movement not only invites the poor to tell their stories of poverty but also invites the poor to be leaders within such movements. The poor's participation in crafting political and policy activism is very important to the integrity, effectiveness, and sustainability of movements oriented toward economic justice." But this effort cannot succeed if it does not take more seriously healthy gender and sexual politics in that work and throughout the life of the church.[6]

SARAH MONROE AND AARON SCOTT

When over one hundred people living along the Chehalis River in Aberdeen, Washington were thrown out of their encampment with no place to go, any belongings they couldn't carry with them or load in a friend's car were bulldozed and trashed. Realizing there was no media present to witness the eviction, campers posted their own livestream of the police arriving to enforce the eviction. The videos broke the isolation and anonymity that so often hides the ways in which life and dignity are violated for the poor across our nation. Among the local clergy who came to stand with the campers and bear witness to the displacement was the Rev. Sarah Monroe of Chaplains on the Harbor. She shared the news online, "Constant trauma and displacement and loss break people in ways that you can't imagine unless you have been through it. I can't adequately describe what I am watching people go through. At the same time, I am still in awe of people's courage and leadership, their ability to hope for a better future. Mother of God, have mercy on your weary children."[7] Later that week those evicted from the Chehalis River encampment, along with nearly homeless and formerly homeless Aberdeen residents, met with the mayor to discuss Aberdeen's housing and land crisis. The campers had been asking for a meeting for over a year, but elected officials, with little sympathy and even fewer solutions to offer, had ignored them. When the city officials in Aberdeen again turned their homeless citizens away empty handed, Chaplains on the Harbor asked the Lutheran church if they could use their parking lot to organize Aberdeen's first self-governed tent city.[8]

Twenty-two homeless people, along with dozens of volunteers, most poor themselves, built a different kind of community in that tiny parking lot. Comparing their faith to that of a mustard seed, Monroe said, "It's not respectable. It's downright scandalous—especially if you talk to some folks in Aberdeen." But, she points out, "the history of the early Jesus movement was pretty scandalous too . . . a community where all were fed and no one was hungry . . . a community that welcomed outcasts." And those Jesus-following outcasts became leaders of a movement. The kingdom of God came in the form of a scrubby mustard plant most would consider a weed and was led by "people that those in power say are nobody . . . coming together to honor the dignity of every human being."[9]

Sarah Monroe is a priest in the Episcopal Church. She grew up in rural Washington on a small farm and is a self-described redneck. Aaron Scott, Chaplains on the Harbor's cofounder, grew up in Upstate New York in areas that are economically and socially similar to Grays County. When Scott first met Monroe, she was just beginning to figure out how to pastor in the communities she came from, starting with being a steady, quiet presence among the homeless and poor in Aberdeen, breaking people's isolation with coffee, cigarettes, and conversation. She showed up when people too poor for church needed pastoral care.

Monroe and Scott spotted an abandoned Episcopal church in Westport, a town of 2,000 people also in Grays Harbor County, and persuaded the diocese to let them use it as a community center, worship space, and base for forming Chaplains on the Harbor. Westport's official unemployment rate is 10 percent, but in reality 71 percent of adults are out of the labor force, including retirees, people living on disability, and those who have given up on finding employment. The official federal poverty rate for the county is 25 percent, but three out of four families depend on some form of social services. The problem is exacerbated by six hundred active municipal arrest warrants in the town of Westport alone, most of which are for poverty-related offenses like failure to pay traffic fines, driving without a license, petty theft, minor drug possession, and what Scott calls, "crimes of economic survival committed in the absence of legitimate employment opportunities."[10]

Chaplains on the Harbor is officially a "mission station" of the diocese. They are clear that they are not a charity. "We are a church. We are a congregation." And they do many of the things that one associates with a church: "a network of people who take care of each other, worship together, eat together, pray together, study the Word and the world together." But they also count among what it means to be church: "dream of ways to transform our community together, and then take action for that transformation together." And they are "a congregation made up almost entirely of poor and homeless people."[11] Scott says that almost everyone there has been hurt by churches in life, the traumas of theological malpractice, and "some love Jesus anyway." Those who don't are just as welcome. Counting those who are in the encampments, RV parks, and jails, Scott estimates that their constituency is 70 percent white, 20 percent Native and 10 percent Latinx.[12] Both Scott and Monroe are white and queer. They have three rules: "no violence, no language that disrespects people, and keep an eye on your own stuff."[13] They openly practice harm reduction for drug users, not waiting for people to get sober or clean, "because God does not wait for that."[14]

Since their founding in 2013 they have established self-governing tent cities in Aberdeen and Hoquiam, fought the town of Westport to win the right to use their church building as a sanctuary space for homeless families, hosted State of the Streets events in Aberdeen and Westport, developed a School of Hard Knocks political education project, and started Harbor Roots farm, a community supported agriculture and job training program. But these successes have been wrested from conditions of great despair. They have buried dozens of people lost to preventable deaths: eviction, suicide, drug overdose, police violence, medical neglect in state prison, and cancer related to timber-pulp industrial waste. One young man died when he was denied medical care for pneumonia by two hospitals. They had flagged him as "drug seeking." When a woman was tased to death by police, the official report cited "natural causes: delirium related to schizophrenia."[15]

Scott introduced the annual State of the Streets event in Westport with the history of the Poor People's Campaign, saying "It's hard to think about yourself as a leader when you are poor, when you are struggling. It's hard to imagine yourself as the next Martin Luther King. But the thing to remember is: Martin Luther King didn't do any of this alone." Scott demystifies that leadership so that the congregation can imagine sharing in it. "It was poor people who made it happen. Some of them could not read, some of them were disabled, some of them were sick, and many of them had been to jail. . . . We believe it'll be those same people who make things happen today."[16] Monroe and Scott have emphasized four themes within their approach to chaplaincy and its relationship to social transformation: pastoral care for the front lines of struggle, building a theological and moral framework of the struggle for human dignity, equipping community leaders to love and protect one another, and nurturing community leaders to "keep their eyes on the horizon"[17]

When the twenty people camping on the church's property were threatened with physical violence, they brought them into the sanctuary. They set up a night security team to keep watch, because the police refused to take the vigilante threats seriously. Those who were publicly threatening the homeless families also began drawing attention to Monroe and Scott's queer identities. Slurs from the vigilantes targeted them as the "fag church." But the attempt to isolate them became an opportunity for conversations within the congregation about queer and transgender justice. The building of this community is not easy, including that they work hard to share the space with each other, always working to make the sanctuary safe and free of interpersonal violence.

Monroe and Scott are not only pastors but producers of ethics, theologies, biblical exegesis, and social theory. Like King they have decided that the vocation of a pastor is to nurture individual and social transformation, and like King, their theologies and political strategies have been shifted by the successes and failures in work to make change real. Scott points out that the dominant models churches have for responding to social and economic concerns are wholly inadequate to the crises they face in Grays Harbor. Even the Episcopal Church, which at times has taken progressive stances on issues before other denominations, often does so within a model where you have guest speakers on an issue after church on Sunday, pass congressional or convention resolutions, and take up special collections. "But the fundamental focus of our worship, education, and faith formation remains unchanged. And in the end, we don't actually make an impact." Monroe points out that that model isolates issues from one another and avoids addressing structural transformation that would require change in relationships of power.[18]

In a time when there is a "culture of impunity" for violence against the poor in all its forms, Chaplains on the Harbor begins with "accompaniment and endurance alongside grassroots freedom fighters—on the streets, at protests, in tent cities, in jail, at ground-zero sites of climate change and in other crisis zones."[19] State violence comes in the form of a "police culture of war against the streets," the use of prisons and fines to fund city budgets, medical neglect, including for the treatment of the disease of addiction, eviction from fallow land, permanent joblessness, poverty wages, and education neglect. In every case people are "regularly treated as if their lives somehow matter so much less." And so when the police hit them with police cars, beat them in their tents in the night, and chase them into the river to drown, it is "as if they deserve to be chased like animals and beaten." The congregation of Chaplains on the Harbor asserts the opposite.

When Monroe visits congregants in jail and prison, between discussing sentencing and transfers, they talk about politics and theology: "They hate the guards. They hate the food. They hate the whole damn system. But they love Jesus." And they confess to Monroe that "they understand Jesus to be a prisoner who was killed by the same empire they're up against." Sermons frequently place biblical stories next to what the community is grappling with and hoping for, drawing parallels that emphasize that biblical texts and stories are full of political content, in particular opposition from a powerless poor against powerful elites.[20] At Chaplains on the Harbor's inaugural Christmas party, Scott preached on "Herod's Lie" in Matthew 1:18–2:23, asking, "Why would a king with a whole army under him be afraid of a newborn baby from a poor, homeless, refugee family?" It was for the same reasons that in Aberdeen the mayor, city council, and police would be afraid of a homeless camp. Like Herod they know that truth comes from the bottom, not the top.

> And God loves the truth. . . . [King Herod's] got all the money and all the guns and yet he's afraid of a homeless baby whose family is squatting in a barn that doesn't belong to them. Because he knows that baby will someday grow up to tell the truth. And the truth is: nobody needs a king. Nobody needs a king, but everybody needs and deserves a place to call home. Nobody needs a king, but everybody deserves all the loaves and fishes they can eat. Nobody needs a king, but everybody deserves healing. Nobody needs a king, but we sure as hell need each other. . . . The King Herods of this world aren't coming to rescue us. We can only rescue each other. And that's kind of scary. But it's also kind of beautiful. . . . What we do together here—that is the manger. We are the manger. Because what we do here together cradles the hope of this whole broken world.[21]

This hard work meets opposition at every turn—material, political, and spiritual—and so the ministry involves nurturing an orientation toward the horizon. Through the cultivation of hope sustained by connectedness to others and increasing clarity about the task ahead and the role they are called to play in transformative social movements. Hope in the midst of hopelessness comes from discerning one's purpose, strength, and partners in long-term struggle. Scott insists, "Nobody is watching this county. If we're not part of something bigger, we will die."[22] But as they cultivate hope in each other, they cultivate their own hope.

> Real hope in hard times requires a belief that the entire structure of our society can be changed—and changed by the very people who have been most shut out of dignity and abundant life. This kind of hope is the height of absurdity in our

dominant values system. It is foolishness. Surely the poor cannot save us as a society, let alone save themselves. Leave that job to the experts with degrees and positions of public office. Leave it to the rich. Except, here is the catch: at Chaplains on the Harbor, we believe in Jesus. We believe that a homeless Palestinian Jewish peasant changed everything under heaven. Even after he is assassinated by the system, we read in today's Gospel that he lives on wherever suffering people are fed abundantly.

Surrounded by dying young people, lost to suicide and overdose, Chaplains on the Harbor "refuse to accept that this present reality is God's will for the world." They insist that poverty-abolitionist chaplaincy is "not merely feeding and praying with people" it is also

raising up prophets. We are raising up street leaders and poverty scholars who are here to teach the world exactly what good news for the poor entails. Our mission is to build a movement for the full abolition of poverty in Grays Harbor, a movement led by poor people themselves for the good of the whole county. An outlandish dream. A resurrection dream. A dream worthy of the Gospel.[23]

When the fiftieth anniversary of the original Poor People's Campaign approached, Chaplains on the Harbor was among those who called for a new campaign. They were joined by two pastors from across the country who also had been organizing in the spirit of the freedom church of the poor.

WILLIAM J. BARBER II AND LIZ THEOHARIS

When seventeen North Carolinians were arrested for civil disobedience on a Monday in 2013 at their state legislative building, their open letter said, "from the moral framework of the Scriptures and our Constitution,[24] we are calling together a coalition of goodwill." Echoing King's freedom church and nonviolent army of the poor, they called themselves "a nonviolent volunteer army of love to oppose this legislature's heartless, ideologically driven agenda. . . . We will become the 'trumpet of conscience' and the 'beloved community' that the Rev. Dr. Martin Luther King Jr. called upon us to be, echoing the God of our mothers and fathers in the faith." The North Carolina NAACP continued in that Jesus tradition with thirteen Moral Mondays during the 2013 legislative season, with 950 arrests.[25] The Rev. Dr. William J. Barber II, then NC NAACP president and architect of the action, points out that the first Moral Monday was when Jesus turned over the tables of the money changers in the Jerusalem temple.[26]

Barber was born in Indiana but grew up in North Carolina's Washington County, where his family helped integrate the faculty, staff, and student body of public schools. He has been pastor at Greenleaf Christian Church (Disciples of Christ) in Goldsboro since 1993. He believes that as clergy, he must tend to the individual and the social. "I'm a pastor. When you deny Medicaid I have to bury. When you deny living wages I have to help pay the light bills."[27] He culls from the Bible a commitment to the power of a moral vision of hope, believing that "part of the moral movement is to develop subversive hope." The work of social transformation is not simply "getting things done" but must "rekindle imagination of what is possible" allowing us to "subvert all of the allegiances we have already committed ourselves to. Prophetic vision unchains us, loosens us, sets us free to dream again." When we forget the longer work of building vision and hope, we leave ourselves vulnerable to manipulation and disunity.[28]

An essential part of that is fusion organizing, coming together across lines of race, ethnicity, creed, and religion around shared interests. Barber argues that across US history, social and political gains have depended on a fusion politics. "Blacks and whites, Jews and Catholics, labor and youth came together," and they achieved the gains of the Civil Rights Movement, the expansion of social security, and expanded opposition to the War in Vietnam.[29] The Poor People's Campaign is among those moments. Fusion organizing can be traced back to the post-Civil War Reconstruction fusion of poor whites and poor Black people. They were able to elect Black people and nonelite whites to state offices, write constitutions that included ideas like "the right to the fruit of one's labor," and free public education.[30] But because fusion politics has such potential to build real power, across history it is always met by a reaction. Reconstruction fusion was met with violence, first directed against everyone who engaged in fusion politics, but then shifted to target Black leaders specifically, with white terrorist militias like the Klan commandeering control of the region without fear of reprisal.[31]

Past and present, that reaction has hidden behind distorted moral narratives. Barber is quick to discern any misapplication of the Bible to hurt the poor. He believes that those who call themselves conservative Christians are not. "To be a true conservative is to conserve love and justice and mercy, which are at the heart of the Gospel."[32] The same is true of the term evangelical, now used as media shorthand for Christians who oppose reproductive rights, queer rights, racial justice, and economic equality. Barber claims the title evangelical and cites the long history of evangelicals who have been motivated by their faith to "proclaim the good news of liberty," including abolitionists, suffragists, and King.[33] Those who believe in social justice and liberation have lost influence and trust by ceding moral ground and moral language. "True spirituality calls us to be suspicious of concentrations of wealth and privilege and power, and to mistrust any kind of rationalism that justifies the subordinating other person to our own benefit. We are called to be sensitive to the poor, the disenfranchised, the stranger, the outsider." These are the "weightier matters of faith."[34]

Barber's theological ethics have a strong commitment to human dignity. It is a theme that unites those who claim a religious tradition and those whose morals and ethics do not come from a religious tradition. For Barber it is a religious conviction based in the doctrine of *Imago Dei*, and moral claims must be evaluated in relationship to it. For example, his critique of voter suppression is more than political. Voter suppression is "a soul-damaging act; it has spiritual dimensions." By rendering human beings, "politically impotent" it "steals his or her agency in the political realm," and when committed against Black and brown people, it is "yet another means of dehumanizing and . . . a means of social control." It is a "form of self worship" on the part of those who deny voting rights. The fulfillment of the right to vote is the restoration of "the God given dignity to human beings equally Created in God's image, equally endowed with God's authority over the earth, equally called to engage their own individual will in concert with God's will." [35] The blasphemous attack on voting rights stems from a fear that if "black, brown, and white humanity" believe in their own humanity and that they share humanity, "they might start voting together in ways that respects the humanity of all people." This possibility is why those who protect the interests of elites, "can't allow these folks to start believing in their humanity." It is a theology of human dignity that reveals that the Citizens United vs. FEC Supreme Court decision that corporations have First Amendment rights to unlimited election spending, "is blasphemy to notion of image of God." It enshrines the ideology that "a corporation without a soul has more clout than a human being."[36] The denigration of human dignity is a powerful tool of extremism, and the celebration of the reality of human dignity is its weakness.

For Barber the implication is that human dignity must be celebrated in public and in policy, not just in private. The appearance of a religious distinction between our private lives and our public lives is part of what has weakened Christian moral witness. "There are those who say our concern as the people of God should be private soul-saving. . . . I'm not against pastoral inner man healing." But when that emphasis on the private is not matched by a social gospel that seeks social and economic structures that honor human dignity, it is disingenuous in its care for the human spirit and dishonest about its distinction between the public and private. Those who claim religion is about the individual often have very public positions on the categories of abortion, homosexuality, and prayer in the schools. Too often the appeal to limit Christian purview to the personal is matched with a theology that "places God on the side of private ownership at the expense of the poor" and gives divine sanction to "rugged individuality, mass gun ownership, and support of the death penalty and war."[37] Behind these religious ideologies are material interests, not simply a battle of ideas. Extremists have found the talk about morality an effective way to maintain power and protect the interests of the few who benefit materially from their policies.[38] These unethical stances and the policies they defend degrade human dignity and are therefore an affront to God. When they parade as faithful Christianity, they expose a weakness of being biblically and doctrinally unfounded. In the work of justice, prophetic leadership is poised to exploit that weakness.

Barber and Liz Theoharis were hearing about each other's work in 2014 and began a series of exchanges. Theoharis's Kairos Center was the hub of a national network of grassroots community and religious leaders that grew out of the history of homeless organizing and welfare rights organizing. They could trace their leadership directly back to the Poor People's Campaign of 1968 and had been organizing around reigniting it. Theoharis brought delegations of grassroots leaders and seminarians down to check out Barber and the Moral Mondays Movement and found a shared vision. She invited Barber to come up to keynote the launch of the Kairos Center for Religions, Rights, and Social Justice at Union Theological Seminary (UTS) in New York City and get to know the leaders who were talking about what a Poor Peoples' Campaign would look like today. By the end of 2016 they had been to thirty states together as a traveling seminary course in public theology. Barber taught history and ethics, and Theoharis taught biblical exegesis. The trainings were an opportunity to bring leaders from their respective networks from the same cities and towns into relationship with each other. Evenings were filled with moral revival mass meetings.[39]

When Theoharis was a teenager, she started organizing with poor and homeless families in the Kensington neighborhood of Philadelphia with homeless organizers who had come out of the National Union of the Homeless. In the 1990s they had built chapters in over twenty-five cities, some with thousands of members, winning the right to vote without a residence and hundreds of units of affordable housing, before its leadership fractured. Leaders from the Philadelphia chapter were living in a tent city when families were starting to reach the new two-year cutoffs for aid in Bill Clinton's 1996 dismantling of welfare. Tent City became a base of operations for poor families, housed and homeless, and together they formed the Kensington Welfare Rights Union (KWRU).

Over the next decade KWRU would connect with a growing network of organized poor people across the United States: grassroots campaigns taking human-rights approaches to raise poverty wages; end farmworker and day-labor abuses; keep rural hospitals open, pass universal single-payer healthcare, block the privatizationof water utilities, shutoffs of household water, and foreclosures for past-due water bills; clean up poisoned water in West Virginia, Louisiana, and Michigan; house the homeless; and stop police violence. The leaders in this network spanned race and ethnicity, gender, age, and geography. They were figuring out how to turn mutual aid projects into politicized survival projects. They took on campaigns to win housing and community services, but they did so in ways that called attention to the inadequacies of what they were winning. Political education was an important part of this distinction. They drew lessons from the history of abolition, labor, Black freedom struggles, and welfare rights.

In 2003, they organized around the thirty-fifth anniversary of the Poor People's Campaign by calling for its revival. They started where the original campaign started, in Marks, Mississippi, and marched to Washington, D.C.. Along the way they met with thousands of poor people, brought attention to the healthcare crisis, the decimation of welfare, growing unemployment due to downsizing, and NAFTA. When they arrived, they set up a new Resurrection City and petitioned the government to protect human rights.

Throughout these years of organizing, Theoharis said not a week would go by without someone quoting the biblical passage, "the poor will be with you always," to her. Sometimes the person wasn't even Christian, but that verse had come to be a universal proof text to justify poverty. She wasn't the only one hearing it. The network of poor leaders from across the country kept running into the same ideological blockade passed off as religion. The pastors that would come around homeless encampments and the organized poor only knew how to treat people as charity cases or souls to save. Seminaries were not equipping clergy to join and lead movements of the poor, even though historically, they assessed, religious leadership had been central to U.S. social movements. So they sent Theoharis to UTS to become a pastor and biblical scholar for the movement. They charged her with thinking about the role of clergy in scaling up a whole movement around the leadership of the poor, bring resources to support campaigns, and sustain the work in the long term.

Her dissertation, not surprisingly, took on "the poor will be with you always," showing how what we often think is Jesus condoning poverty is actually just the opposite.

When Jesus says, "the poor will always be with you" he is actually quoting Deuteronomy 15, which says that there will be no poor person among you if you follow the commandments God is giving today—to forgive debts, release slaves, pay people fairly and lend money even knowing you won't get paid back. Deuteronomy 15 continues that because people will not follow those commandments, the poor will never cease to be in the land.

Jesus isn't condoning poverty—he is reminding us that God hates poverty, and has commanded us to end poverty by forgiving debts, raising wages, outlawing slavery, and restructuring society around the needs of the poor. He is reminding the disciples that charity and hypocrisy will not end poverty but keep poverty with us always. He is reminding his followers that he is going to be killed for bringing God's reign here on earth, and it is their responsibility to continue the quest for justice.[40]

While she was a student at UTS, her classmates were hungry to connect with the network of poor people taking on the evils of society. Many had come to seminary looking to put their faith into action on the question of poverty, but charity continued to be the only offering. Theoharis started researching what was being taught across the country and found no seminary or divinity school had a course on poverty. She and several other seminarians founded the Poverty Initiative at UTS in 2004 (which later became the Kairos Center). They partnered with UTS faculty to teach courses or class sessions on poverty in almost every field. And they started offering poverty immersion courses, like the KWRU poverty reality tours, taking seminarians and social work students to Appalachia, the Mississippi Delta, and post-Katrina New Orleans, not to commit acts of charity, but to learn from the organized and organizing poor. Students witnessed not only the deep crisis of poverty and racism, but also saw grassroots leaders winning significant campaign victories.

Kairos also partnered with UTS to bring formerly homeless organizer Willie Baptist to be the seminary's Poverty Scholar in Residence. Baptist had been politicized by the Watts Rebellion in 1964 and had been organizing the poor and dispossessed ever since, including the United Steelworkers and the National Union of the Homeless. Theoharis and Baptist met in Philadelphia's tent city. When he was the education director of KWRU, Theoharis became an assistant education director. Baptist has focused on the importance of education and leadership development as organizing work. Among his sources for this emphasis is King's campaign to unite the poor across racial lines as a "new and unsettling force."[41] As coordinator of Kairos' Poverty Scholars Program, Baptist built a hub for education and leadership development for grassroots human rights organizations and future religious leaders.

Theoharis's organizing work, combined with the experience of studying the text "the poor will be with you always," led to the development of a new methodology for biblical exegesis. She saw over and over again how the organized poor were reading the Bible together differently in the context of their work to end poverty, with implications that radically changed the meaning of the text. Their insights sharpened the argument that the heart and center of the Bible is how society meets the needs of the poor, the immigrant, and the marginalized. "Exodus is a founding story of God being on the side of the poor and oppressed, the Deuteronomic Code offers commandments of how you care for your neighbor is how you honor God, the prophets denounce oppressing the poor, the gospels proclaim bringing good news to the poor, and Paul's epistles instruct the followers to offer mutual solidarity through the collection for the poor." The method draws from the contributions of empire critical and contextual Bible-study methodologies as it posits "the organized poor are the epistemological, political, and moral change agents in our society." As such the organized poor, past and present, are the makers and interpreters of good news. Jesus's anointing as Christ was to a mission and ministry of organizing against the empire of Caesar and for the empire of God.[42]

When Theoharis first sought ordination in the Presbyterian Church (USA), she was turned away for the heretical belief that God wants us to end poverty. The ordination committee cited Jesus, "the poor will be with you always." Theoharis returned year after year to make her case, and finally was ordained to the work of the Kairos Center in 2014. Within three years she had won two national denominational leadership awards and her book was that year's recommended read for the entire denomination.

Theoharis's father and sister both showed up in footnotes several chapters ago. Jeanne Theoharis is a Black freedom struggles historian who wrote the definitive biography of Rosa Parks. Athan Theoharis is the foremost authority on the FBI and contributed to the passing of the Freedom of Information Act. But it was her mom, Nancy Theoharis, whose days as a full-time activist in Milwaukee and galvanizer of the Presbyterian Church nationally, that started Liz Theoharis's journey to a calling as a pastor, organizer, and scholar.

POOR PEOPLE'S CAMPAIGN: A NATIONAL CALL FOR MORAL REVIVAL

Barber and Theoharis had both come to the history of the 1968 Poor People's Campaign through their own organizing and study. Theoharis was introduced to it by the homeless organizers and welfare rights leaders who trained her, some of whom were there in 1968. Barber came to it as he was looking to history for models of fusion organizing, trying to solve real problems in his community, like how racism was keeping Black and white people from winning better wages in North Carolina. When Theoharis introduced him to the grassroots human rights organizations that had started calling for its revival, he also saw the opportunity to draw from that history politically and theologically to impact the national conversation and shift what is politically possible electorally and legislatively across the country. They became cochairs of the Poor People's Campaign: A National Call for Moral Revival (PPC:NCMR). This taking up on the fiftieth anniversary was not a commemoration. It was a reclaiming of a vision and strategy, because the racism, poverty, and militarism of 1968 had deepened. And PPC:NCMR expanded those triple evils to include environmental devastation and distorted moral narratives. Barber and Theoharis called for a "broad and deep national moral movement—led by the poor, impacted, clergy and moral agents—to unite our country from the bottom up."

In the spring of 2018, the campaign engaged in the longest sustained wave of nonviolent direct action and civil disobedience in the United States in this century. Forty days of action lined up with the dates of Resurrection City's launch and shuttering, from Mother's Day to June 23, fifty years later. In Washington, D.C., and state capitals across the country there were 219 actions with five thousand people risking arrest in acts of nonviolent direct action. Most arrests happened on Moral Mondays, which were followed by a week of mass meetings, teach-ins, and cultural events. On the fiftieth anniversary of Solidarity Day, tens of thousands of people gathered around a stage on the National Mall against the backdrop of the Capitol building. It was flanked by two twenty-six-foot banners that read simply, "Fight Poverty, Not the Poor." The slogan came from welfare rights organizing in the 1980s.

The PPC:NCMR didn't start with a list of policy demands. It started with a set of principles. Those fundamental commitments articulated a strategy, a tactics, and a moral grounding. Out of that grew a set of comprehensive, visionary demands, and from those demands grew a poor people's budget that included policies and programs. The PPC:NCMR also didn't start as a list of national organizations. It started with people forming organizing committees in their states, many of whom had been organizing their community, congregation, or state for years. That nascent leadership included poor and impacted people, clergy, and people moved to take sides with the poor—those the campaign called moral agents. Out of that grew state coordinating committees, and eventually, once the campaign was established in dozens of states, drew in what they call "mobilizing partners"—labor unions, major denominations, faith bodies, social justice and environmental organizations, and social organizations.

What's significant about both of these starting points—a set of principles and a state-based leadership—is that it isn't a traditional campaign of disparate allies coming together around a lowest-common-denominator demand and disbanding when it's been accomplished. It's an organizing model designed to grow a nonpartisan, bottom-up fusion movement. The depth of the organizing is what supports the breadth of the organizing, and the breadth of the organizing draws an increasing number of people into deeper relationships with the campaign. The policy demands similarly refused to be hemmed into transactional or partisan relationships. They articulate a big but realizable vision that calls broad sections of people away from the pessimism of piecemeal partisanship and toward a hope and confidence that something profoundly different is possible.

Among the fundamental principles that ground the campaign are ideas that pick up King's articulation of the need to organize in new ways in the era of human rights. It includes a commitment to "lifting up and deepening the leadership of those most affected by systemic racism, poverty, the war economy, and ecological devastation and to building unity across lines of division." With that comes a clear articulation of "the centrality of systemic racism in maintaining economic oppression" and that "unjust criminalization systems . . . exploit poor communities and communities of color." It also insists that "people should not live in or die from poverty in the richest nation ever to exist." As with King's vision for a campaign of the poor. These principles are not only assessments of conditions. They are articulations that imply strategy and tactics that respond to those conditions. The principles go on to articulate a direct commitment to "build up the power of people and state-based movements to serve as a vehicle for a powerful moral movement" and "to transform the political, economic, and moral structures of society." Within that there's a commitment to nonviolence, nonpartisanship, state-based organizing, and moral direct action.

During the forty days of action on the fiftieth anniversary of Resurrection City, the campaign took part in a congressional hearing on poverty. Poor people addressing elected officials with testimony and demands echoed the tactics of 1968. No Republicans showed up, but it wasn't a cozy conversation with Democrats. Even progressive House and Senate leaders were pushed back on when they claimed their voting records proved they are allies of the poor. Scott from Chaplains on the Harbor was watching and said,

> We staged a full-on narrative takeover . . . young black moms from Flint keeping them on the ropes. Generations of Appalachians eviscerating the myth that you can't organize for revolution in the coal fields. Apache Stronghold women grieving for their sacred sites buried under concrete. Undocumented moms with their children in their arms closing us out in deafening chants. What I saw yesterday made it very clear that we have what it takes to build a politically independent force.[43]

As Scott suggests, the action was not only about pressuring elected officials, but also about building cohesion and confidence among the leaders of the campaign. Theoharis describes, "The idea is to shine a light on both the conditions in marginalized communities—pollution, climate change, the war economy—and also the creative tactics people are using to bring the issues and their work to the forefront."[44]

A year later, that initial launch translated into coordinating committees in forty states sending a thousand delegates to a Moral Action Congress, convening poor people, impacted people, clergy, and moral leaders. An audit of economic and social conditions and comprehensive demands around all five evils had been translated into a Poor People's Moral Budget. And leaders from the campaign testified again at an official hearing, this time before the House Budget Committee. By 2020 the PPC:NCMR was able to use its growing state leadership to respond to the rapidly unfolding crises of economic meltdown, public health pandemic, and the escalating response and counter-reaction to the systemic racism of state violence.

Leaders in the campaign expose the breadth and depth of poverty in one of the richest nations. They make connections between dumping of human waste in people's yards because of the lack of sewer systems, to poisoned water in Flint because of austerity in public utilities, to the inability of homeless families to wash their hands during pandemics like that caused by COVID-19. In most testimonies by leaders coming from poverty, they point to how the crises in their life can't be slotted into one of the evils. There's poverty, systemic racism, state violence, and environmental crisis in stories about dying for lack of health care, prisons instead of jobs or adequate welfare, and homelessness in cities full of vacant houses. The PPC:NCMR brings those stories together, engages in moral and political reflection on their significance, and takes action together in the streets and legislature. Their target is the "misappropriated funds of an immoral federal budget" that funnels funding into the war economy, buying weapons and passing old ones to domestic police forces, while leaving people hungry, without health care, and homeless. They call this policy violence.

Like the 1968 Poor People's Campaign, this new effort takes on the triple evils of poverty, racism, and militarism. Already in the original campaign the poor were seeing environmental crisis, because the poor are always the front lines of disasters. Farmers raised questions about agricultural chemicals, and young people testified that that their air and water were polluted.[45] The PPC:NCMR puts environmental devastation alongside the triple evils. It also added distorted moral narratives that lie about the poor, pose charity as a solution, and hide inequality as the real source of poverty. And like the original campaign, poverty is known to cross race and ethnic lines, with poor whites continuing to be the largest group of poor people and with poor people of color being dramatically disproportionately impacted by poverty.

Like in 1968 the poor themselves are leaders, contributing their stories and their organizing skills. Today's campaign takes the idea of education and study further than was possible in Resurrection City, with study of public policy and social and economic conditions. They undergo training in nonviolence, theomusicology and movement arts, digital organizing, documentation, media outreach, storytelling, and fundraising.

Unlike the 1968 Poor People's Campaign, this new effort is based in growing state leadership. This is a lesson learned from the successes of the North Carolina Moral Mondays, out of which Barber comes, and the welfare rights and homeless organizing, out of which Theoharis comes. It avoids the pitfalls of Resurrection City, where the massive occupation not only pinned down leaders with cumbersome logistics but also failed to nurture local organizing structures for when people returned home. The mobilizing of the PPC:NCMR is tied to organizing sustained networks of leaders. And as in North Carolina, where they learned they were fighting extremist policies that took root at the local and state level, "the center of gravity is in the local work that people are doing to build a deep and broad and strong foundation for an actual movement for the long haul."[46]

While the 1968 Poor People's Campaign did not lift up its religious diversity, PPC:NCMR is intentionally interreligious. Campaign materials cite the Qu'ran and Bhagavad Gita alongside Jewish and Christian scriptures. Often it's paired with language from the Declaration of Independence and US Constitution, a connection King had often made in talking about both civil and human rights. And religious and civil language is paired with broader language of "moral values, because the campaign includes people who do not identify as religious." Theoharis and Barber both draw deeply from their Christian tradition and its biblical sources. They often wear matching stoles, quilted by Kansas campaign leader Rev. Jessica Williams, that read "Jesus was a poor man," echoing one of the mule train wagons from 1968. But the campaign's contribution to ethics comes not just from Theoharis and Barber. Moral leaders across the country, as individuals and as a whole, contribute to the theological vision. The poor taking action together itself objectively poses the ethical questions, What type of society denies its people the right to live? What is the measure of our nation when our children die because we cannot afford health care? Why are we homeless when houses are empty? Why we are hungry when food is thrown away? The poor taking action together heralds that our nation is in labor to become a new creation. Moral leaders from across the states have taken up the PPC:NCMR for Moral Revival because we hope for something we cannot yet see. We are told that poverty will always be with us, but we have a different vision for the world. It is a vision that knows from history that transformation is possible.

After coming to Washington, D.C., during the forty days of action, Mashyla Buckmaster, a leader from Chaplains on the Harbor, wrote,

> I never would have imagined people would want to put me in front of a crowd to speak. Who would want to hear from my awkward ex-junkie mouth? . . . I feel so lucky to have been given the chance to make a new proper family. And on top of all that the feeling of being on the right side of history is chilling. My soul is smiling. . . . And I will pray every day for people to hear us, I will pray for long cool breezes, and I will pray for justice. I am finally hopeful that my daughter or her daughter's future will turn out alright and not some Terminator Mad Max bullshit.[47]

Ashley Hufnagel has helped build the Maryland PPC:NCMR. She is part of the Oak Hill Center for Education and Culture, a school that draws from creative practices to develop organizers, educators, and artists for human rights movement work. Hufnagel argues art and culture make unique contributions to building a "different value system" and challenging the existing value system. She says,

> Even liberals and progressives replicate the dominant value system without even knowing it. We don't say, 'we deserve this because we're human beings and our lives are valuable and matter just from the basic point of being alive.' Rather we try to prove we will be productive members of this society if you just give us a chance to be productive. It's a productivist ethos that says my life is valuable only when I give back profit because I'm able to work. It needs to be completely undermined.

Even well-paid workers play into a system that, in the word of King, "thingifies" them.[48]

A strong theological conception of human dignity brings into sharp relief that it is the economy and not the poor themselves who are to blame for poverty. Breaking past the idea that to be poor is to be criminal, incompetent, and a failure is a step that cannot be circumvented. This makes the organization of the poor a contribution to an expanded conception of human dignity. Nijmie Dzurinko is a founder of Put People First–Pennsylvania, a statewide membership organization that believes in leadership development through political education, policy campaigns, and care for one another and community. They are organizing in the geographically, racially, and politically divided state of Pennsylvania, and they have helped build the Pennsylvania Poor People's Campaign. They are clear that their campaigns are contributing to a united movement for human rights. Dzurinko identifies the contribution of organizing and education to our conception of human dignity.

> The dehumanization of the system is a roadblock. When we're subject to dehumanization from a variety of different levels. It has an impact on how we see ourselves, treat ourselves, and see other people. Because of this, looking around at our families, friends and neighbors, we don't trust people or see them as actually capable of leading something. There is disconnect between the aspiration of leadership of the poor and most directly impacted and the way we learn to think about ourselves and each other. Political education and leadership development process can get to the root causes of why people's lives are in such disarray, why our lives look like they do, and how dehumanization teaches us to treat each other. Lifting up the idea that we deserve better can clash with our lived experience.[49]

Claire Chadwick, a licensed Baptist preacher and leader of the Kansas PPC:NCMR, testified about contracting COVID-19 as an essential worker at a big box store during a PPC:NCMR press conference. She pointed to some of the same themes as Hufnagel in the valuing of people only as producers of wealth. Chadwick said,

> It is wrong for companies to treat workers as expendable instead of as essential. Our work has always been essential. People are just now acknowledging that. But will they forget again? I need more than Facebook posts telling me how great my sacrifice is. I need living wages, paid sick and leave time, a union, and universal healthcare that isn't tied to my job.

King's push for the 1968 Poor People's Campaign to emphasize jobs and income similarly argued that these fundamental questions have implications that would transform every aspect of society, "bringing the whole of society under judgement the way that lunch counters did all of segregation."50

Chadwick again echoed King's 'church within a church" and "freedom church" conceptions when she described the significance of the poor coming together in the PPC:NCMR: "When Jesus speaks in Matthew about giving us the keys to the kingdom of heaven, this time I spent with you all is, I believe, what he was thinking of. We were more than a beloved community standing up for ourselves and for our brothers and sisters. For me, we were doing church. Praying with our feet and taking a stand in the heat and the rain and regardless of the consequences."51

Following King's insight that "in order for the evils of racism, poverty and war to end, new values must be born," Barber believes that "our moral witness is to call people evangelically to listen to heart of the gospel, which is love and justice and mercy" as an alternative to the values and theologies that have buttressed austerity, inequality, and racism. The task of religious leadership is to "work and pray to exorcise that thinking and seek to redeem the soul of America. The heart of public evangelicalism is an insistence that our nation must be born again."52

NOTES

1. Keri Day, *Religious Resistance to Neoliberalism: Womanist and Black Feminist Perspectives* (New York: Palgrave Macmillan, 2015), 48–49, 54, 76, 77, 112; Keri Day, "Global Economics and US Public Policy: Human Liberation for the Global Poor," *Black Theology* 9, no. 1 (April 2011): 12, 13.

2. Day, *Religious Resistance to Neoliberalism*, 13, 54.

3. Keri Day, *Unfinished Business: Black Women, the Black Church, and the Struggle to Thrive in America* (Maryknoll, NY: Orbis Books, 2012), 44, 98–100, 107.

4. Day, *Unfinished Business*, 68, 151.

5. Day, *Unfinished Business*, 8, 47, 53–54.

6. Day, *Unfinished Business*, 9, 47, 59, 61–62, 150, 151. Day also calls for the incorporation of asset-building approaches to poverty as "an invitation to converse about how to give the poor fair access into the wealth-producing structures of our society." Similarly the promotion of socially conscious capitalism is an opportunity to displace profit maximization as the primary value in society. The task is similar for global poverty. Global capital proposes that the poor are best served by incorporation into expanding capitalist markets. Day argues that neoliberal values make the distribution of the gains from globalization nearly impossible. Day, "Global Economics and US Public Policy," 14, 27, 32.

7. Sarah Monroe, Facebook, October 15, 2016.

8. Churches are allowed to use their property for three months free of local ordinances, and so the tent city moved in rotation every three months to a new church host, some congregations with unease and others with surprising grace. But it was the camp residents themselves who really made the tent city possible.

9. Sarah Monroe, "The Kingdom of God Comes in a Parking Lot," *A Wandering Minister* (blog), June 20, 2015, http://awanderingminister2.blogspot.com/2015/06/the-kingdom-of-god-comes-in-parking-lot.html.

10. Aaron Scott, "Real Hope," *Aaronheartsjesus* (blog), April 10, 2016, https://aaronheartsjesus.wordpress.com/2016/04/10/sermon-third-sunday-in-easter-2016/. Monroe calculates that even though some people have multiple warrants, at least four hundred residents have at least one outstanding warrant. Aberdeen used to be the lumber capital of the world. But as the lumber and mill industries left in the 1970s, little came to replace it. In 1989 the state created a TIDES program to turn unemployed loggers into prison guards, part of a larger cultivation of the prison industry as a source of employment and city revenues. This was a malicious partner to the criminalization of those dependent on the activities of the underground economy. The city of Hoquiam receives a million dollars a year from Washington State Department of Corrections, but only if it keeps the beds of the local jail full. This trading of human life for profit has not actually lowered unemployment rates, but it has increased incarceration rates. The prison industry is "consuming the lives of poor white local youth." Monroe says, "It continues to be impossible, in the short-term, to protect my young adults from incarceration. There are no living-wage jobs. Most of our young leaders have been in the system since they were fifteen." Aaron Scott, "Radical Rednecks: The Necessity of Organizing Poor Whites for Poverty Abolition Movements, from Slavery to the Prison-Industrial Complex" (unpublished, 2016).

11. They formally describe themselves as "a ministry of presence in Grays Harbor County, a developing worshiping congregation, and a faith-based center for rural leadership development in the movement to end poverty."

12. Scott, "Radical Rednecks."

13. Aaron Scott, Facebook, October 26.

14. Aaron Scott, "The God of Secrecy," *Aaronheartsjesus* (blog), January 22, 2017, https://aaronheartsjesus.wordpress.com/2017/01/26/sermon-third-sunday-after-the-epiphany-2017/.

15. Aaron Scott, "A Call for the New Poor People's and Poor Children's Campaign" (Repairers of the Breach National Political Organizing Leadership Institute and Summit, Raleigh, NC, March 16, 2017).

16. Aaron Scott, "Introduction to the Poor People's Campaign" (State of the Streets, Westport, WA, July 14, 2016). Scott noted that campaign organizer Hank Adams was from the Quinault reservation in Grays Harbor County.

17. Aaron Scott, Sarah Monroe, and Lindsey Krinks, "Radical Chaplaincy: Reflections on the Northwest Solidarity Tour," *Aaronheartsjesus* (blog), October 2, 2015, https://aaronheartsjesus.wordpress.com/2015/10/02/radical-chaplaincy-reflections-on-the-northwest-solidarity-tour/.

18. Aaron Scott and Sarah Monroe, "Dialogue on the Suburbanization of Poverty."

19. Scott, Monroe, and Krinks, "Radical Chaplaincy."

20. Scott preached, "The Roman Empire of Jesus' time, like our own, was a murderous ransacking plague. 'The nations,' the Gentiles, overwhelmingly did not fare well when they were invaded by the Roman army. A handful of puppet dictators and elites did ok, the rest were dispossessed of their land, labor, and liberty." Aaron Scott, "Fred Hampton's Jesus Movement," *Aaronheartsjesus* (blog), April 23, 2016, https://aaronheartsjesus.wordpress.com/2016/04/23/sermon-fifth-sunday-in-easter-2016/.

21. Aaron Scott, "King Herod Is a Liar," *Aaronheartsjesus* (blog), December 19, 2015, https://aaronheartsjesus.wordpress.com/2015/12/19/sermon-chaplains-on-the-harbor-inaugural-christmas-party/.

22. Scott, "Call for a New Poor People's Campaign."

23. Scott, "Real Hope."

24. William J. Barber II and Barbara Zelter, *Forward Together: A Moral Message for the Nation* (St. Louis: Chalice Press, 2014), 9.

25. Barber II and Zelter, *Forward Together: A Moral Message for the Nation*, 4, 21–22. Ninety-six percent of those arrested are North Carolinians, coming from all regions of the state, including Western North Carolina, a largely white region in the Appalachian Mountains.

26. William J. Barber II and Liz Theoharis, "Call to Action" (Repairers of the Breach National Political Organizing Leadership Institute and Summit, Raleigh, NC, March 16, 2017). Al McSurely, who had led the Appalachian delegation to the 1968 Poor People's Campaign, was asked by Barber to serve as the NAACP's legal redress chair when Barber became president and was part of developing HKonJ and the Forward Together Movement (William J. Barber II and Jonathan Wilson-Hartgrove, *The Third Reconstruction: Moral Mondays, Fusion Politics, and the Rise of a New Justice Movement* [Boston: Beacon Press, 2016], 51). In reflecting on the lessons of the Poor People's Campaign, McSurely points out that King's lieutenants did not understand King's strategy and therefore were unable to implement it without him. This was a lesson Barber took seriously, and the leadership of the Moral Mondays Forward Together Movement were aware that to be totally dependent on Barber's leadership leaves them vulnerable and limits their capacity. The development of religious leaders who can work simultaneously within and beyond North Carolina is a priority. McSurely said that leadership must be cultivated through practice. One might be a great organizer, but to be an effective strategist takes intentional development.

Barber says from the first year he was NC NAACP president, he "practiced doing nothing alone." McSurely, interview.; Barber II and Wilson-Hartgrove, *The Third Reconstruction*, 48.

27. William J. Barber II, "Moral Framework for Movement-Building in This Time" (Repairers of the Breach Political Organizing Leadership Institute and Summit, Philadelphia, PA, June 14, 2016).; Barber II and Wilson-Hartgrove, *The Third Reconstruction*, xiii.

28. While Barber was president of the NAACP North Carolina Conference it grew to be the largest State Conference in the South and second nationally only to New York. William J. Barber II (Historic Thousands on Jones Street Seminar, Raleigh, NC, February 15, 2015); (Barber II and Zelter, *Forward Together: A Moral Message for the Nation*, 4).

29. William J. Barber II, "A Third Reconstruction? Rev. William Barber Lifts the Trumpet," interview by Peter Laarman, January 14, 2016, http://religiondispatches. org/a-third-reconstruction-rev-william-barber-lifts-the-trumpet/.

30. Barber II and Zelter, *Forward Together: A Moral Message for the Nation*, 9. The NC Constitution, a product of Reconstruction-era fusion politics, which declares as "self-evident that all persons are created equal" and "endowed by their Creator with certain inalienable rights." Those rights include not only life, liberty and the pursuit of happiness, but also "the enjoyment of the fruits of their own labor" (Article 1, Section 1). It also holds that "all political power" is "for the good of the whole" (Article 1, Section 2).

31. Barber II and Wilson-Hartgrove, *The Third Reconstruction*, 116.

32. William J. Barber II, "The Call to Be Positioned as Powerful Prisoners of Prophetic Hope" (Keynote, 2015 Martin Luther King, Jr. Commemoration, Duke University, January 18, 2015), https://www.youtube.com/watch?v=-vbSA2RxRrE.

33. William J. Barber II, "Evangelicals Are Not for Trump or Carson, but for the Gospel," *News & Observer*, November 7, 2015, http://www.newsobserver.com/ opinion/op-ed/article43492335.html.

34. Barber II, "Prisoners of Prophetic Hope." Seeing that they were outmatched in terms of a clear and connected prophetic religious leadership, Barber formed Repairers of the Breach. Its purpose is to develop a national network of "thousands of clergy and lay leaders who will dedicate their lives to rebuilding, raising up and repairing our moral infrastructure." Citing Isaiah 58:12, they call the leadership in formation, "the repairers of the breach and the restorers of our communities." Foster Pinkney points out that the first verse of this chapter was a favorite citation of Benjamin Mays during the early stirrings of the Civil Rights Movement and that Barber applies it similarly: "Shout out, do not hold back! Lift up your voice like a trumpet! Announce to my people their rebellion, to the house of Jacob their sins" (Isaiah 58:1) (Foster Pinkney, "Moral Leadership for Today's Freedom Movements," Kairos, March 5, 2015, https:// kairoscenter.org/moral-leadership-for-todays-freedom-movements/).

35. William J. Barber II, "Challenging & Changing the Moral Climate in America" (Union Theological Seminary, New York, NY, April 20, 2016).; The Forward Together Moral Movement, "Voter Rights Lectionary," 2016, 3.

36. Barber II, "Challenging & Changing the Moral Climate in America."

37. Barber II, "Prisoners of Prophetic Hope."

38. William J. Barber II and Jonathan Wilson-Hartgrove, "Extremists Also The Ugly History Behind 'Religious Freedom' Laws," *The Washington Spectator*, May 1, 2015, http://washingtonspectator.org/the-ugly-history-behind-religious-fr eedom-laws/.

39. The Moral Political Organizing Leadership Institute and Summit (MPOLIS) traveling seminary for moral and religious leaders included lessons in political strategy and tactics learned from the Moral Monday Movement. MPOLIS trainings were one to two days, with fifty to one hundred local clergy, young adults, and grassroots campaign leaders (Barber II, "Moral Framework for Movement-Building in This Time"). At most of the trainings, Yara Allen taught theomusicology, which includes the study of the theological content of music and the role of music in movements. She argues music helps participants communicate with each other and with the larger society through cultural expression. Cultural work is communication, not entertainment. Mahalia Jackson was a movement leader, not an entertainer. Music moves people from being individuals to collectivity (Yara Allen [Historic Thousands on Jones Street Seminar, Raleigh, NC, February 15, 2015]). These sessions are complemented by case studies that focus on social, economic and political issues as they manifest in that city or region, with an imperative that the case studies feature leadership and testimony from those directly affected by the problem. Many but not all MPOLIS sites included a revival. Between April and November 2016, Repairers of the Breach and the Kairos Center, held twenty-two moral revivals across the United States.

40. Theoharis is the author of *Always with Us?: What Jesus Really Said about the Poor* (Eerdmans, 2017). She is coauthor with Barber of *Revive Us Again: Vision and Action in Moral Organizing* (Beacon, 2018).

41. Baptist is the author of *Pedagogy of the Poor* with Jan Rehmann (New York: Teachers College Press, 2011); co-author of *A New and Unsettling Force: Reigniting Rev. Dr. Martin Luther King, Jr.'s Poor People's Campaign* (Poverty Initiative, 2009); and *It's Not Enough to Be Angry* (University of the Poor Press, 2015).

42. Liz Theoharis, *Always with Us?: What Jesus Really Said about the Poor*, 2017; Willie Baptist and Liz Theoharis, "Reading the Bible with the Poor," in *Reading the Bible in an Age of Crisis*, ed. Bruce Worthington (Minneapolis, MN: Fortress Press, 2015), 21–51.

43. Ashley Hufnagel, "Rearticulating a New Poor People's Campaign: Fifty Years of Grassroots Anti-Poverty Movement Organizing," Feminist Formations 33, no. 1 (Spring 2021): 209.

44. Erik Gunn, "'The Center of Gravity is in the Local Work': Liz Theoharis on the Poor People's Campaign," *The Progressive*, May 1, 2019.

44. Wright, "Civil Rights 'Unfinished Business,'" 510–11; "Meeting Minutes of the Minority Group Steering Committee," 5.

46. Erik Gunn, "'The Center of Gravity Is in the Local Work.'"

47. Clinton Wright, "Reflections from the delegates," May 23, 2018, unpublished document, 2.

48. King, "'Where Do We Go from Here?' (SCLC Convention)," 24.

49. Liz Theoharis et al., "'Questions Must Be Raised': Who Are the Poor? Why Are We Poor?," 2016, https://kairoscenter.org/who-are-the-poor/; Put People First! PA, www.putpeoplefirstpa.org.

50. King, "See You in Washington," 6–7.

51. Clinton Wright, "Reflections from the delegates," 3.

52. William J. Barber II and Jonathan Wilson-Hartgrove, "The True Heart of Public Evangelicalism," Beacon Broadside: A Project of Beacon Press, February 12, 2016, https://www.beaconbroadside.com/broadside/2016/02/the-true-heart-of-public-evangelicalism.html.

Conclusion

The Poor People's Campaign of 1968 is an unfinished story. The problems it sought to resolve not only continue to plague our world, they have escalated. But those whose lives are threatened by poverty, racism, war, and environmental crisis are poised to be a force of revolutionary transformation, if we can come together as a class across the lines that divide us.

We are confronted by the enormity of the task before us. Scholars, ethicists, and organizers have wrestled with the horizon of what is possible and offered their conclusions to the poor. Frances Fox Piven and Richard A. Cloward assess the history of poor people's movements and contend, "Protesters win, if they win at all, what historical circumstances has already made ready to be conceded."[1] Reinhold Niebuhr argued, "We must strive as best we can to attain decency, clarity and proximate justice in an ambiguous world."[2] And organizer Saul Alinsky taught, "If you start with nothing, demand 100 percent, then compromise for 30 percent, you're 30 percent ahead."[3] These realist insights were culled from experience and study. But King's experience and study led him to something different. He discerned more was possible. He fought for that conviction and began planning to make it real.

As the wins of the Civil Rights Movement were implemented in the late 1960s, King realized that civil rights would never be secure in a society structured around systemic racism, economic exploitation, and state violence. He started seeking leaders who might join a broad human rights movement to deal a devastating blow to those evils. He assessed that they should begin with a campaign of the poor, because if they could take action together across racial lines, the poor were poised to be a "new and unsettling force." In a deeply racist society the challenge of unity would be formidable, but King argued the experience of taking action together would lead to new possibilities. "In dangerous moments people begin holding hands that didn't know they could hold them. . . . It's a way to unite forces."[4] They could bring even greater numbers of people toward a revolution of values. They could become a "freedom church of the poor," the hope of the world, theologically and politically. To take shape they would need to learn organizing tactics and political strategy. And then he was assassinated.

The Poor People's Campaign did convene a broad, multiracial leadership from among the poor. But it couldn't move beyond the model where the poor petition Washington to concede budget allotments and bureaucratic adjustments to existing programs. In this conception Washington was the savior of the poor, offering proximate justice along the lines of what they were ready to concede, a small percentage of what is necessary for life. But there was another vision where the poor were capable of becoming a transforming force for moral and structural change, the saviors not only of themselves but the entire nation, and, if they could unite with those like them around the globe, the world itself.

Keri Day, Sarah Monroe and Aaron Scott, William J. Barber II and Liz Theoharis, and the leaders of the Poor People's Campaign: A National Call for Moral Revival have taken up this history and vision. They draw unique but related theological and ethical themes that respond to the enmeshed crises that King sought to resolve more than a half century ago. Each assert that poverty is a material crisis and a theological one. Each are ethicists and producers of Christian ethics, even if it is not in their official title. Like King, they find new insights as they go about the work of forming other religious and community leaders—through campaigns, chaplaincy, and scholarship. Their ethics hold in tension the process of social change and the realized society transformed, refusing to sacrifice one to the other.

Each of these ethicists is from and for what King might have called the freedom church of the poor. As their communities imagine new social and economic relationships, they gain insights into how we get there. They demonstrate that theological, biblical, and ethical inquiry must be done by scholars of all vocations, including those engaged in the "nettlesome task" of organizing campaigns and developing leaders. The poor contribute not only the data for analysis, but are interpreters and theorizers as well, bringing valuable contributions to the field. And each of these ethicists clings to hope, not because change is easy, but because despite having "little or nothing to lose," they know the communities from which they come have everything to gain. Their hope comes from what Scott calls "a costly orientation toward this world."

> Real hope that the real world might really get better is a terrifying thing to consider, because it forces us to acknowledge just how much needs to change. . . . Hope is not cheap. It is dangerous. . . . It will get you in trouble. It will get you laughed at. It will get you punished. . . . What better teachers can we ask for on enduring all this, for the sake of real hope, than those who are at the forefront of punishment and trouble in our society already?[5]

This is the cross that King said would leave "marks of Jesus Christ on your body and on your soul."[6] And it is a cross that can only be known by carrying it.

Movements start with a small, dissenting leadership, and only later do they win the rest of the church and nation. So the first task of religious leaders is to win themselves to this work and become deeply committed—to wake up thinking about it and orient all they do towards it. Studying the role of religious leadership in the history of social change is important in discerning that task. That leadership has taken many forms—public speakers, writers, insurrectionists, organizers, pastors, chaplains—with names known and unknown to history. What they had in common was that they responded to the spiritual needs of others, sustaining them and emboldening them for the work of social change. To fight for your freedom, you have to believe you are worthy of freedom. Today we are told all day every day that we are only worth what we're paid, and if we're unpaid, we're worth even less. We only deserve health care if we can afford it. We only deserve to be safe on the streets if we don't spend our time on the streets. In the face of this denigration of our dignity, dissenting religious leaders and people of faith proclaim that God promised abundance and provided abundance. They assert that we are all children of God, full of dignity and freedom. Their organizing work is true to the gospel, and they are helping give form to new freedom churches of the poor that are indeed good news. The way forward will be a difficult and precarious path, full of suffering, but that is a price that has been paid before.

NOTES

1. Frances Fox Piven and Richard Cloward, *Poor People's Movements: Why They Succeed, How They Fail* (Vintage, 1979), 36.

2. Reinhold Niebuhr, "The Problem of a Protestant Social Ethic," *Union Seminary Quarterly Review* 15, no. 1 (November 1959): 10–11.

3. Saul Alinsky, *Rules for Radicals: A Practical Primer for Realistic Radicals* (New York: Vintage Books, 1989), 59.

4. Martin Luther King Jr., "See You in Washington" (SCLC Staff Retreat, Atlanta, GA, January 17, 1968), 9, King Speeches, Series 3, Box 13, King Center Archives.

5. Aaron Scott, "Famine of the Word," *Aaronheartsjesus* (blog), July 17, 2016, https://aaronheartsjesus.wordpress.com/2016/07/17/sermon-ninth-sunday-after-pentecost-2016/.

6. Martin Luther King Jr., "To Minister to the Valley" (Ministers Leadership Training Program, Miami, FL, February 23, 1968), 16, King Speeches, Series 3, Box 15, King Center Archives.

Bibliography

Abernathy, Ralph. *And the Walls Came Tumbling Down: An Autobiography*. New York: Harper & Row, 1989.

Aboulhosn, Angelica. "'His Camera Is Guided by His Heart': On Robert Houston's Photographs of the Poor People's Campaign." National Museum of African American History & Culture, January 8, 2018. https://nmaahc. si.edu/blog-post/%E2%80%9Chis-camera-guided-his-heart%E2%80%9D-robert-houston%E2%80%99s-photographs-poor-people%E2%80%99s-campaign.

Alexander, Michelle. *The New Jim Crow: Mass Incarceration in the Age of Colorblindness*. New York: New Press, 2012.

Alinsky, Saul. *Rules for Radicals: A Practical Primer for Realistic Radicals*. New York: Vintage Books, 1989.

Allen, Yara. "Theomusicology." Presented at the Historic Thousands on Jones Street Seminar, Raleigh, NC, February 15, 2015.

Allott, Patricia, Bernie Boston, Edgar Cahn, and George De Vincent. "This Was Resurrection City." Southern Christian Leadership Conference, 1968.

Anderson, Carol. *Eyes Off the Prize: The United Nations and the African American Struggle for Human Rights, 1944-1955*. New York: Cambridge University Press, 2003.

Anderson, Jervis. *Bayard Rustin: Troubles I've Seen*. New York: HarperCollins, 1997.

"Arrested Development." *The Economist*, October 4, 2014. http://www.economist. com/news/special-report/21621158-model-development-through-industrialisation-its-way-out-arrested-development.

Asch, Christopher Myers. *The Senator and the Sharecropper: The Freedom Struggles of James O. Eastland and Fannie Lou Hamer*. New York: W.W. Norton, 2008.

Associated Press. *Cuts for Story: Wa15023 "Welfare."* Washington, D.C.: AP Archive, 1968. https://www.youtube.com/watch?time_continue=50&v=IFP4hdp4 4h0&feature=emb_logo.

Atkins, Oliver F. *Atkins_92_cs_10*. 1968. Photograph. Oliver F. Atkins photograph collection, Box 12, Folder 21. George Mason University, Special Collections and Archives. http://sca.gmu.edu/finding_aids/atkins.html.

———. *Atkins_92_cs_20*. 1968. Photograph. Oliver F. Atkins photograph collection, 1943-1975. George Mason University, Special Collections and Archives. http://sca.gmu.edu/finding_aids/atkins.html.

Babones, Salvatore. "The Minimum Wage Is Stuck at $7.25; It Should Be $21.16." Institute for Policy Studies, July 24, 2012. http://inequality.org/minimum-wage/.

Baker-Fletcher, Garth. "Somebodyness and Self-Respect: Themes of Dignity in Martin Luther King and Malcolm X." *Union Seminary Quarterly Review* 48, no. 1–2 (1994): 7–18.

Baldwin, Lewis. *The Voice of Conscience: The Church in the Mind of Martin Luther King, Jr.* New York: Oxford University Press, 2010.

Baptist, Willie. *It's Not Enough to Be Angry*. University of the Poor Press, 2015.

Baptist, Willie, and Jan Rehmann. *Pedagogy of the Poor*. New York: Teachers College Press, 2011.

Baptist, Willie, and Liz Theoharis. "Reading the Bible with the Poor." In *Reading the Bible in an Age of Crisis*, edited by Bruce Worthington, 21–51. Minneapolis, MN: Fortress Press, 2015.

Barber II, William J. "The Call to Be Positioned as Powerful Prisoners of Prophetic Hope." Keynote presented at the 2015 Martin Luther King, Jr. Commemoration, Duke University, January 18, 2015. https://www.youtube.com/watch?v=-vbSA2RxRrE.

———. "Challenging & Changing the Moral Climate in America." Union Theological Seminary, New York, NY, April 20, 2016.

———. "Evangelicals Are Not for Trump or Carson, but for the Gospel." *News & Observer*, November 7, 2015. http://www.newsobserver.com/opinion/op-ed/article43492335.html.

———. "Moral Framework for Movement-Building in This Time." Presented at the Repairers of the Breach Political Organizing Leadership Institute and Summit, Philadelphia, PA, June 14, 2016.

———. "Moral Fusion Organizing." Presented at the Historic Thousands on Jones Street Seminar, Raleigh, NC, February 15, 2015.

———. "A Third Reconstruction? Rev. William Barber Lifts the Trumpet." Interview by Peter Laarman, January 14, 2016. http://religiondispatches.org/a-third-reconstruction-rev-william-barber-lifts-the-trumpet/.

Barber II, William J., and Liz Theoharis. "Call to Action." Presented at the Repairers of the Breach National Political Organizing Leadership Institute and Summit, Raleigh, NC, March 16, 2017.

Barber II, William J., and Jonathan Wilson-Hartgrove. "Extremists Also Remember Selma: The Ugly History Behind 'Religious Freedom' Laws." *Washington Spectator*, May 1, 2015. http://washingtonspectator.org/the-ugly-history-behind-religious-freedom-laws/.

———. *The Third Reconstruction: Moral Mondays, Fusion Politics, and the Rise of a New Justice Movement*. Boston: Beacon Press, 2016.

————. "The True Heart of Public Evangelicalism." Beacon Broadside: A Project of Beacon Press, February 12, 2016. https://www.beaconbroadside.com/broadside/2016/02/the-true-heart-of-public-evangelicalism.html.

Barber II, William J., and Barbara Zelter. *Forward Together: A Moral Message for the Nation*. St. Louis: Chalice Press, 2014.

Beadenkopf, Brenda. "Part XVIII: Poor People's Campaign, Assassination of Dr. Martin Luther King," (unpublished manuscript, n.d.).

Belafonte, Harry. Interview by Blackside, Inc. "Eyes on the Prize II: America at the Racial Crossroads 1965 to 1985." May 15, 1989. Henry Hampton Collection. Washington University Libraries, Film and Media Archive. http://digital.wustl.edu/e/eii/eiiweb/bel5427.0417.013harrybelafonte.html.

Bender, Steven W. *One Night in America: Robert Kennedy, Cesar Chavez, and the Dream of Dignity*. New York: Routledge, 2015.

Bivens, Josh, and Lawrence Mishel. "Understanding the Historic Divergence Between Productivity and a Typical Worker's Pay." *Economic Policy Institute* (blog), September 2, 2015. http://www.epi.org/publication/understanding-the-historic-divergence-between-productivity-and-a-typical-workers-pay-why-it-matters-and-why-its-real/.

Blanchard, Eric. Interview by the author. Digital audio recording. Phone. July 24, 2015.

————. "The Poor People and the 'White Press.'" *Columbia Journalism Review*, Fall 1968, 61–65.

Bland, Ben. "China's Robot Revolution." *Financial Times*, June 6, 2016. https://www.ft.com/content/1dbd8c60-0cc6-11e6-ad80-67655613c2d6.

Branch, Taylor. *At Canaan's Edge: America in the King Years, 1965-68*. New York: Simon & Schuster, 2007.

————. *Parting the Waters: America in the King Years 1954-63*. New York: Simon & Schuster, 1989.

Bronson, Jennifer, and Ann Carson. "Prisoners in 2017." Bureau of Justice Statistics, April 2019. https://www.bjs.gov/index.cfm?ty=pbdetail&iid=6546.

Bureau of Labor Statistics. "1-Month Net Change, Total Nonfarm Labor, 1968." United States Department of Labor. Accessed January 19, 2017. https://data.bls.gov/pdq/SurveyOutputServlet.

————. "Unemployment Rate (1948-2017)." Accessed May 14, 2017. https://data.bls.gov/pdq/SurveyOutputServlet.

Burns, Stewart. *To the Mountaintop: Martin Luther King's Mission and Its Meaning for America*. 2nd edition. Charleston, SC: CreateSpace, 2018.

Burris, Bertha. Interview by Colleen Wessel-McCoy, Derrick McQueen, Juli Bertalan, and John Wessel-McCoy. Digital audio recording. Marks, Mississippi. May 19, 2008.

Burrow, Rufus. *Extremist for Love: Martin Luther King Jr., Man of Ideas and Nonviolent Social Action*. Minneapolis: Fortress Press, 2014.

Carson, Clayborne. *In Struggle: SNCC and the Black Awakening of the 1960s*. Cambridge, MA: Harvard University Press, 1995.

Chan, Kenyon. Poor People's Campaign Oral History. Interview by John Alexander, September 16, 2015. https://pages.shanti.virginia.edu/ResurrectionCity/oral-histories/kenyon-chan/.

Chase, Robert T. "Class Resurrection: The Poor People's Campaign of 1968 and Resurrection City." *Essays in History*, 40 (1998).

Chaudry, Ajay, Christopher Wimer, Suzanne Maccartney, Lauren Frolich, Colin Campbell, Kendall Swenson, Don Oellerich, and Susan Hauan. "Poverty in the United States: 50-Year Trends and Safety Net Impacts." U.S. Department of Health and Human Services, March 2016.

Cobb, Daniel M. *Native Activism in Cold War America: The Struggle for Sovereignty.* Lawrence, KS: University Press of Kansas, 2008.

Cocco, Federica. "Most US Manufacturing Jobs Lost to Technology, Not Trade." *Financial Times*, December 2, 2016. https://www.ft.com/content/dec677c0-b7e6-11e6-ba85-95d1533d9a62.

The Colbert Report. Season 4, Episode 10, "Andrew Young." Aired January 22, 2008, on Comedy Central. http://www.cc.com/video-clips/xw3v9i/the-colbert-report-andrew-young.

Collier, Jimmy, and Frederick Douglass Kirkpatrick. *Everybody's Got a Right to Live.* LP. New York: Broadside Records, 1968.

Collins, Chuck, and Josh Hoxie. "Billionaire Bonanza." Institute for Policy Studies, November 2017.

Collum, Danny Duncan. *Black and White Together: The Search for Common Ground.* Maryknoll, NY: Orbis Books, 1996.

Cone, James H. "Black Theology and Black Liberation." In *Black Theology: A Documentary History, Vol. 1*, edited by James H. Cone and Gayraud S. Wilmore, 2nd ed. Maryknoll, N.Y: Orbis Books, 1993.

———. *A Black Theology of Liberation*. Maryknoll, NY: Orbis Books, 1986.

———. *The Cross and the Lynching Tree*. Orbis Books, 2011.

———. *God of the Oppressed*. Maryknoll, NY: Orbis Books, 1997.

———. *Martin & Malcom & America: A Dream or a Nightmare*. Orbis Books, 1992.

———. "Systematic Theology 393: Malcolm and Martin." Lecture, Union Theological Seminary, New York, NY, March 28, 2006.

———. "The Theology of Martin Luther King, Jr." *Union Seminary Quarterly Review* 40, no. 4 (1986): 21–39.

Copeland, M. Shawn. "Wading through Many Sorrows." In *A Troubling in My Soul: Womanist Perspectives on Evil and Suffering*, edited by Emilie Maureen Townes, 109–24. The Bishop Henry McNeal Turner Studies in North American Black Religion. Maryknoll, NY: Orbis Books, 1993.

Crawford, Vicki L., Jacqueline Anne Rouse, and Barbara Woods. *Women in the Civil Rights Movement: Trailblazers and Torchbearers, 1941-1965.* Bloomington: Indiana University Press, 1990.

Crosby, Emilye. *Civil Rights History from the Ground Up: Local Struggles, a National Movement.* Athens: University of Georgia Press, 2011.

Day, Keri. "Global Economics and US Public Policy: Human Liberation for the Global Poor." *Black Theology* 9, no. 1 (April 2011): 9–33.

————. *Religious Resistance to Neoliberalism: Womanist and Black Feminist Perspectives*. New York: Palgrave Macmillan, 2015.

————. *Unfinished Business: Black Women, the Black Church, and the Struggle to Thrive in America*. Maryknoll, NY: Orbis Books, 2012.

Debnam, Jewell. "Black Women and the Charleston Hospital Workers' Strike of 1969." Dissertation, 2016. Michigan State University.

Department of Health and Human Services. "Annual Update of the HHS Poverty Guidelines." January 18, 2018. https://www.federalregister.gov/documents/2018/01/18/2018-00814/annual-update-of-the-hhs-poverty-guidelines.

Desmond-Harris, Jenée. "The Poor People's Campaign: The Little-Known Protest MLK Was Planning When He Died." *Vox*, January 16, 2017. http://www.vox.com/2017/1/16/14271074/the-poor-peoples-campaign-the-little-known-protest-mlk-was-planning-when-he-died.

Dickson, Paul, and Thomas Allen. "Marching on History." *Smithsonian*, February 2003. http://www.smithsonianmag.com/history/marching-on-history-75797769/.

Dorrien, Gary. *Breaking White Supremacy: Martin Luther King Jr. and the Black Social Gospel*. New Haven: Yale University Press, 2017.

————. *The Making of American Liberal Theology: Crisis, Irony, and Postmodernity 1950-2005*. Louisville: Westminster John Knox Press, 2006.

————. *The New Abolition: W. E. B. Du Bois and the Black Social Gospel*. New Haven: Yale University Press, 2015.

————. *Social Ethics in the Making: Interpreting an American Tradition*. Chichester, U.K.; Malden, MA: Wiley-Blackwell, 2008.

"Dr. King's Error." *New York Times*, April 7, 1967. Page 36.

Edelman, Marian Wright. Interview by Henry Hampton. "Eyes on the Prize II: America at the Racial Crossroads 1965 to 1985." December 21, 1988. Washington University Libraries, Film and Media Archive, Henry Hampton Collection. http://digital.wustl.edu/e/eii/eiiweb/ede5427.0676.044marianwrightedelman.html.

Elliott, Larry. "World's Eight Richest People Have Same Wealth as Poorest 50%," *The Guardian*, January 15, 2017. https://www.theguardian.com/global-development/2017/jan/16/worlds-eight-richest-people-have-same-wealth-as-poorest-50?CMP=twt_a-world_b-gdnworld.

Fager, Charles. *Uncertain Resurrection: The Poor People's Washington Campaign*. Grand Rapids, MI: Eerdmans, 1969.

Fairclough, Adam. *To Redeem the Soul of America: The Southern Christian Leadership Conference and Martin Luther King, Jr.* Athens: University of Georgia Press, 1987.

Federal Reserve Bank of St. Louis, "Households and Nonprofit Organizations; Net Worth." January 19, 2020. https://fred.stlouisfed.org/graph/?graph_id=369801.

————. "Wealth Inequality in America: Key Facts & Figures," August 14, 2019. https://www.stlouisfed.org/open-vault/2019/august/wealth-inequality-in-america-facts-figures.

Fisher, Gordon. "The Development and History of the Poverty Thresholds." *Social Security Bulletin* 55, no. 4 (1992). https://www.ssa.gov/history/fisheronpoverty.html.

Foner, Eric. *Reconstruction: America's Unfinished Revolution, 1863-1877*. New York: History Book Club, 2005.

Fox, Liana. "The Supplemental Poverty Measure: 2018." The United States Census Bureau, October 2019.

Freeman, Roland L. *The Mule Train: A Journey of Hope Remembered*. Nashville, TN: Thomas Nelson, 1998.

Frost, Jennifer. *An Interracial Movement of the Poor: Community Organizing and the New Left in the 1960s*. New York: New York University Press, 2001.

Gabler, Neal. "The Secret Shame of Middle-Class Americans." *The Atlantic*, May 2016. http://www.theatlantic.com/magazine/archive/2016/05/my-secret-shame/476415/.

Garrow, David J. *Bearing the Cross: Martin Luther King, Jr., and the Southern Christian Leadership Conference*. New York: Quill, 1999.

———. *The FBI and Martin Luther King, Jr.: From "Solo" to Memphis*. New York: W.W. Norton, 1981.

George, Carol V. R. *Segregated Sabbaths; Richard Allen and the Emergence of Independent Black Churches 1760-1840*. New York: Oxford University Press, 1973.

Giddings, Paula. *When and Where I Enter: The Impact of Black Women on Race and Sex in America*. New York: Bantam Books, 1985.

Gilbert, Ben W. *Ten Blocks from the White House: Anatomy of the Washington Riots of 1968*. New York: F. A. Praeger, 1968.

Glaude, Eddie S. *Exodus!: Religion, Race, and Nation in Early Nineteenth-Century Black America*. Chicago: University of Chicago Press, 2000.

Goldsmith, William, and Edward Blakely. *Separate Societies: Poverty and Inequality in U.S. Cities*. 2nd Edition. Philadelphia: Temple University Press, 2010.

Goldstein, Alyosha. *Poverty in Common: The Politics of Community Action during the American Century*. Durham: Duke University Press, 2012.

———. "The Violence of Poverty: A 'Living Memorial' for MLK." *Counterpunch* (blog), April 26, 2012. http://www.counterpunch.org/2012/04/26/the-violence-of-poverty/.

Gollin, Albert E. "The Demography of Protest: A Statistical Profile of Participants in the Poor People's Campaign." Bureau of Social Science Research, Inc., August 5, 1968.

Gunn, Erik. "'The Center of Gravity Is in the Local Work': Liz Theoharis on the Poor People's Campaign." *The Progressive*, May 1, 2019.

Hampton, Henry, Steve Fayer, and Sarah Flynn. *Voices of Freedom: An Oral History of the Civil Rights Movement from the 1950s through the 1980s*. New York: Bantam Books, 1991.

Harding, Vincent. "Introduction." In *Where Do We Go From Here: Chaos or Community?*, by Martin Luther King, Jr. Boston: Beacon Press, 2010.

———. *Martin Luther King, the Inconvenient Hero*. Maryknoll, NY: Orbis Books, 2008.

Harrington, Michael. Interview by Blackside, Inc. "Eyes on the Prize II: America at the Racial Crossroads 1965 to 1985." May 15, 1989. Washington University Libraries,

Film and Media Archive, Henry Hampton Collection. http://digital.wustl.edu/cgi/t/ text/text-idx?c=eop;cc=eop;rgn=main;view=text;idno=har5427.0719.063.

Harrison, Mark, and Nikolaus Wolf. "The Frequency of Wars." *Economic History Review* `65, no. 3 (July 22, 2011): 1055–76.

Higginbotham, Evelyn Brooks. *Righteous Discontent: The Women's Movement in the Black Baptist Church, 1880-1920.* Cambridge, MA: Harvard University Press, 1993.

Hing, Alex. Remembering Resurrection City. Interview by John Alexander, October 2017. University of Virginia. https://eastwindezine.com/remembering-resurrection-city/.

Hinshaw, Cecil. "FBI Requests for Information of the Poor People's Campaign," May 28, 1968. CRD Administration 32557. The Archives of the American Friends Service Committee.

Honey, Michael K. *Going Down Jericho Road: The Memphis Strike, Martin Luther King's Last Campaign.* 1st ed. New York: W.W. Norton & Co, 2007.

Horsley, Richard A., ed. *Hidden Transcripts and the Arts of Resistance: Applying the Work of James C. Scott to Jesus and Paul.* Semeia Studies, no. 48. Atlanta: Society of Biblical Literature, 2004.

Horton, Myles. Letter to Andrew Young, April 5, 1968. SCLC Papers, Series VIII, 177:20. King Center Archives.

Houston, Robert, and Aaron Bryant. "Most Daring Dream: Robert Houston Photography & the 1968 Poor People's Campaign." *Callaloo* 31, no. 4 (2008): 1272–74.

Hufnagel, Ashley. "Rearticulating a New Poor People's Campaign: Fifty Years of Grassroots Anti-Poverty Movement Organizing," *Feminist Formations* 33, Issue 1 (Spring 2021): 189–220.

Hunter, Charlayne. "On the Case in Resurrection City." In *Black Experience: The Transformation of Activism*, edited by August Meier, 2d ed. New Brunswick, NJ: Transaction Books, 1973.

———. "On the Case in Resurrection City." In *The Eyes on the Prize Civil Rights Reader: Documents, Speeches, and Firsthand Accounts from the Black Freedom Struggle, 1954-1990*, edited by Clayborne Carson, David J. Garrow, Gerald Gill, Vincent Harding, and Darlene Clark Hine, 426–38. New York: Viking, 1991.

Jackson, Jesse. "Resurrection City: The Dream, The Accomplishments." *Ebony*, October 1968.

Jackson, Thomas F. *From Civil Rights to Human Rights: Martin Luther King, Jr., and the Struggle for Economic Justice.* Philadelphia: University of Pennsylvania Press, 2007.

Jenkins, Willis. "Conclusion: Christian Social Ethics After Bonhoeffer and King." In *Bonhoeffer and King: Their Legacies and Import for Christian Social Thought*, edited by Willis Jenkins and Jennifer M. McBride. Minneapolis: Fortress Press, 2010.

Kelley, Robin D. G. *Hammer and Hoe: Alabama Communists during the Great Depression.* Chapel Hill: University of North Carolina Press, 2015.

King, Coretta Scott. *My Life with Martin Luther King, Jr.* New York: Holt, Rinehart and Winston, 1969.

King Jr., Martin Luther. "Address at Mass Meeting." Eutaw, AL, March 20, 1968. King Speeches, Series 3, Box 13. King Center Archives.

———. "Address at Mass Meeting." Albany, GA, March 22, 1968. King Speeches, Series 3, Box 13. King Center Archives.

———. "Advice for Living." *Ebony*, April 1958.

———. "Honoring Dr. DuBois." *Freedomways* 8, no. 2 (Spring 1968).

———. "Meaning of Hope." Dexter Ave. Baptist Church, Montgomery, Alabama, December 10, 1967. King Speeches, Series 3, Box 13. King Center Archives.

———. "Negroes Are Not Moving Too Fast." *The Saturday Evening Post*, November 7, 1964.

———. "Press Conference on Washington Campaign." Ebenezer Baptist Church, Atlanta, GA, December 4, 1967. King Speeches, Series 3, Box 13. King Center Archives.

———. "SCLC Staff Retreat Speech." Frogmore, SC, November 14, 1966. King Speeches, Series 3, Box 13. King Center Archives.

———. "See You in Washington." SCLC Staff Retreat, Atlanta, GA, January 17, 1968. King Speeches, Series 3, Box 13. King Center Archives.

———. "Speech at Staff Retreat." Frogmore, SC, May 1967. King Speeches, Series 3, Box 13. King Center Archives.

———. "State of the Movement." Frogmore, SC, November 28, 1967. King Speeches, Series 3, Box 13. King Center Archives.

———. "Suffering and Faith." *Christian Century*, April 27, 1960.

———. "A Testament of Hope." *Playboy*, April 1969.

———. *A Testament of Hope: The Essential Writings and Speeches of Martin Luther King, Jr.* Edited by James M. Washington. San Francisco: HarperOne, 1991

———. "The Other America: Address at Local 1199." Hunter College, New York, NY, March 10, 1968. King Speeches, Series 3, Box 15. King Center Archives.

———. *The Radical King.* Edited by Cornel West. Boston: Beacon Press, 2015.

———. "The Three Evils of Society." National Conference for New Politics, Chicago, IL, August 31, 1967. King Speeches, Series 3, Box 13. King Center Archives.

———. *The Trumpet of Conscience.* New York: Harper & Row, 1968

———. "To Charter Our Course for the Future." Address. Frogmore, SC, May 22, 1967. King Speeches, Series 3, Box 13. King Center Archives.

———. "To Minister to the Valley." Ministers Leadership Training Program, Miami, FL, February 23, 1968. King Speeches, Series 3, Box 15. King Center Archives.

———. "What Are Your New Year's Resolutions?," January 7, 1968. King Speeches, Series 3, Box 13. King Center Archives.

———. "'Where Do We Go From Here?,' Address to the 11th Annual SCLC Convention." King Encyclopedia at Stanford, August 16, 1967. http://kingencyclo-pedia.stanford.edu/encyclopedia/documentsentry/where_do_we_go_from_here_delivered_at_the_11th_annual_sclc_convention.1.html.

———. *Where Do We Go from Here: Chaos or Community?* New York: Harper & Row, 1967.

————. *Where Do We Go from Here: Chaos or Community?* Boston: Beacon Press, 2010.

————. "Who Is My Neighbor?" Ebenezer Baptist Church, Atlanta, GA, February 18, 1968. King Speeches, Series 3, Box 13. King Center Archives.

————. "Why We Must Go to Washington." Atlanta, GA, January 15, 1968. King Speeches, Series 3, Box 13. King Center Archives.

Kramer, Marian. Interview by the author. Digital Recording. Phone. September 15, 2015.

Kroll, Luisa. "Forbes Billionaires 2018." *Forbes*, March 6, 2018. https://www.forbes.com/sites/luisakroll/2018/03/06/forbes-billionaires-2018-meet-the-richest-people-on-the-planet/#bd719c06523d.

Lawson, Max, Man-Kwun Chan, Francesca Rhodes, Anam Parvez Butt, Anna Marriott, Ellen Ehmke, Didier Jacobs, Julie Seghers, Jamie Atienza and Rebecca Gowland. "Public Good or Private Wealth." Oxfam International, January 2019. https://indepth.oxfam.org.uk/public-good-private-wealth/.

Lincoln, C. Eric, and Lawrence H. Mamiya. *The Black Church in the African American Experience.* Durham: Duke University Press, 1990.

Listing of Those to Be Invited to the Minority Group Meeting. Atlanta, GA, nd. SCLC Papers, Series VIII, 179:11. King Center Archives.

Lohr, Kathy. "Poor People's Campaign: A Dream Unfulfilled." NPR.org. Accessed June 19, 2008. http://www.npr.org/templates/story/story.php?storyId=91626373.

Long, Michael G. *Against Us, But for Us: Martin Luther King, Jr. and the State.* Macon: Mercer University Press, 2002.

Lumet, Sidney, and Joseph L. Mankiewicz. *King: A Filmed Record. . . Montgomery to Memphis.* Documentary, 1970.

Mantler, Gordon. "Black, Brown and Poor: Martin Luther King Jr., The Poor People's Campaign and Its Legacies." Dissertation. Duke University, 2008.

————. *Power to the Poor: Black-Brown Coalition and the Fight for Economic Justice, 1960-1974.* Chapel Hill: University of North Carolina Press, 2013.

————. "'The Press Did You In': The Poor People's Campaign and the Mass Media." *The Sixties* 3, no. 1 (June 1, 2010): 33–54. https://doi.org/10.1080/17541321003771128.

Matthews, Dylan. "Are 26 Billionaires Worth More than Half the Planet? The Debate, Explained." *Vox*, January 22, 2019. https://www.vox.com/future-perfect/2019/1/22/18192774/oxfam-inequality-report-2019-davos-wealth.

Matthews, Ethel Mae. Interview with Blackside, Inc. "Eyes on the Prize II: America at the Racial Crossroads 1965 to 1985." February 23, 1989. Washington University Libraries, Film and Media Archive, Henry Hampton Collection. http://digital.wustl.edu/cgi/t/text/text-idx?c=eop;cc=eop;rgn=main;view=text;idno=mat5427.0331.105.

McKnight, Gerald. *The Last Crusade: Martin Luther King, Jr., the FBI, and the Poor People's Campaign.* Boulder, CO: Westview Press, 1998.

McSurely, Al. Interview by the author. Digital audio recording. New York City, January 30, 2015.

"Meeting Minutes of the Minority Group Steering Committee." April 1968. Southern Christian Leadership Conference Records, Subseries 10.3, Poor People's Campaign, Box 571. Emory University.

Meier, August, John H. Bracey, and Elliott Rudwick, eds. *Black Protest in the Sixties*. New York: M. Wiener, 1991.

Minchin, Timothy J. *From Rights to Economics: The Ongoing Struggle for Black Equality in the U.S. South*. Gainesville: University Press of Florida, 2007.

Moffett, Barbara. Letter to Eleanor Eaton. "Minority Leaders Conference Washington's Poor People's Campaign," April 2, 1968. CRD Administration 32557. The Archives of the American Friends Service Committee.

Monroe, Sarah. "The Kingdom of God Comes in a Parking Lot." *A Wandering Minister* (blog), June 20, 2015. http://awanderingminister2.blogspot.com/2015/06/the-kingdom-of-god-comes-in-parking-lot.html.

Moynihan, Daniel Patrick. "The Negro Family: The Case for National Action." In *Welfare: A Documentary History of U.S. Policy and Politics*, edited by Gwendolyn Mink and Rickie Solinger, 226–38. New York: New York University Press, 2003.

Murrow, Edward. *Harvest of Shame*. DVD. Docurama, 2005.

Nadasen, Premilla. *Welfare Warriors: The Welfare Rights Movement in the United States*. New York: Routledge, 2005.

National Employment Law Project. "A Strong Minimum Wage Can Help Working Families, Businesses and Our Economy Recover." New York, NY, January 2011.

National Welfare Rights Organization. "Proposals for a Guaranteed Adequate Income." In *Welfare: A Documentary History of U.S. Policy and Politics*, edited by Gwendolyn Mink and Rickie Solinger, 373–79. New York: New York University Press, 2003.

"Newsletter for the Poor People's University." May 29, 1968. SCLC Papers, Series VIII, 179:23. King Center Archives.

"Newsletter for the Poor People's University." May 31, 1968. SCLC Papers, Series VIII, 179:23. King Center Archives.

Niebuhr, Reinhold. "The Problem of a Protestant Social Ethic." *Union Seminary Quarterly Review* 15, no. 1 (November 1959): 1–11.

O'Dell, Jack. *Climbin' Jacob's Ladder: The Black Freedom Movement Writings of Jack O'Dell*. Berkeley: University of California Press, 2010.

Payne, Charles. "'Men Led, But Women Organized': Movement Participation of Women in the Mississippi Delta." In *Women and Social Protest*, edited by Guida West and Rhoda Lois Blumberg, 156–65. New York: Oxford University Press, 1990.

Payne, Charles M. *I've Got the Light of Freedom: The Organizing Tradition and the Mississippi Freedom Struggle*. Berkeley: University of California Press, 1995.

Pepper, William F. *An Act of State: The Execution of Martin Luther King*. New York: Verso, 2003.

———. *Orders to Kill: The Truth behind the Murder of Martin Luther King*. New York: Carroll & Graf, 1995.

Pinkney, Foster. "Moral Leadership for Today's Freedom Movements." *Kairos: The Center for Religions, Rights, and Social Justice (blog)*, March 5, 2015. https://kairoscenter.org/moral-leadership-for-todays-freedom-movements/.

Piven, Frances Fox, and Richard Cloward. *Poor People's Movements: Why They Succeed, How They Fail*. New York: Vintage, 1978.

Podair, Jerald. *Bayard Rustin: American Dreamer*. Lanham, MD: Rowman & Littlefield, 2009.

"Poor People in America: Economic Fact Sheet for the Poor People's Campaign." January 1968. Southern Christian Leadership Conference Records, Subseries 10.3, Poor People's Campaign, Box 573, Folder 28. Emory University.

"Poor People's Campaign Committees." n.d. SCLC Papers, Series VIII, 177:19. King Center Archives.

"Poor People's Campaign Gains." September 1968. Southern Christian Leadership Conference records: Subseries 10.3: Poor People's Campaign records, Box 572, Folder 25. Emory University.

"Poor People's Campaign Informational Pamphlet," 1968, document image in Jaid Jilani, "Dr. King Wanted 'Grand Alliance' of Blacks and Whites to Build Economic Justice," Alternet, August 19, 2015. http://www.alternet.org/2015/08/dr-king-wanted-grand-alliance-blacks-and-whites-build-economic-justice/.

"Poor People's University Proposed Curriculum." n.d. SCLC Papers, Series VIII, 179:23. King Center Archives.

Poverty Initiative. *A New and Unsettling Force: Reigniting Rev. Dr. Martin Luther King, Jr.'s Poor People's Campaign*. New York City, 2009.

"A Proposed Plan of Structure of the Poor People's University." n.d. SCLC Papers, Series VIII, 179:23. King Center Archives.

Raboteau, Albert J. *Canaan Land: A Religious History of African Americans*. Oxford; New York: Oxford University Press, 2001.

Rabuy, Bernadette, and Daniel Kopf. "Prisons of Poverty: Uncovering the Pre-Incarceration Incomes of the Imprisoned." Prison Policy Initiative. July 9, 2015.https://www.prisonpolicy.org/reports/income.html.

Rank, Mark R., and Thomas A. Hirschl. "Estimating the Risk of Food Stamp Use and Impoverishment During Childhood." *Archives of Pediatrics & Adolescent Medicine* 163, no. 11 (November 2, 2009): 994–99. https://doi.org/10.1001/archpediatrics.2009.178.

Ransby, Barbara. *Ella Baker and the Black Freedom Movement: A Radical Democratic Vision*. Chapel Hill: University of North Carolina Press, 2003.

———. "Ella Baker's Legacy Runs Deep. Know Her Name." *The New York Times*, January 20, 2020, sec. Opinion. https://www.nytimes.com/2020/01/20/opinion/martin-luther-king-ella-baker.html.

Rasmussen, Larry L. "Life Worthy of Life: The Social Ecologies of Bonhoeffer and King." In *Bonhoeffer and King: Their Legacies and Import for Christian Social Thought*, edited by Willis Jenkins and Jennifer M. McBride. Minneapolis: Fortress Press, 2010.

"Resurrection City, Part 2." *Spokane Daily Chronicle*, June 28, 1968, Final edition, sec. A.

Sarkar, Saurav, and Shailly Gupta Barnes. "The Souls of Poor Folks: Auditing America 50 Years After the Poor People's Campaign Challenged Racism, Poverty, the War Economy/Militarism and Our National Morality." Washington, D.C.: Institute for Policy Studies, April 2018.

Scott, Aaron. "A Call for the New Poor People's and Poor Children's Campaign." Presented at the Repairers of the Breach National Political Organizing Leadership Institute and Summit, Raleigh, NC, March 16, 2017.

———. "Famine of the Word." *Aaronheartsjesus* (blog), July 17, 2016. https://aaronheartsjesus.wordpress.com/2016/07/17/sermon-ninth-sunday-after-pentecost-2016/.

———. "Fred Hampton's Jesus Movement." *Aaronheartsjesus* (blog), April 23, 2016. https://aaronheartsjesus.wordpress.com/2016/04/23/sermon-fifth-sunday-in-easter-2016/.

———. "The God of Secrecy." *Aaronheartsjesus* (blog), January 22, 2017. https://aaronheartsjesus.wordpress.com/2017/01/26/sermon-third-sunday-after-the-epiphany-2017/.

———. "The 'Indian Trail': The Poor People's Campaign of 1968 in the Pacific Northwest." *Kairos: The Center for Religions, Rights and Social Justice* (blog), n.d. http://kairoscenter.org/wp-content/uploads/2014/11/PacNWPPC.pdf.

———. "Introduction to the Poor People's Campaign." Presented at the State of the Streets, Westport, WA, July 14, 2016.

———. "King Herod Is a Liar." *Aaronheartsjesus* (blog), December 19, 2015. https://aaronheartsjesus.wordpress.com/2015/12/19/sermon-chaplains-on-the-harbor-inaugural-christmas-party/.

———. "Radical Rednecks: The Necessity of Organizing Poor Whites for Poverty Abolition Movements, from Slavery to the Prison-Industrial Complex." unpublished, 2016.

———. "Real Hope." *Aaronheartsjesus* (blog), April 10, 2016. https://aaronheartsjesus.wordpress.com/2016/04/10/sermon-third-sunday-in-easter-2016/.

Scott, Aaron, and Sarah Monroe. "Dialogue on the Suburbanization of Poverty." Conference Call presented at the Religious Leaders Group, January 29, 2015.

Scott, Aaron, Sarah Monroe, and Lindsey Krinks. "Radical Chaplaincy: Reflections on the Northwest Solidarity Tour." *Aaronheartsjesus* (blog), October 2, 2015. https://aaronheartsjesus.wordpress.com/2015/10/02/radical-chaplaincy-reflections-on-the-northwest-solidarity-tour/.

Seeger, Pete, Frederick Douglass Kirkpatrick, and Jimmy Collier. *Everybody's Got a Right To Live*. Vol. Pete Seeger Now. Columbia, 1968.

Selby, Gary S. *Martin Luther King and the Rhetoric of Freedom: The Exodus Narrative in America's Struggle for Civil Rights*. Waco: Baylor University Press, 2008.

Sellers, Clevland. Interview by Blackside, Inc. "Eyes on the Prize II: America at the Racial Crossroads 1965 to 1985." October 21, 1988. Washington University Libraries, Film and Media Archive, Henry Hampton Collection. http://digital.wustl.edu/cgi/t/text/text-idx?c=eop;cc=eop;rgn=main;view=text;idno=sel5427.0215.148.

Sidy, Richard. Poor People's Campaign Oral History. Interview by John Alexander, August 5, 2015. https://pages.shanti.virginia.edu/ResurrectionCity/oral-histories/richard-sidys-reflections/.

"Solidarity Day: In Support of the Poor People's Campaign." June 19, 1968. SCLC Papers, Series VIII. King Center Archives.

Solle, Dorothee. *Choosing Life*. Philadelphia, PA: Fortress Press, 1981.

Sonnie, Amy, and James Tracy. *Hillbilly Nationalists, Urban Race Rebels, and Black Power: Community Organizing in Radical Times*. Brooklyn, N.Y.: Melville House, 2011.

"The Souls of Poor Folk: Auditing America Fifty Years After the Poor People's Campaign." Poor People's Campaign: A National Call for Moral Revival, 2018. https://www.poorpeoplescampaign.org/resource/the-souls-of-poor-folk-audit/.

Southern Christian Leadership Conference. "Black and White Together: American Indians, Poor Whites, Spanish-Americans Join Poor People's Washington Campaign," March 15, 1968. SCLC Papers, Series VIII, 179:11. King Center Archives.

———. "Poor People's Campaign Declaration," April 28, 1968. SCLC Papers, Series VIII, 177:25. King Center Archives.

———. "The Poor People's Campaign: A Photographic Journal." 1968. SCLC Papers, Series VIII, 179:19. King Center Archives.

———. "Statement of Demands for Rights of the Poor Presented to Agencies of the U.S. Government by the Poor People's Campaign and Its Committee of 100," May 29, 1968. SCLC Papers, Series VIII, 177:24. King Center Archives.

Steering Committee of the Arden House Conference on Public Welfare. "Governor's Conference on Public Welfare." In *Welfare: A Documentary History of U.S. Policy and Politics*, edited by Gwendolyn Mink and Rickie Solinger, 280–81. New York: New York University Press, 2003.

Teeple, Gary. *Globalization and the Decline of Social Reform: Into the Twenty-First Century*. Aurora, Ontario: Garamond Press, 2000.

Theoharis, Athan G. *Spying on Americans: Political Surveillance from Hoover to the Huston Plan*. Philadelphia: Temple University Press, 1978.

Theoharis, Jeanne, and Komozi Woodard, eds. *Groundwork: Local Black Freedom Movements in America*. New York: New York University Press, 2005.

Theoharis, Liz. *Always with Us?: What Jesus Really Said about the Poor*, Grand Rapids, MI: Eerdmans, 2017.

Thurman, Hy. Interview by author. Digital audio recording. Telephone, July 15, 2015.

———. *Revolutionary Hillbilly: Notes from the Struggle on the Edge of the Rainbow*. Berkeley, CA: Regent Press, 2020.

Tillmon, Johnnie. "Welfare Is a Women's Issue." In *Welfare: A Documentary History of U.S. Policy and Politics*, edited by Gwendolyn Mink and Rickie Solinger, 373–79. New York: New York University Press, 2003.

Torres, Sasha. *Black, White, and In Color: Television and Black Civil Rights*. Princeton, NJ: Princeton University Press, 2003.

"A Tragedy." *Washington Post*, April 6, 1967. Sec. A, page 20.

United Nations. "Ending Poverty," December 3, 2018. https://www.un.org/en/sections/issues-depth/poverty/.

United Nations High Commissioner for Refugees. "Figures at a Glance." January 19, 2020. https://www.unhcr.org/figures-at-a-glance.html.

The United States Census Bureau. "2017 American Community Survey 1-Year Estimates."2017. https://factfinder.census.gov/faces/tableservices/jsf/pages/productview.xhtml?src=bkmk.

United States Congress Senate Committee on Government Operations Permanent Subcommittee on. *Conference on Problems Involved in the Poor Peoples' March on Washington, D.C. April 25, 1968.* Washington: U.S. Govt. Print. Off, 1968.

United States Federal Bureau of Investigation. "Memorandum: Counterintelligence Program Black Nationalist-Hate Groups Racial Intelligence (Poor People's Campaign)," May 22, 1968. The COINTELPRO Papers. https://en.wikipedia.org/wiki/File:FBI_PPC_1.pdf.

Untitled drawing of Resurrection City. Southern Christian Leadership Conference, n.d. SCLC Papers, Series VIII, 177:19. King Center Archives.

Untitled report on the Poor People's University. Southern Christian Leadership Conference, n.d. SCLC Papers, Series VIII, 180:4. King Center Archives.

Warnock, Raphael Gamaliel. *Churchmen, Church Martyrs: The Activist Ecclesiologies of Dietrich Bonhoeffer and Martin Luther King, Jr.* New York: Union Seminary, 1994.

———. "Preaching and Prophetic Witness." In *Bonhoeffer and King: Their Legacies and Import for Christian Social Thought*, edited by Willis Jenkins and Jennifer M. McBride. Minneapolis: Fortress Press, 2010.

West, Guida. *The National Welfare Rights Movement: The Social Protest of Poor Women.* New York: Praeger, 1981.

West, Guida, and Rhoda Lois Blumberg. "Reconstructing Social Protest from a Feminist Perspective." In *Women and Social Protest,* edited by Guida West and Rhoda Lois Blumberg, 3–36, New York: Oxford University Press, 1990.

Williams, Delores S. *Sisters in the Wilderness: The Challenge of Womanist God-Talk.* Maryknoll, NY: Orbis Books, 1993.

Williams, Hosea. Letter to Staff of the SCLC. "Memorandum: Weekly Report and Doctor King's People to People Tours," March 8, 1968. Southern Christian Leadership Conference Records, Subseries 10.3, Poor People's Campaign, Box 571. Emory University.

Williams, Jakobi. *From the Bullet to the Ballot: The Illinois Chapter of the Black Panther Party and Racial Coalition Politics in Chicago.* Chapel Hill: University of North Carolina Press, 2013.

Wilmore, Gayraud S. *Black Religion and Black Radicalism: An Interpretation of the Religious History of Afro-American People.* Maryknoll, NY: Orbis Books, 1983.

Wolff, Edward. "Recent Trends in Household Wealth in the United States: Rising Debt and the Middle-Class Squeeze—an Update to 2007." Annandale-on-Hudson, NY: Levy Economics Institute of Bard College, March 2010. http://www.levyinstitute.org/pubs/wp_589.pdf.

Wright, Amy Nathan. "Civil Rights 'Unfinished Business': Poverty, Race, and the 1968 Poor People's Campaign." Dissertation. The University of Texas at Austin, 2007.

X, Malcolm. *Malcolm X Speaks: Selected Speeches and Statements.* New York: Pathfinder Press, 1965.

Yellen, Janet. "Perspectives on Inequality and Opportunity from the Survey of Consumer Finances." Board of Governors of the Federal Reserve System, October 17, 2014. https://www.federalreserve.gov/newsevents/speech/yellen20141017a.htm.

Yen, Hope. "4 in 5 in USA Face Near-Poverty, No Work." *USA Today*, September 17, 2013. http://www.usatoday.com/story/money/business/2013/07/28/americans-poverty-no-work/2594203/.

Yglesias, Jose. "Dr. King's March on Washington, Part II." In *Black Protest in the Sixties*, edited by August Meier, John H. Bracey, and Elliott Rudwick, 269–82. New York: M. Wiener Pub., 1991.

Young, Andrew. *An Easy Burden: The Civil Rights Movement and the Transformation of America.* New York: HarperCollins Publishers, 1996.

Youngblood, Doug. "Letter from Youngblood." In *The Movement: 1964-1970*, edited by Clayborne Carson and Martin Luther King, Jr. Papers Project, 434. Westport, CT: Greenwood Press, 1993.

Zikode, S'bu. "The Political and Economic Challenges Facing the Provision of Municipal Infrastructure in Durban." Durban University of Technology, 2016.

Index

Abernathy, Ralph, 14, 36, 45–46, 55, 56, 57, 60n28, 71, 74, 76, 77–79, 98, 99
abolition of slavery, 95, 98, 101–4, 109n32, 109n40, 110n44, 114, 132, 147, 150
Acts (book): 2:41, 99–102
Adams, Hank, 37n12, 44, 59n12, 81, 82, 84, 160n16
AFL-CIO, 25, 79
African Methodist Episcopal Church, 98, 101, 108n26, 109n39
African Methodist Episcopal Church–Zion, 101, 103, 108n26, 108n27
agricultural labor, 6, 19n39, 24, 25, 43, 46, 56, 69, 149, 155
Aliauja Federal de Pueblas Libres, 25
American Friends Service Committee, xxi, 24, 25, 74, 96
Amos (book), 99, 133
Appalachia, xii, 25, 44, 46–47, 48, 49, 55, 59n18, 60n26, 61n35, 81, 82, 154, 160n25
Armenian Orthodox Church, 98
Army (US), 37n10, 72, 73, 74, 75, 87n19, 89n36, 109n40
art and culture. *See* organizing
Asian Americans, xxiv n32, 45, 62n54
atheists, 98
Austin, Ernest, 24, 44

automation, xviii, 12, 15, 20n51, 115, 122

Baker, Ella, 32–33, 51, 62n56
Baker-Fletcher, Garth, 114
Baldwin, Lewis, 101, 111n58, 124n27, 129
Baptist, Willie, 151, 162n41
Baptists, 98, 100, 102, 107n15, 108n28, 109n32, 109n40, 128, 137n11, 158
Barber, William J., II, xx, 139, 146–49, 152–53, 156, 158, 160n26, 160n28, 161n34, 162n39, 166
Barbour, J. Pius, 128, 134
Belafonte, Harry, 4, 14, 35, 45, 80
beloved community, xv, 35, 70, 113, 118–20, 146, 158
Bevel, James, 9, 27
The Bible, 21n63, 102, 103, 104, 105, 117, 128, 130, 134, 139, 146, 147, 151–53, 158, 167
black church, xiv-xv, 95, 100–106, 108n28, 109n32, 109n40, 110n57, 111n58, 115, 128, 145n6, 140–41
black freedom struggles, 13, 20n55, 23, 24, 34, 44, 51, 101, 121, 150
Black Panther Party, 42, 47, 63n62, 82
black power, 2, 3, 14–15, 16n6
Black Theology, 110n57, 140

Blakey, Doug, xi, 25
Bonus Army, 72–73, 88
Braden, Ann, 44
Braden, Carl, 25, 44
Brethren Peace Fellowship, 98
Brown, John, 101
Browne, Borden Parker, 122n2
Bryant, Aaron, 76
Buckmaster, Mashyla, 156
Burris, Bertha, 43, 51, 67

capitalism, xv, xviii, 5, 6, 24, 64n71, 80,
    84, 95, 136n4, 140, 159n6
Casa Puerto Rico, 25
Catholics, 25, 82, 96, 98, 137n11, 147
Chadwick, Claire, 158
Chambers, Annie, 51
Chan, Kenyon, 62n54
chaplaincy, 144, 146, 166
Chaplains on the Harbor, 139, 142–
    46, 154, 156
charity, xvii, 31, 85, 115–16, 117, 118,
    143, 150, 151, 155
Charleston hospital worker strike, 78–79
Chavez, Cesar, 25, 35, 86n10
Christian realism, xiv, xv, 118, 165
civil disobedience, xi, xx, 98,
    130, 146, 153
civil religion, xv, 97, 115, 146, 156
civil rights, xii, xx, 4, 7–8, 12, 15n3,
    24,27, 30, 91n62, 114, 148, 165
Civil Rights Movement, xii, xiv–xv, xvi,
    2, 3, 4, 7–11, 14, 15n3, 20n55, 23,
    32–33, 35, 42, 45, 58n7, 75, 76–77,
    79, 81, 82, 91n61, 91n62, 95, 106,
    120–22, 124n30, 127, 128, 129, 131,
    133, 135, 136n6, 147, 161n34, 165
Civil War (US), 101, 103
Clark, Jim, 14
Clark, Michael, 47, 81
Clark, Ramsey, 36, 40n53,
    58n5, 75, 89n36
Clark, Septima, 78

class, xvii–xix, 6, 11, 13–14, 18n26,
    19n47, 26, 54–55, 77, 80–81, 83,
    87n17, 96, 113, 139–41
Clinton, Bill, 149
Cloward, Richard A., 71, 165
Coleman, Dovie, 25, 44, 51
Collier, Jimmy, 49
Collins, Dora, 67
Colossians (book): 2:15, 105
Committee of 100, 47, 54, 55,
    83, 86n6, 97
Cone, James, xiv, 106, 110n57,
    130, 137n22
Congress (US), xi, 33, 47, 51, 56, 57,
    68, 70–71, 99, 154
Congress on Racial Equality (CORE),
    30, 64n71, 91n62
Constitution (US), 8, 48, 97, 99, 156
Corona, Bert, 27
Cotton, Elizabeth, 49
crucifixion, 105, 120, 122n2, 130–31,
    132, 134, 137n22, 138n36, 145, 167
Crusade for Justice, 25, 37n12, 43, 82

Daniel (book): 3:130, 98–99
Day, Keri, xxii, 71, 140–41
democracy, xix, 32–33, 45, 83
Department of Agriculture, xxiv, 69
Department of Health, Education, and
    Welfare, 47, 48, 50, 56, 69, 98
Department of the Interior, 69, 83
Department of Justice, 36, 56, 57, 58n7,
    69, 74, 89n30, 89n36
Department of Labor, 47
Deuteronomy (book), 150; 15:1–11, 148
DeWolf, L. Harold, 122n2, 129
Dorrien, Gary, 122n2, 123n15, 124n30,
    125n39, 127, 129
DuBois, W.E.B., xiv, 35, 111n58
Dzurinko, Nijmie, 157

Ebenezer Baptist Church, 17n17,
    95, 99, 132
Edelman, Marian Wright. *See*
    Wright, Marian

education, xx, 5, 7, 8, 11, 35, 47, 51, 56, 67, 82, 84, 144, 147, 155. *See also under* King, Martin Luther, Jr.; organizing; Poor People's Campaign. *See also* Resurrection City: Poor People's University
environmental devastation, xx, 27, 62n55, 153, 155, 165
Episcopalians, 25, 96, 98, 137n11, 142–44
Exodus (book), 98, 105, 132, 151–53

Fager, Chuck, 56, 70, 76, 98
Farm Labor Organizing Committee, 25
FBI, xxi, 35, 44, 52, 73–75, 87n19, 88n28, 89n36, 96, 136n6, 152
feminism, 29, 71, 140
Fort Hood Three Committee, 25, 37n12
food, xi, xxiv n28, 5, 17n21, 43, 45, 51, 54, 57, 64n78, 69, 70, 82, 83, 84, 85, 97, 100, 156
Franklin, C. L., 98–99
Freedman, Jill, 76
freedom, xiii, xiv, 2, 34, 81, 82, 98, 102, 103, 104, 105, 110n44, 110n45, 110n57, 116–17, 124n30, 133–35, 167
freedom church, 95, 100–106, 133
"freedom church of the poor," xiii, 33–34, 36, 95–96, 100, 106, 116–17, 128, 133–35, 139, 146, 158, 165, 166–67
Freeman, Roland, 76

Gandhi, Mahatma, xiv, xv, 120, 125n39
Garrow, David, 36, 88n28
Genesis (book):37: 19–20
Giddings, Paula, 27
Givens, Cornelius, 41
Goldstein, Alyosha, 19n50, 63n69
Gonzales, Nita Jo, 51
Gonzales, Rodolfo "Corky," 27, 37n12, 43, 46
guaranteed annual income, xv, 4, 11, 12, 13, 19n50, 53, 55, 98, 115

Hamer, Fannie Lou, 15, 21n63, 91n62
Harding, Vincent, 6, 17n16, 26, 32, 36, 80, 92n82, 127
Harrington, Michael, 21n58, 70
Hawthorne School, 41, 46–47, 49, 51, 53, 61n35, 61n39, 75, 80, 81, 82, 97
Hayden, Tom, 25
healthcare, 5, 31, 43, 45, 47, 143, 144, 147, 149, 150, 158
Highlander Folk School, 25, 44, 49, 78, 81, 82
homelessness, 1, 83, 141–46, 149, 150, 151, 152, 155, 156
Hoover, Herbert, 72–73
Hoover, J. Edgar, 72, 74
hope, 104, 105–6, 116–17, 121, 124n30, 129, 134–35, 142, 145, 147, 153–54, 156, 165, 166
Horn, Etta, 28, 29, 51
Horton, Myles, 35, 40n48, 49
Houck, Tom, 24, 54
housing, xx, xxiv n28, xxvi n41, 2, 7–8, 11, 17n22, 23, 51, 53, 55, 57, 68, 69, 83, 84, 85n7, 142, 149, 150
Houston, Robert, 76
Hufnagel, Ashley, 157, 158
human dignity, xii, xv, xviii, xix, 14, 76, 95–96, 97, 105, 110n44, 113–17, 119, 122, 124n27, 128, 135, 138n27, 140, 141, 142, 144, 145–46, 148–49, 157, 167
human rights, xiii, xv, xvi, xxi, 2, 8, 13, 14, 18n34, 20n52, 20n55, 23, 24, 27, 30, 31, 33, 68, 83, 97, 115, 118, 121, 124n27, 133, 136n6, 149–50, 151, 154, 156, 157, 165
Hunter, Charlyne, 46, 52, 76

image of God (*imago dei*), 95, 114, 116, 117, 146
immigration, 69, 86n6, 117, 151
incarceration, xx, xxiv n32, xxvii n44, 1, 45, 48, 49, 79, 99, 143–44, 145, 157n10

indigenous peoples. *See*
Native Americans
inequality, xvii–xix, xxv n35, xxvi n38,
xxvi n41, 3, 10, 12, 63n69, 64n72,
119, 136 n4, 155, 159
inner church, 129–30, 134
internationalism, xv, xvi, xviii–xix, xxiii
n17, xxvi n42, 1, 5, 18n34, 80, 84,
114, 159n6
Isaiah (book), 97; 58:1, 12, 161n34
Islam, 98, 156

Jacobs, Harriet, 102
Jeremiah (book): 8:22, 106
Jackson, Jesse, 9, 21n56, 79, 81, 83
Jesus, 23, 96, 97, 100, 105, 120,
125n39, 127, 129–30, 131, 132, 134,
138n25, 142, 143, 145–46, 149–50,
152, 156, 158, 160n20, 167
John (book): 1:42, 100; 3:1–21, 131
Johnson, Click, 61n35
Johnson, Lyndon B., 2, 4, 5, 10, 23, 30,
36, 55, 59n12, 67, 71, 72–73
Johnson, Mordecai, 125n39, 128
JOIN Community Union, 25, 37n12, 82
Judaism, 25, 96, 98, 146, 147, 156
justice, xvi, 99, 100, 113, 119, 120–22,
135, 140, 141, 144, 147, 151,
158, 165, 166

Kairos Center for Religions, Rights,
and Social Justice, xx, 149, 151,
152, 162n39
Kennedy, Robert, 9, 28, 86n10
Kensington Welfare Rights Union,
149–50, 151
King, Coretta Scott, xiv, 41, 45,
51, 57, 78–79
King., Martin Luther, Jr., xiv–xv;
assassination, xi, xv, 35–36,
40n48, 40n53, 72, 87n19, 125,
132; education, xiv, 127–28, 129;
misremembrance, xv, 36, 127;
"revolution of values," xiii, xv–xvi,
xx, 2, 122, 139, 165; "triple evils,"
xii–xiii, xv, xvi, 2–7, 8, 17n20, 66,
93, 121, 152–53, 153
King, Martin Luther, Sr., xiv, 128
kingdom of God, 16n13, 95, 100, 117–
18, 120, 129, 130, 135, 142, 152, 158
Kirkpatrick, Frederick, 49

La Raza Unida, 82
Latin American Defense Fund, 25
Lawson, James, 30, 63n62
leadership of the poor, xv, xiii, xx, 4, 10,
13, 26–29, 31, 32–5, 50, 54, 56, 68,
78, 81, 85, 117, 128, 133–35, 141,
143–44, 150, 153, 154, 157, 166
liberalism, xiii, 4, 10, 11, 55, 56, 63n69,
64n71, 82, 118, 157
Logan, Marian, 9
Lomax, Alan, 49
love, 113, 119–22, 122n2, 130–31,
137n22, 140, 144, 146, 147, 158
Luke (book):3:15–17, 125; 4:4, 100;
10:30–37, 115–16; 13:18–19, 142
Lumbee Indian Citizens Council, 25

Maggard, Buck, 48
Mantler, Gordon, 61n39,
71–72, 75, 87n17
Mark (book):1:15, 100; 2:1–9, 127;
4:30–32, 142
mass meetings, xii, 29–30, 98–99, 128,
129, 149, 153
Matthew (book):1:18–2:23, 145;
3:1–12, 127; 4:4, 100; 6:11, 97;
13:31–32, 142; 16:19, 158; 26:6–13,
150–51, 152
Matthews, Ethel Mae, 67, 85n2
Mays, Benjamin E., 111n58, 127–27,
134, 161n34
McCollough, Marrell, 87n19
McKnight, Gerald, 72–73
McSurely, Al, 44, 48, 59n18, 61n35, 73,
81, 82, 160n26
media, xiv, 4, 9–10, 32, 47, 48, 51, 52,
55, 56, 61n42, 69–70, 73, 74, 75–77,
82, 141, 155

Memphis Invaders, 52, 63n62
Methodists, 98, 102, 109n32, 109n40, 137n11. *See also* African Methodist Episcopal Church
Mexican American Youth Organization, 25
Mexican Americans, xii, 13, 21, 24, 25, 27, 41, 43, 45, 46, 49, 54, 69, 75, 80–81, 82
migrant labor, 19n39, 24, 25, 46, 69
militarism, xxvii n44, 4, 6, 119, 144, 148–49, 153, 155. *See also under King, Martin Luther, Jr.*
Minority Group Leaders Conference, 24–27, 28, 29, 35, 44, 47, 54, 96
Monroe, Sarah, 139, 141–46, 159n10, 166
Montes, Carlos, 80–81
Moral Mondays Forward Together Movement, 146, 149, 153, 155, 160n26, 162n39
Moultrie, Mary, 78

NAACP, xiv, 9, 30, 64n71, 79, 91n62, 146, 160n26, 161n28
National Council of Churches, 25, 98
National Indian Youth Council, 25
National Union of the Homeless, 147, 149
National Welfare Rights Organization, xxi, 19n50, 20, 24, 25, 27–29, 41, 44, 48, 51, 54, 71
Native Americans, xii, 21n63, 24, 25, 37n12, 41, 42, 43, 44, 45, 46, 47–48, 53–54, 58n12, 60n26, 61n35, 69, 75, 83–84, 86n10, 143
Newman, Grace Mora, 37n12, 51
Nixon, Richard, 19n50, 64n72, 86n10
nonviolence, xiv, xv, 2, 3, 31, 33, 34, 35, 39n47, 42, 52, 61n35, 72, 85, 92n82, 119–20, 121, 125n39, 131, 133, 143, 154, 155

O'Dell, Jack, 91n61
Office of Economic Opportunity, 5, 69

Omeja, Aleah, xii
organizing, xiii, xv, 7–8, 27–29, 29–30, 31, 32–33, 47, 51, 53–54, 68, 71, 118, 119–20, 152–53, 155, 167; arts and cultural, 42, 49–50, 98, 105–46, 107n15, 110n56, 153, 162n39; and education, xiii, 31–32, 33–35, 50, 103, 143, 150, 151, 155, 157, 162n39; fusion, 147, 160n26; labor, 25, 54, 55, 57, 69, 78–79, 91n61, 91n62, 147, 153, 158; multi-racial, xii, xiii, 13–14, 20n56, 21n63, 24–27, 43, 48, 56, 68, 71–72, 75, 79, 81, 82, 83, 84, 103, 147, 149–50, 154, 155, 165; religious, 2, 57, 95–96, 98, 99–100, 103–5, 110n56, 127, 129–30, 132, 134, 142, 147–48, 151, 161n34

Parks, Rosa, xiv, 152
Payne, Larry, 52
Pentecost, 99–100
Personalism, xv, xiv, 100, 113–15, 122n2, 124n31
police, xiv, xx, xxvii n44, 15n3, 42, 43, 48, 49, 51–53, 58n4, 57, 72–75, 76, 79, 83, 87n19, 125n41, 141, 143–45, 155. *See also* incarceration; FBI
political strategy, xv, 3, 8, 14–15, 26, 32–34, 35–6, 68, 71, 83, 121, 122,131, 153, 154
Poor People's Campaign: accomplishments, 67–71, 80–83; caravans, xi, 42–44, 46, 52, 58n6, 58n7, 61n35; demands, 11–12, 20n52, 27, 47, 53–57, 68–69; direct action, 47–48; Mule Train, 43, 58n4, 58n6; political education, xiii, 31, 33, 35, 42, 49–50, 67; Solidarity Day, 36, 41, 55–57, 98, 153. *See also* Resurrection City; leadership of the poor
Poor People's Campaign: A National Call for Moral Revival, xx, 139, 152–58, 166

Poor People's Coalition and Embassy, 79–80

poor whites, xi, 2, 6, 13–4, 21n57, 24, 25, 26, 44, 46, 49, 53, 60n26, 81, 83, 103, 133, 147, 155, 159n10

poverty, xvi–xix; 1960s, xi, xvii, 1, 5–6, 12, 13, 30, 46, 52, 84–85, 133; contemporary, xvi, xvii, xxiv, n28, xxv n35, 1, 142–43, 155; and gender, xxiv n32, 27–29, 140–41; global, xviii–xix, xxvi n42, 159n6; and incarceration, xxv n32, 144–45, 159n10; official measure, xxiv n28, 17n22, 19n50, 142–43; and race, xvii, xxiv n32, xxvi n41, 1, 13–14, 46, 53–54, 91n62, 140–41; and work, xvii–xviii, xxv n35, 11–13, 19n50, 20n52, 30, 21n57, 21n62, 55, 56, 78–79, 91n62, 115, 122, 132, 147, 157, 158. *See also* leadership of the poor; King, triple evils

power, xiii, xv, xvi, 3, 8, 10, 13, 15, 26, 33–34, 65–66, 113, 120–22, 129, 147, 154

Presbyterians, 111n39, 137n11, 152

Prosser, Gabriel, 103

Puerto Ricans, xii, 13, 24, 25, 35, 37n12, 41, 45, 54, 75, 78, 81, 82

racism, xix, xxiv n32, 2–3, 6–7, 14, 23–24, 29, 43, 77, 80–81, 83–84, 91n62, 101–2, 114, 119, 120–21, 128, 133, 136n4, 140–41, 147, 152, 154, 155. *See also under King, Martin Luther, Jr.*

Rainbow Coalition (original), 71, 79, 82, 86n10

Ransby, Barbara, 32

Reagon, Bernice, 49

Reconstruction, xiv, 7, 147, 161n30

Repairers of the Breach, 161n34, 162n39

Resurrection City, 31, 41, 44–47, 48–50, 51, 52, 57, 73; demographics, 45, 60n26, 75, 98; Many Races Soul Center, 45, 49; marshals, 51–53, 57, 75–76; Poor People's University, 35, 39n47, 45, 49–50, 70; violence, 51–52, 70, 72, 73, 75–76, 96

Romasco, Anne, 49

Roosevelt, Franklin D., 73

Ross, Esther, 44

Rustin, Bayard, xiv, 55–56, 79, 125

Rutherford, William, 9, 70

salvation, 105, 106, 108n26, 128, 130–33, 136n6, 138n27

Sanders, Beulah, 29, 51

sanitation workers strikes, 30, 52, 63n61, 79, 132, 134

Scott, Aaron, 139, 141–46, 154, 160n16, 166–67

Seeger, Pete, 49

segregation, xii, xv, 2, 7, 12, 15n3, 24, 30, 77, 86n10, 91n62, 114, 116, 119–21, 128, 129

sexism, xvii, xxiv n32, 29, 50–51, 78–79, 140

Sidy, Richard, 46, 49, 98, 107n15

Sioux Indian Council, 25

slavery, 101–2, 114, 132, 150. *See also* abolition

Smiley, Glenn, xiv, 125n39

Social Gospel, xiv, xv, 100, 101, 115, 117, 122n2, 127, 136n4, 148

Solle, Dorothee, 138n27

Southern Christian Leadership Conference, xiv, 2, 6, 9, 10, 11, 24, 28, 32, 33, 36, 46–47, 48, 51, 54, 57, 69, 78, 80

Southern Conference Education Fund, 25, 44

Student Nonviolent Coordinating Committee, 17n17, 18n34, 25, 30, 49, 52

Sullivan, William, 63n62, 74, 96

suffering, xv, 2, 5, 7, 21, 106, 121, 130–31, 133, 138n25, 138n27, 146

technology, xvi, xviii, xxv n36, 12, 15, 20n51, 115, 118, 122
Terry, Peggy, 24, 37n12, 51, 57, 83
Theoharis, Liz, 139, 149–56
Thom, Mel, 25
Thurman, Dovie, 81
Thurman, Howard, xiv, 128, 133
Thurman, Hy, 82
Tijerina, Reies Lopez, 27, 37n12, 43, 47, 54, 81
Tillmon, Johnnie, 28–29, 38n23, 51, 57
Tucker, Sterling, 56
Turner, Albert, 42
Turner, Nathaniel, 103

Udall, Stewart, 59n12, 84, 88n20
uprisings, 2–3, 34, 51, 72, 75, 79, 103
unemployment, xx–xxi, 5, 6, 10, 12, 13, 21n57, 21n62, 51, 84, 127, 142–43, 150, 159n10
Union Theological Seminary, 149, 150, 151
United Church of Christ, 24
United Farm Workers, 25, 86n10

Vesey, Denmark, 103
Vietnam War, xii, xiii, 4, 8, 13, 16n12, 16n13, 17n16, 17n17, 20n54, 24, 25, 48, 55–56, 59n18, 63n68, 75, 86n10, 87n19, 132–33, 147
Vigil, Ernesto, 49
violence, xv, xix, xxvii n44, 2, 3, 4, 17n17, 31, 34, 48, 76, 121, 129, 130, 143, 144, 147, 155
voting rights, xx, 7, 8, 9, 30, 79, 148, 149

Walker, Tillie, 43, 51, 59n12, 83–84
War on Poverty, 4, 5, 20n53, 25, 28, 30, 43, 53, 63n69, 69, 89n30, 113
Ware, Florestine, 44
Warnock, Raphael, 130
Washington, D.C., xi, xii, 9, 10, 11, 23, 28, 31, 41, 47–48, 72, 78, 96, 150, 153, 156
wealth, xviii, xix, 1, 5, 6, 21n58, 26, 68, 117–18, 122, 133, 140, 147, 155, 158, 159n6; global, xix, 1; and race, xxvi n38
welfare rights, 25, 67, 81, 86, 149, 150, 151, 152, 153, 156. *See also* National Welfare Rights Organization
white church, 95, 101–3, 128, 129, 137n11
Wilkins, Roger, 56, 58n7
Williams, Delores, 131
Williams, Hosea, 45, 57
Williams, Jessica, 156
Womanism, 71, 131, 138n25, 140–41
working class, xvii-xviii, xix, 56, 11–12, 21n57, 91n61, 96, 115, 119, 122, 142, 147
World Council of Churches, 24
Wright, Marian, 9, 51, 56, 69, 70

Yglesias, Jose, 11, 13
Young, Andrew, 9, 28, 35, 53, 57, 73, 97, 80, 96, 97
Young Lords, 82
Young Patriots, 82

About the Author

Colleen Wessel-McCoy is the Neeley Visiting Professor of Religion and Public Policy at Arizona State University's School of Public Affairs. Previously she was lecturer at Union Theological Seminary and coordinator of Poverty Scholarship and Leadership Development at the Kairos Center for Religions, Rights, and Social Justice. She is an educator with the Poor People's Campaign: A National Call for Moral Revival.

Made in the USA
Coppell, TX
06 November 2023

23882986R00132